Essentials of Health Behavior

Social and Behavioral Theory in Public Health

Mark Edberg, PhD

Associate Professor

The George Washington University

School of Public Health

Washington, DC

JONES & BARTLETT
LEARNING

d Headquarters
Jones & Bartlett Learning
40 Tall Pine Drive
Sudbury, MA 01776
978-443-5000
info@jblearning.com
www.jblearning.com

Jones & Bartlett Learning
Canada
6339 Ormindale Way
Mississauga, Ontario
L5V 1J2
CANADA

Jones & Bartlett Learning
International
Barb House, Barb Mews
London W6 7PA
UK

Jones & Bartlett Learning books and products are available through most bookstores and online booksellers. To contact Jones & Bartlett Learning directly, call 800-832-0034, fax 978-443-8000, or visit our website www.jblearning.com.

Substantial discounts on bulk quantities of Jones & Bartlett Learning publications are available to corporations, professional associations, and other qualified organizations. For details and specific discount information, contact the special sales department at Jones & Bartlett Learning via the above contact information or send an email to specialsales@jblearning.com.

Production Credits
Publisher: Michael Brown
Associate Editor: Katey Birtcher
Production Director: Amy Rose
Associate Production Editor: Daniel Stone
Associate Marketing Manager: Sophie H. Fleck
Cover Design: Kristin E. Ohlin
Manufacturing Buyer: Therese Connell
Composition: Shawn Girsberger
Senior Photo Researcher and Photographer: Kimberly Potvin
Printing and Binding: D.B. Hess
Cover Printing: John P. Pow Company
Cover Images: Upper left corner: © Alvaro Pantoja/Shutterstock, Inc.
            Upper right corner: © Emin Kuliyev/Shutterstock, Inc.
            Lower left corner: © Photos.com
            Lower right corner: © Ximagination/Shutterstock, Inc.

Library of Congress Cataloging-in-Publication Data
Edberg, Mark Cameron, 1955-
  Essentials of health behavior : social and behavioral theory in public health / Mark Edberg.
    p. ; cm.
  Includes bibliographical references and index.
  ISBN-13: 978-0-7637-3796-2
  ISBN-10: 0-7637-3796-8
  1. Social medicine. 2. Public health. 3. Health behavior. I. Title.
  [DNLM: 1. Health Behavior. 2. Attitude to Health. 3. Health Promotion--methods.
W 85 E21e 2007]
  RA418.E3389 2007
  362.1--dc22
                        2007006449

6048
Printed in the United States of America
14 13 12 11 10   10 9 8 7 6

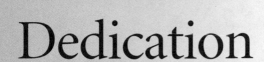

Dedication

*This book is dedicated to my family for their support and tolerance,
to all those at The George Washington University and at Jones & Bartlett Publishers
who were behind the Essentials of Public Health series, and, importantly,
to all those already working or planning to work on the front lines to help improve
the lives and health of so many people in the United States and around the world.
Your work is a testament to humanity at its best.*

Mark Edberg, PhD
The George Washington University

Table of Contents

Prologue

From cigarette smoking, to eating habits, to our daily routine, our every day behaviors affect our health in ways that we often fail to appreciate or even notice. Beyond our individual behaviors, there are larger social and population forces at play in all of our lives, which serve to mold and further reinforce our individual behavior.

Essentials of Health Behavior skillfully combines an emphasis on individual behavior with a clear focus on the social factors that influence the "big picture", population health perspective. Mark Edberg's approach grounds the practical everyday behaviors within key theories of human behavior drawn from the social sciences. Building on this understanding of health behavior, *Essentials of Health Behavior* examines a range of methods for changing behavior and applies these to programs in health promotion and disease prevention.

Edberg brings to his writing the lessons of extensive teaching experience at both the undergraduate and graduate levels—at The George Washington University School of Public Health and Health Services and its Columbian College of Arts and Sciences he taught health behavior courses, as well as courses that focus on the impact of culture on health—as well as his training and experience as an anthropologist, and social researcher with a public health focus. As an anthropologist he has a unique understanding of the impact culture and social organization have on individual behavior.

Essentials of Health Behavior is a key book in the **Essential Public Health** series. Like the other books in the series it has been written to fulfill competencies expected from public health education, which will form the basis for the certifying examination of the National Board of Public Health Examiners.

Essentials of Health Behavior can be used in social science curriculum that looks at the many factors that affect health behavior. Health behavior is also a key building block for health education. Health professional educators in the clinical disciplines are increasingly coming to appreciate that good outcomes rest on understanding the social and economic factors that affect individual behavior. As the social and behavioral sciences become more integrated into the clinical curriculum, *Essentials of Health Behavior* will provide a structured curriculum designed to fulfill these needs.

The *Essentials of Health Behavior* text will be complemented by a Reader, which emphasizes the interdisciplinary approach needed to understand and change behavior. Background readings will provide students and faculty with a range of approaches to reinforcing and expanding upon the key concepts in the main text. The full list of materials in the **Essential Public Health** series can be found at http://www.jbpub.com/essentialPublicHealth/.

I am confident that you will benefit from the *Essentials of Health Behavior,* whether you are using this book for a course in public health, psychology, sociology, anthropology, heath education, communications, or the range of other fields that are affected by health behavior.

Richard Riegelman, MD, MPH, PhD
Series Editor—*Essential Public Health*

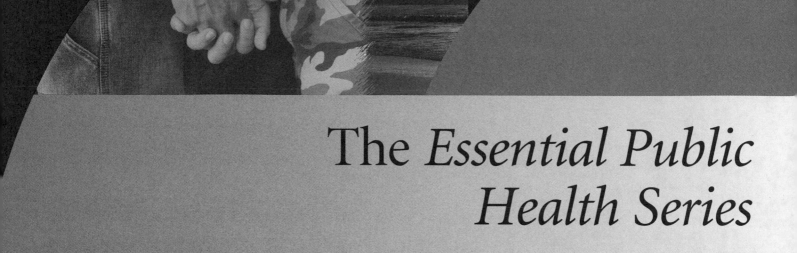

The *Essential Public Health Series*

Log on to www.essentialpublichealth.com for the most current information on availability.

CURRENT AND FORTHCOMING TITLES IN THE ESSENTIAL PUBLIC HEALTH SERIES:

ABOUT THE EDITOR:
Richard K. Riegelman, MD, MPH, PhD, is Professor of Epidemiology-Biostatistics, Medicine, and Health Policy, and founding dean of The George Washington University School of Public Health and Health Services in Washington, DC. He has taken a lead role in developing the Educated Citizen and Public Health initiative which has brought together arts and sciences and public health education associations to implement the Institute of Medicine of the National Academies' recommendation that ". . .all undergraduates should have access to education in public health." Dr. Riegelman also led the development of George Washington's undergraduate public health major and minor and currently teaches "Public Health 101" and "Epidemiology 101" to undergraduates.

Preface

Health promotion, education, and prevention programs ultimately focus on changing health behavior. But what do we mean when we say "health behavior"? Is health-related behavior really different than any other behavior? There is no reason to think it is. To help us understand it, then, we can draw from the fascinating, multidisciplinary, and ongoing quest to try and understand human behavior in general. That of course, is a big task, and no one book can cover that in any adequate way. What we can do, though, is provide an introduction to the kinds of theoretical approaches that are used, or could be used, in developing and implementing health promotion programs, and to show how such approaches are applied to real-life settings.

It is my hope that combining these elements together in one book will fill an important gap for undergraduate programs in public health, and will provide an important piece of the foundation necessary for understanding the field. It is important that students in public health have a solid grounding in social/behavioral theory, and particularly important that they gain a general understanding in this subject area before they proceed to a graduate program or move to direct involvement in prevention and health education programs that apply such theory. Why? Because proper use of theory in public health means, in part, the ability to place particular theoretical approaches in context, to have some sense of their origins, their underlying assumptions, their strengths and weaknesses, and the programs/situations for which they might or might not be most applicable.

More and more, public health interventions and their evaluations are guided by theoretical frameworks. Program goals, program components, and the types of data used as evidence of program success are thus built on specific theoretical underpinnings. Without at least a general background, application of theory can all too easily become formulaic and inappropriate—form without substance. A key aim of this book, in that sense, is to provide the groundwork for understanding, assessing, and effectively applying theory.

In that spirit, *Essentials of Health Behavior* is designed to:

1) introduce students to the relationship between behavior and a selection of major health issues;

2) provide an introductory background to the kinds of social and behavioral theories that guide our understanding of health-related behavior, and that form the background for health promotion and prevention efforts; and

3) explore some of the ways in which these theories and approaches are used in applied health promotion efforts.

In the first section, we will introduce the relationship of behavior to health, review a sample of current and ongoing health problems (domestic and international), and, in a broad sense, discuss the relationship of behavior to those health problems. In the second section, we will provide a context from which to understand theory, and survey theoretical perspectives from psychology, social psychology, sociology, and anthropology that offer explanations of human behavior, keeping in mind that health behavior is one domain of human behavior in general—thus linking the field of health promotion/prevention to the broader context of social/behavioral theory. The third section will introduce students to theory-based program planning and application, providing real-world examples across a range of settings – including community, school, and workplace programs, global health, mass media/communications, and programs targeting special populations. This section will also show how theory links program design, implementation, and evaluation. In the fourth section, current issues in the applied field of health behavior/health promotion will be reviewed, and we will present some of the occupational and career possibilities for which material in the book is relevant.

Mark Edberg, PhD

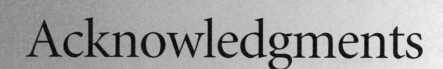

Acknowledgments

One can never attempt to do a book alone, and with that in mind, I am deeply grateful to a number of individuals who provided invaluable support and assistance in preparing this book: .

- Dr. Richard Riegelman, for his leadership in compiling the series and for shepherding everyone through the process.
- Heather Jordan, MPH, Izetta Simmons, MPH, and Elizabeth Collins, MPH, for providing knowledgeable and outstanding research support, editing, and shaping up the manuscript.
- Dorothy Biberman, MPH, and Kennedy Watkins, MPH candidate, for invaluable support with literature research.
- Kristen Corey, MA, for literature research support on obesity in Chapter 2
- Deborah Galvin PhD and Julia Lear, PhD for providing expert critique and assistance on Chapter 9
- Lorien Abroms, PhD, for expert critique and assistance on Chapter 10
- Laurie Krieger, PhD, for expert critique and assistance on Chapter 11
- The Department of Prevention and Community Health, School of Public Health and Health Services at the George Washington University, for overall support and expertise.

And of course, thanks to my wife Haykham and children Eleazar and Jordana for tolerating my ever-present box of book-related materials and work that have accompanied me everywhere over the past year.

Mark Edberg, PhD

About the Author

Mark Edberg, PhD is an applied and academic anthropologist by training with over 18 years' significant experience in public health, social and community research, as well as public health program development and evaluation. He is currently Associate Professor in the Department of Prevention and Community Health at The George Washington University School of Public Health and Health Services, with a joint appointment in the Department of Anthropology. Dr. Edberg has been Principal Investigator, or Co-Principal Investigator, on numerous studies; for the Centers for Disease Control and Prevention, National Institutes of Health, Department of Health and Human Services, and other agencies, focusing on HIV/AIDS, violence, and substance abuse prevention, minority health/disparities in health, and marginalized and at-risk populations. Currently, Dr. Edberg is Principal Investigator (PI) on a four-year research effort to develop and evaluate a youth violence prevention intervention targeting community-modifiable factors (funded by CDC) in a Latino community in the Washington, DC metropolitan area. He is also Co-PI on an effort to evaluate a sexual exploitation/trafficking prevention program, and lead consultant on a community assessment of HIV, STI/STD, and hepatitis risk among Latino youth. For the U.S. Office of Minority Health (OMH), he is a Co-Project Director on an effort to develop an evaluation framework for efforts by states and U.S. territories to eliminate minority health disparities, and Project Director on the continuing implementation of a Uniform Data Set (evaluation) for all OMH-funded activities.

Recently, Dr. Edberg was Co-PI on an innovative quantitative/qualitative study for the National Institute on Drug Abuse (NIDA) on substance abuse and HIV risk among three Southeast Asian populations in the Washington, DC metro area. Dr. Edberg also directed an effort to develop an evaluation data system for all grant programs funded by the U.S. Office of Minority Health (Department of Health and Human Services). This system is now Internet-based, and was the result of two previous projects for the same agency involving in-depth evaluation of agency programs. The Department of Health and Human Services gave this project a Best Practices in Evaluation award. Other recent research efforts include: ethnographic research in the U.S.-Mexico border region on the public image of narcotraffickers, and the relationships between this public image to violence and other risk behaviors (this work is documented in a recent book published by the University of Texas Press); Co-PI for the Washington, DC site under the NIDA Cooperative Agreements to Evaluate HIV/AIDS Risk Behavior Interventions with injection drug and crack users; PI for two small NIH-funded efforts to research and develop strategies for reaching out-of-treatment drug users (for HIV testing) and to reach low-income Hispanic/Latino women towards the goal of increasing use of prenatal care and reducing infant mortality; field ethnographer for a NIDA study on risk behavior among runaway youth; and evaluator, trainer and other positions on a range of community intervention and social marketing projects concerning substance abuse, smoking, HIV/AIDS, and violence. Dr. Edberg has also worked, under USAID contract, in Honduras and Puerto Rico as part of a democracy development project.

With respect to his faculty role, Dr. Edberg was recently Health Promotion Track Director within the Department of Prevention and Community Health. At the graduate level he teaches Health Behavior and Health Education and Qualitative Research Methods; at the undergraduate level he developed and has taught two new courses in Social and Behavioral Theory for Health Education/Promotion and the Impact of Culture on Health. He has also has taught Research Methods in Sociocultural Anthropology and Psychological Anthropology for the Department of Anthropology.

Dr. Edberg's outside interests include music—he is founder, songwriter, lead guitar and vocals for an original modern-rock group called the Furies. In addition to performing at clubs and other venues, the Furies have performed at benefit and social issue-related events.

Photo Credits

SECTION I

On Health and Behavior—
An Introduction

CHAPTER 1

Introduction:
The Links Between Health and Behavior

LEARNING OBJECTIVES

By the end of this chapter, the reader will be able to:

- Understand that there are multiple influences on health behavior
- Define what is meant by the *ecological model*
- Explain the types of factors influencing health that are covered in an ecological model

"Life is a voyage . . ."

—VICTOR HUGO, 1866, FROM *THE TOILERS OF THE SEA*

THE SETTING: DAILY LIFE

Any in-depth discussion of health behavior is, of necessity, going to involve a certain amount of wrestling with abstractions about motives, causal and contributing factors, contexts, cues, and other issues related to why people do what they do. To help make sense of such discussions, it may help to begin with a simple scenario about a "health behavior" that would seem to be very mundane—brushing teeth. It's the sort of thing that would *not* ordinarily be the object of much introspection, to say the least. It's the kind of behavior that is for the most part habit, far below the radar of our thinking selves, which makes it an ideal starting point for considering the issues raised in this book.

Suppose a friend of yours—we'll call him Sam—was brushing his teeth, and doing so very vigorously. If you asked him why he was doing this, your conversation might go as follows:

YOU: Hey Sam, why are you brushing your teeth like that?

SAM: What do you mean, why am I brushing my teeth? Don't you brush yours? I don't wanna get cavities or have my teeth fall out, okay? What kind of a question is that?

Well that's that, then, right? End of story. Sam is brushing his teeth (and doing it well) to maintain healthy teeth. Makes perfect sense.

But now suppose, as you continue watching Sam perform his tooth-brushing ritual, you see, lying conveniently on the sink, a copy of GQ magazine with a cover photo showing what appears to be the model of hip maleness—a chiseled figure leaning nonchalantly against a wall, comfortably worn leather jacket open and loose, hair just right even while a few strands display a defiant anarchy, and a carefully casual, unshaven jaw and chin. Punctuating this icon's studied hip gestalt is a set of perfect, strong, gleaming white teeth.

Hmm. The plot thickens. So maybe he is also trying in his own way to look like Mr. Ultimate Male. By brushing his teeth?

Whatever.

Now suppose, after completing the tooth-brushing scene, Sam, looking intense and preoccupied, digs through his closet for some clothes to wear. Clearly, he is not looking for just any clothes. He is looking through his meager and often rumpled wardrobe for something that will display just the right sense of *je ne sais quoi.**

---

* French phrase meaning, literally, "I don't know what," but used to refer to someone who is cool and has a "special something" about them.

By this time, your curiosity can no longer be contained.

YOU: Okay, Sam, out with it. You going somewhere (heh, heh)?

SAM (trying to pretend that nothing out of the ordinary is going on): Uh, whaddya mean?

YOU: C'mon, Sam. What am I, an idiot? Going out? To dinner? A movie? A party? Whatever it is, it looks to me like it's no ordinary party.

SAM (letting down his guard): Okay, Okay. I was invited to this party, alright? And it's actually at her parent's house.

YOU (interrupting): Wait a minute. *Whose* parent's house?

SAM: Well, you remember a few weeks ago I mentioned that I met someone I think is . . . kinda special.

YOU: Okay, now I understand. The tooth brushing, all of it.

SAM: Here's the thing. I'm not exactly going to be the only person there, ya know what I mean? She didn't just invite me.

YOU: So you want to . . . stand out.

SAM: Yeah.

YOU: Got it. Lookin' sharp. Good luck.

After this, the plot is now more complete. If you were asked to explain the motivations behind Sam brushing his teeth (vigorously), you now have at least three possibilities:

1. For health reasons
2. To look as much as possible like the male icon in the magazine (a cultural factor)
3. (Related to #2) To stand out from the crowd and be as attractive as possible to a person of the opposite sex, and a special person at that

We can get more complicated with another question: Which of these three motivations do you think was dominant in the scenario we just described? Probably number 2 or 3, right? This time, anyway. But if you ask Sam the same question tomorrow, when, for example, he is barely awake and perhaps on his way to work, you might find that motivation number 1 is actually the most important, or even another one yet unnamed (e.g., "habit," or "so my breath won't smell bad").

Or, suppose Sam was the first person to go to college from his small rural town, and his family had little income

and no health insurance. Because of the precariousness of his (and his family's) position, he was very concerned about maintaining his health lest he have to go to a doctor with no money to pay. And a dentist? That would be out of reach. So, as a result, he was very, even overly, concerned with preventing such a situation.

In yet one more wrinkle, suppose Sam's mother instructed him, when he was very young, to brush his teeth religiously after every meal. Every day, his mother drilled into Sam's head that he just was not *clean* or presentable to the world without doing so. The reason for her intense dental vigilance was that she herself lost most of her teeth at an early age because, as a child, neither she nor her parents knew much about teeth or the role of brushing. Of course Sam would not likely know the reasons behind her admonitions—all he would know was that it was a big thing for his mother, and that he had grown up not feeling very presentable somehow, unless his teeth were brushed.

THE QUESTIONS

The moral of the story is this: There is an entire field of study and practice concerned with the complex nature of health behavior, with a goal of implementing programs and interventions that seek to promote *change* in behavior in order to improve the health of the public or a segment of the public. You are undoubtedly familiar with these kinds of programs—campaigns to stop smoking, warnings on advertisements and on cigarette packaging, and lawsuits against tobacco companies; television advertisements and school programs warning young people about drug and alcohol use, or about drinking and driving; public campaigns, including billboard ads, metro and bus ads, and television ads, about the risks of transmitting HIV and the benefits of HIV testing; and public campaigns about cardiovascular health and diet, about low-carb diets or about low cholesterol food choices. There are many more such examples.

Most of these programs and interventions rely on a body of knowledge about *what motivates and influences human behavior*. In other words, if the public health question is:

Why do people behave in healthy (or unhealthy) ways?

This question is really just a more focused version of the following:

Why do people do what they do?

Thus, in order to understand something about human behavior as it relates to health, we have to think about this subset of behavior in the context of what generally motivates or influences human behavior. Moreover, as you saw in the example of Sam and brushing teeth, behavior that is often categorized as "health behavior" is not necessarily motivated or influenced by concerns about health. It may be in some cases. Or it may be health concerns mixed together with other concerns. Or it may be based on concerns that have nothing to do with "health" per se. Or it may be based on ideas about being healthy that are different than the standards of health common to Western medicine. A case in point: For many cultures, being thin is not viewed as healthy. A large man—one that we might call overweight—is viewed as healthy and "doing well." This is particularly true for peoples who have experienced food shortages throughout their history.[1] Being thin is a reminder, a symbol, of starvation.

And that is only part of the story. Often, what people do or don't do related to health has more to do with socioeconomic circumstances, or environmental conditions, or public policies and regulations. A woman may not get routinely screened for breast cancer simply because she lives in a rural area and health care providers who do the screenings are not easily accessible. This doesn't have as much to do with her motivation as it does her social and geographic situation. People living downstream from a factory that is polluting the waterway may suffer health consequences from eating fish or other animals contaminated by the pollutant, or from contaminated drinking water. It may be the case that they are not sufficiently aware of the risk. Yet they may also be heavily dependent on fishing for their livelihood, and may have been dependent on fishing for many generations—enough to build up a local culture related to the fishing life. If you were trying to pinpoint where to start in reducing the health risk for these people, what would you address first?

In some parts of the rapidly developing world, economies and societies that were once rural and agrarian have experienced a dramatic shift to urban and more industrialized economies. This process has many implications for health and social conditions in general. In their former rural life-pattern, people may have lived in small villages that did not put much pressure on the local environment, and food may have been relatively easy to obtain. Once in the urban context, the picture changes. Living conditions are more crowded (see Figure 1-1). Food is not as easily obtained.

FIGURE 1-1 Shanty town in Manila, Philippines.

Copyright Flat Earth/FotoSearch. Retrieved from "Shanty town," http://en.wikipedia.org/wiki/Shanty_town.

Water and sanitary systems may be overwhelmed by the number of people. Housing is hard to come by. Diseases like tuberculosis spread more easily. Women may come to the cities from the rural areas and find themselves forced to engage in the sex trade in order to survive, placing themselves and their partners at great risk for HIV/AIDS or other sexually transmitted infections (STIs). Knowledge about some of these risks may be limited. In the latter case, attitudes about gender roles may restrict women from seeking other types of work. Where, then, would you begin to address the health problems that arose? What would you point to as key influencing factors?

THE COMPLEX SOCIAL-ECOLOGICAL WEB

These examples illustrate the complexity of factors that influence human behavior with respect to health and other issues. Until the late 1970s/early 1980s, health promotion professionals and programs focused primarily on the knowledge, attitudes, and motivations of *individuals,* without much attention devoted to the social, cultural, and economic circumstances that are also major determinants of behavior.[2] The more recent focus on the multiplicity of influences on behavior is called the *ecological model.*[2] Under this model or approach to understanding health behavior, it is assumed that no one factor influences people's behavior; instead, the complex interaction between individuals and an environment is a process that, taken together, influences behavior. In other words, *behavior doesn't exist in a vacuum.*

So, for example, think of the following factors as a sampling of potential contributors to the behavior of individuals:

Individual factors

- Awareness and knowledge (about health risks, ways to prevent health problems, etc.)
- Biophysical characteristics (e.g., genetics, systemic vulnerabilities)
- Personal attitudes and motivations
- Developmental stage (e.g., adolescent, adult)
- Behavior/habit socialization (e.g., from parents, family)

Social/cultural/group factors

- Social/peer group lifestyle patterns
- Cultural attitudes/beliefs (and their implications for health)
- Level of social support

Socioeconomic and structural factors

- Poverty
- Education

- Access to health care and prevention services/information
- Social stressors such as civil strife, neighborhood violence, racial and other discrimination
- Access to clean water

Political factors

- Policies and funding for health promotion programs
- Health insurance (policies, cost, availability)
- Regulations that impact health risk (e.g., prohibiting sale of cigarettes to minors)

Environmental factors

- Presence of an environmental risk, such as air and water pollution
- Disasters
- Conditions for spread of an infectious disease

This list of factors, however, doesn't operate in the world as simply a collection of separate items. The factors tend to operate *together.* The term *ecology* is thus useful to describe this system of relationships. Its origin is in biology, where it generally refers to:

- A system of interactions between organisms and an environment
- The complex relationships between organisms in the system (e.g., niches)
- The dependent relationships between members/components of the system, where if one part of the system is disturbed, other parts will be affected

Although the concept originates in biology, the basic idea is useful in thinking about human behavior in context. The diagram in Figure 1-2 may help. It shows the linkages and connections among people, an environment,[†] and behavior.

That does make the task of understanding behavior more complicated, doesn't it?

Clearly, answering the question "Why do people do what they do?" or its public health version "Why do people behave in healthy (or unhealthy) ways?" is no easy matter. Yet to know this is good. Gaining a certain respect for the complexity of the task is, well, *healthy.* Because if you think it's simple, then you are more likely to implement a standardized or cookie-cutter program without much thought as to whether it is appropriate to the situation. And it is one goal of this book that you emerge with more wisdom than that.

---

† Here we are defining *environment* as that which exists outside the individual, so it could mean the social as well as the physical environment.

FIGURE 1-2 Diagram of linkages and connections among people, an environment, and behavior.

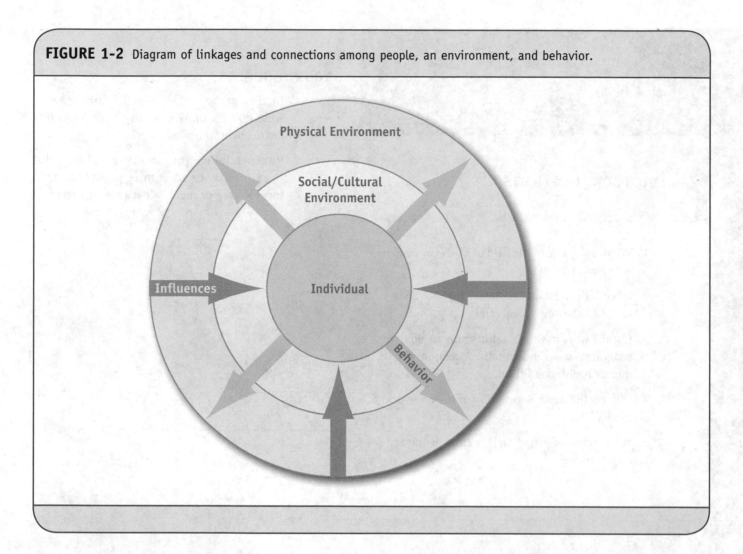

However, lest you throw up your hands and claim that behavior is just too complicated to do anything about, consider that a long tradition of researchers and practitioners have built up a considerable store of scientific knowledge, interpretive understanding, and practical application with respect to changing human behavior. There are, of course, many different schools of thought, many different applied traditions, and, in keeping with the complexity of the endeavor, many disagreements about basic scientific truths, approaches, strategies, and just what should be the focus of attention.

IN THIS BOOK

In this book, we are going to review some of these different approaches and theoretical traditions (to understand and change human behavior), with an eye toward providing you with enough tools so that you can make informed judgments about what theories and approaches make sense in a given situation. In doing this, we want you to understand some of the assumptions underlying the theory, and to take a look at where the various theories come from. Second, we are going to present you with a general planning approach for assessing a public health or social problem and, based on your assessment, tools to make a decision about what kind of program might work best to change it, and how to determine whether you have succeeded. Third, you will become acquainted with a range of settings in which you can apply social/behavioral theory to address a spectrum of health problems both in the United States and worldwide, including smoking, cancer, cardiovascular disease, HIV/AIDS, maternal and child health, youth violence, and obesity.

Treat this book not as a compendium of answers to all the questions posed, but as a resource that can help guide you in the ongoing search for answers—a resource that is based on a sampling of what is currently known in the field.

Chapter Questions

1. In the example of Sam and brushing teeth, what do you think were the most important factors behind his behavior?

2. Pick five things you do that could be called "health behavior." List three possible motivators for each of them. What's your pattern?

1. What is the goal of the field of study concerned with health behavior?

2. What is the relationship between health behavior and behavior in general?

3. List the ways in which a shift from an agrarian economy to an industrialized economy may impact health conditions.

4. What is the main assumption of the ecological model?

5. What types of broad factors exist in the ecological model?

REFERENCES

1. Brown PJ, Konner K. An anthropological perspective on obesity. In: Brown PJ, ed. *Understanding and Applying Medical Anthropology.* Mountain View, CA: Mayfield Publishing; 1998.

2. Green LW, Kreuter MW, eds. *Health Promotion Planning: An Educational and Environmental Approach,* 3rd ed. Mountain View, CA: Mayfield Publishing; 1999.

CHAPTER 2

Health Issues and Behavior

By the end of this chapter, the reader will be able to:

- Describe behaviors related to obesity and its consequences (e.g., diabetes, cardiovascular health problems), and factors influencing those behaviors
- Describe behaviors related to youth violence and its consequences (e.g., injury), and factors influencing those behaviors
- Describe behaviors related to HIV/AIDS transmission, and factors influencing those behaviors

---

"He had had much experience of physicians, and said 'the only way to keep your health is to eat what you don't want, drink what you don't like, and do what you'd druther not.'"

—MARK TWAIN (1835–1910)

To give you a clearer sense of why an understanding of human behavior is important in addressing public health problems, let's take a look at a few selected health issues and how they are related to behavioral factors—remembering, as presented in the introductory chapter, that *behavior* (as understood within an ecological model) is just one factor that determines the nature of a given health problem. And, in turn, remembering that there are many factors that influence behavior.

OBESITY*

It is by now well-known that obesity and its consequences (e.g., diabetes, heart disease) have become a serious health concern in the United States and other industrialized countries,[*][1][2] a concern that has received considerable attention from both the mass media and research journals. A recent edition of the *Journal of the American Medical Association*,[3] for example, reported that poor diet and physical inactivity caused 400,000 deaths in the United States in 2000, accounting for 16.6% of all deaths, second only to tobacco (18.1%). Recent estimates also suggest that 97 million adults in the United States are overweight or obese.[4] The trend has clearly been upward; in the last two decades mean body weights have increased by nearly 10%, and clinical obesity has nearly doubled in prevalence.[5] Overweight and obesity are risk factors for coronary heart disease, non-insulin-dependent diabetes, hypertension, certain cancers, and other conditions. If the trend is not reversed over the next few years, some say it may overtake tobacco as the leading preventable cause of mortality.[3]

Where does behavior factor in? Because these trends in overweight/obesity are recent, most agree that interactions between people's behavior and the environment are the primary cause, rather than biological factors.[5][6] In other words, the situation is viewed as *preventable.* Explanations for these sudden and "epidemic" increases in body weight among Americans and populations in other countries generally emphasize *lifestyles* associated with increased overall energy

---

* The author wishes to acknowledge the contribution of, and material provided by, Kristen Corey, M.A., in compiling this descriptive section on obesity.

[handwritten note: !Change environment to promote behavior chng!]

consumption and inactivity. A short list combining behavioral and environmental causes includes the following[5,6]:

- Extensive marketing of unhealthy food products (including fast food)
- Overeating
- Lack of exercise
- Increased reliance on vehicle transportation
- A sedentary lifestyle related in part to the ubiquity of television, computers, and other labor-saving technologies
- Changes in the quality of available foods
- Increased portion sizes
- Trends towards eating out
- The growth of the convenience food industry
- Increased advertising by the food industry

Think about it. How often do you eat out? When you do, what do you have? How often do you exercise?

For a while, public health efforts to address overweight and obesity concentrated on increasing awareness through education about healthy behaviors. Guidelines for exercise/diet and the health consequences of overweight and obesity aimed to change behavior by arming people with personal knowledge and skills. Despite moderate short-term successes, these approaches have not proved effective in the long term.[6,7] This issue is a good example of the ecological model at work, because the problem appears to be related to environmental factors that shape behavior, that *encourage* the overconsumption of food, and that *discourage* physical activity.[6]

Many of these earlier efforts also relied on the use of individual behavior change theories—including those we will be discussing in this book—that emphasize the individual as the target of change, and address knowledge, attitudes, decision-making processes, and skills. Critics of these efforts have cited the over-reliance on what individuals can and cannot do over sociocultural and physical environmental factors that play a role in their decision making. This can't necessarily be "fixed" simply by adding an intervention focusing on individual behavior to an intervention that targets an environmental cause, because behavior and the environment interact.[8]

Interact: "To act upon one another."[9]

This is where ecological models come in.[10] Ecological models integrate the various influences on health behavior, including interpersonal, organizational, community, and public policy factors, to name a few. So, you could say that obesity-related behavior is influenced by:

- Individual factors (e.g., genetics, taste/food preferences, attitudes, beliefs, knowledge, hunger)
- Social factors (e.g., interpersonal processes, relationships, social status)
- Cultural factors (shared beliefs/values related to food, the body, eating practices)
- Physical environment (availability/cost of food types or exercise options, physical layout of environment)

These factors interact, and to understand behavior, it is important to understand that interaction. An ecological intervention (with a goal of changing behavior) can then include components that address several factors where, for example, an environmental change supports behavior change.[11] For example, closing down vending machines, or altering the products they sell (an environmental change), will cut down on the eating of high fat snacks (a behavior).

Food, Eating, and Obesity

We all know that eating involves choices about what to eat. So it is no surprise that taste, cost, convenience (availability), and individual food preferences are key influences on dietary choices.[12,13] This, however, does not say much in itself. A lot of factors go into the process of choice, including:

- *Availability of healthy food:* Many studies have documented the lack of supermarkets, farmers markets, and grocery stores in low-income areas.[14,15] These kinds of stores are more likely to have fresh fruits and vegetables. In other words, choice of food is limited by where one lives in some cases.
- *Attitudes, beliefs, and sociocultural norms related to diet:* The cross-cultural literature suggests that dietary choices also are shaped by social and cultural factors.[16,17] Foods are associated with individual or group identity and with ideas about "how daily life should be." Conceptions of what constitutes food or a meal, as well as how foods should be consumed and prepared, vary by ethnicity, geographic region, gender, age, and social class.[18-20] An important issue is demonstrated in this example: Peoples' ideas about *what constitutes a good or acceptable meal* differ. Typically, across cultures, definitions of the ideal meal include a meat or other protein source and a "starchy" food such as bread, rice, or one of numerous root crops. In many cases, the starchy food is the main component of the meal in part because it is more available or accessible.[17,18,21]

The cross-cultural literature also highlights many meanings associated with food and eating, and many of these have social implications. Food sharing is commonly associated with strong individual, family, and group ties and often

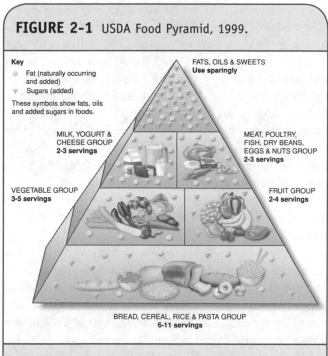

FIGURE 2-1 USDA Food Pyramid, 1999.

Key
- ○ Fat (naturally occurring and added)
- ▽ Sugars (added)

These symbols show fats, oils and added sugars in foods.

FATS, OILS & SWEETS
Use sparingly

MILK, YOGURT & CHEESE GROUP
2-3 servings

MEAT, POULTRY, FISH, DRY BEANS, EGGS & NUTS GROUP
2-3 servings

VEGETABLE GROUP
3-5 servings

FRUIT GROUP
2-4 servings

BREAD, CEREAL, RICE & PASTA GROUP
6-11 servings

Source: U.S. Department of Agriculture Center for Nutrition Policy and Promotion.

FIGURE 2-2 USDA Food Pyramid, 2006.

Source: U.S. Department of Agriculture Center for Nutrition Policy and Promotion.

invokes values of hospitality, mutual caring, group solidarity, and common goals, as well as social and even political obligations.[17,18,22-25] Failure to share when it is socially expected or offering inappropriate foods is identified with negative values or used to express dissatisfaction with social relationships.[26-28] In contrast to nutritional models that determine the healthiness of foods based on their composition, investigations of local models suggest that the most commonly eaten foods that leave the consumer feeling full are often considered the most healthful.[17,29]

People may also be at risk for obesity-related problems because they do not know the relationship between diet and disease.[18,29] Remember that calling obesity a "disease" is a very recent phenomenon; until recently, many people would not have thought of it that way. In fact, "being large" has positive value in a number of societies. Weight gain, good appetite, and large stature have been considered signs of good physical and social health. By contrast, weight loss, poor appetite, and thinness have been considered signs of poor health.[30-35] Decisions about whether to choose low fat/healthy foods are affected by people's beliefs about how much benefit those foods will have and their "confidence" (usually referred to as *self-efficacy*—we'll talk about that in Chapter 5) that they can in fact manage their choices.[6] Obese individuals may also

Uneducated!

FIGURE 2-3 Family meal.

Source: Ryan McVay/PhotoDisc/Getty Images.

feel that obesity is not preventable given the social pressures surrounding eating, or they may expect a "cure" for the condition, rather than dietary advice.[36,37]

Finally, it is just hard for people to take risks seriously if they are not meaningfully connected to lifestyle, personal experience, and ideas of lifelong health status.[38-41] Although many behaviors may threaten long-term health, the immediate benefits of risky behavior may be seen to enhance one's state of well-being. This has been demonstrated with respect to smoking and adolescent self-image;[38] with risky needle sharing among injection drug users, in relation to its perceived practical as well as social benefits;[42] with perceptions of alcohol use among American Indian adolescents;[43] and with other risky activities. Thus, if there are "positive" social/normative benefits associated with unhealthy eating habits, these may affect subjects' perceptions of risk in the same manner.

Physical Exercise and Obesity

Cost, time, safety, and access are major factors affecting an individual's decision to take on or increase regular physical activity. In the course of day-to-day life, the possibility of incorporating exercise as a common routine varies widely depending upon an individual's circumstances related to their job, the amount of free time, the availability of space or facilities, and the physical characteristics of the neighborhood, worksite, or school (commonly referred to as the "built environment").

> The *built environment* can be defined as, "the manmade surroundings that provide the setting for human activity, ranging from the large-scale civic surroundings to the personal places."[44]

A number of research studies have identified links between the built environment and physical activity.[45,46] If there are changes in the built environment that remove barriers, it may, for example, be more possible to walk or bike to destinations, to exercise on lunch breaks, and simply to take the stairs.[47] People will be more likely to do this on their own without the use of an actual intervention. Several promising studies support the idea that changing the built environment across different settings has an effect on behavior. Adding signs to increase stair use among shoppers,[48] providing showers and changing rooms for employees,[49] and increasing access to trails in rural communities[50] are examples of interventions that have increased physical activity.

YOUTH VIOLENCE

When we talk about youth violence as a public health problem in relation to behavior, the concern is the *injury and personal trauma* that violence causes—because, of course, violence is already a behavior and for youth, it has truly been

a serious situation. In recent years, among young people ages 10–24, homicide was the *second leading cause of death* overall in the United States.[51] Specifically, in that age group, it was the leading cause of death for African Americans, the second leading cause of death for Hispanics/Latinos, and the third leading cause of death for American Indians, Alaskan Natives, and Asian/Pacific Islanders.[51] In 2001, 79% of homicide victims ages 10–24 were killed by firearms.[52] In the same year, 5,486 people ages 10–24 were murdered, about 15 every day.[52] Eighty-five percent of these people were young men, while 15% were young women. In addition, a study of 8th and 9th graders showed that 25% had been victims of nonsexual dating violence and 8% had been victims of sexual dating violence.[53]

Violence is clearly a problem with many variations— from intimidation and threat, to situational violence, to intentional violence—and it is largely a problem of young people. Research on youth violence has indicated that serious acts of violence generally begin between ages 12 and 20, with only a very small percentage initiating any violence before age 10 or after age 20.[54-57] Thus, the peak period for violence involvement (engaging in acts of violence) coincides with the developmental stage of adolescence.

Why is there so much violence among young people? There are biological and developmental explanations concerning aggressive behavior[54] and a range of social and psychological explanations that have to do, again, with behavior as it relates to interactions between youth and their personal, family, community, and school environments. Many of the latter explanations address violence as one of a number of adolescent "risk behaviors," including delinquency, substance abuse, sexual risk, school dropout, and others.

Let's take a look at a few of the explanations for youth violence.

Risk and Protective Factor Explanations

This kind of explanation describes violence-related behaviors by parents, peers, the community, and others that may *influence* or shape violent behavior engaged in by young people. These influences are said to be "risk factors" and include family problems, family conflict and violence, absence of positive role models, being a victim of violence, witnessing violence when young, poverty, living in a crime-ridden community where weapons are easily available, social norms that support violence, and other such factors.[58-62] Typically, many of these risk factors are present as influences on violence as a behavior. It has been argued, however, that these risk factors can be offset by the presence of positive or *protective* factors like an adult who is present and cares about the youth, or connections to school or other youth who are not involved in violence.[58,59,63-67] This complex and fluid interaction between an individual and risk/protective factors in one or more domains has been described as a "web of influence," and draws from the *ecological* perspective of Brofenbrenner[68] that we have already referred to as a key concept within public health.[69]

Problem Behavior Syndrome, Behavioral Cluster, and Self-Concept Approaches

In these approaches, violent behavior and its influencing factors are understood to be related to a coherent pattern of risk-taking. (This will be discussed more fully in Chapter 12.) Risk for substance abuse, delinquency/violence, early sexual activity, and other behaviors is viewed as a "problem behavior syndrome" of one form or another, where the risk factors and trajectories are similar and/or overlapping.[70–75] Hawkins and Catalano, for example, note that of the 19 risk factors they have identified for adolescent problem behavior, 16 are common for both delinquency and substance abuse, 11 are common for violence and substance abuse, and 9 are common for all three.[76]

The "coherent pattern" may reflect a kind of conflicting or antagonistic relationship between youth involved in violence and the conventional world, that is, the segment of society for which the risk behaviors are viewed as negative or antisocial,[†] a conflict with the values, goals, institutions, and socializing forces of conventional society. Adolescents who, for a wide variety of reasons including the frustration of aspirations due to poverty, school failure, social disorganization in the community or family, or other such factors, are said to have a low commitment to conventional society and do not endorse its values, are more likely to engage in delinquent or violent behavior and substance abuse, and are more likely to have stronger bonds to other youth who are involved in the same behavior patterns.[74,77,78]

Self-concept can be defined as "the mental image one has of oneself."[9]

Moving beyond the idea of a "problem behavior" syndrome is another approach that seeks to understand a little more about how that antagonistic relationship operates on an individual level. This approach focuses on *self-concept*, particularly what an adolescent views as a "possible self" in the world that he or she can envision as relevant to his or her life.[79,80] If a "task of adolescence" is to experiment with and resolve social roles,[81] the possible selves factor is very important. If an adolescent can think of a satisfactory possible self in the "conventional domains" of family, friends, or school, this will help motivate him or her in making a successful transition to adulthood. If not, adolescents may seek alternative ways to define themselves. Delinquency and violence are alternative routes towards positive self-definition and prestige,[81(p114),82,83] particularly if there is a significant peer group that views these kinds of behaviors as valued.[84] Drawing from the theories of Ogbu[85] and Bourdieu[86,87] among others, Oyserman and Packer note that the identity-formation process is connected to specific social contexts as well.[84] So, for example, in high poverty situations where academic success may not be perceived as related significantly to available life-paths, the behavior patterns and meanings associated with academic success may not be valued, whereas others patterns (e.g., those including violence or other risk behaviors) will be.

Socioecological Models

In the spirit of an ecological approach, youth risk behaviors such as violence have also been viewed as related to social position, that is, where involvement in violence and the causes of involvement differ by socioeconomic status of particular groups. For example, it has been argued that drug use/involvement is motivated more powerfully by economic factors for minority youth than for nonminority youth. Research has shown that there is more experimental drug use among adolescents from higher socioeconomic brackets, while youth from lower socioeconomic groups tend to do less experimenting and more selling.[88-90] Clearly, drug trafficking/selling places youth at much higher risk for violence,[91-94] because violence is so often a part of trafficking. W. J. Wilson, in his seminal work on "underclass" communities, described the isolated and uniformly poverty-ridden nature of inner city underclass communities, where economic opportunities are so limited and there is a historical pattern of disconnection from mainstream economic activity, that drug selling and other aspects of the "street economy" become the dominant playing field for achievement and status,[95] and thus have a strong role in the development and perpetuation of norms and attitudes about violence.[96-102] Some of the work in this area describes "codes of the street" that govern violent or potentially violent interactions, with reference to the immediate social context of such codes.

Data on homicide patterns offer strong support for socioecological arguments about youth violence. The steep rise in *juvenile* homicide from the mid-1980s to the mid-1990s was closely tied to two factors: the volatile crack cocaine epidemic, which entailed the recruitment of urban

---

† See Hirschi T. *Causes of Delinquency*. Berkeley: University of California Press; 1969, and other social control theory.

youth into the "business," and the consequent increase in gun use[103-106] and the subsequent incorporation of guns as part of the norm for violent interaction even well after the decline of the crack boom.[101] Thus the codes or culture of the street now include the use of guns as routine. Some research on youth gang violence follows this approach. Spergel, for example, outlined a comprehensive gang intervention model that views the presence of gangs as largely related to a lack of socioeconomic opportunities, social disorganization, poverty, institutional racism, social policy deficiencies, and a lack of or misdirected social controls.[107]

Social-Cognitive Models

Lastly, while focusing on related aspects of violent behavior, social-cognitive models of violence focus on decision making, reasoning, and other cognitive processes surrounding acts of aggression. In this social information processing model of aggression,[108-110] aggressive behavior happens when a youth evaluates social/behavioral "cues" (like a facial grimace or insult), interprets those cues based on what he or she understands them to mean in a particular context, and then chooses a potentially violent response. Aggressive behavior is said to result from difficulties in coding and interpretation of social cues or to a limited repertoire of nonaggressive behavioral responses. Interpretation of cues and selection of responses is, not surprisingly, related to beliefs about aggression. In numerous studies, aggressive behavior in youth has been related to beliefs about the legitimacy of aggression,[111-114] and positive beliefs about aggression have been associated with perceived neighborhood danger.[115] Furthermore, such approaches also intersect with other approaches discussed thus far. For example, several aspects of the environmental context, such as prevalence of violence in the community, utility of violence for achieving desired outcomes, significant others' (e.g., peers) perceptions of violence, and consequences of violence involvement, are viewed as having implications for youth beliefs about aggressive behavior and their involvement in violence.

HIV/AIDS

By the end of 2004, an estimated 34 to 46 million people around the globe were living with HIV/AIDS,[116] with a nearly incomprehensible additional toll in orphaned children, decimated families and workforces, and stigmatization. Well over 20 million people have died from HIV/AIDS, and there are approximately 5 million or more new infections annually,[117] indicating that the pandemic continues to expand. Since the 1980s, when the disease was first identified, the global HIV/AIDS pandemic has become one of the worst global health crises in history. It is an epidemic that affects the well-being of societies, not just with respect to health. These impacts have included a decrease in average life expectancy, significant reduction in household income (because fewer household members work, and medical expenses may be high), decimation of educational system capacity and school attendance, a general decrease in economic production and increase in poverty, and, as previously noted, a generation of children without parents.

HIV/AIDS has also been a crisis filled with ambiguity and controversy, precisely because its epidemiology—the way in which it spreads—is so clearly tied to behavior and because even though anti-retroviral drugs (administered in multiple forms, known as highly active anti-retroviral therapy or HAART) can treat the condition, there is still no cure. This places a huge burden on prevention which is largely about behavior.[118] There are essentially three major routes of transmission: sexual transmission (either heterosexual or same-sex), sharing intravenous drug equipment, and mother-to-child (perinatal) transmission; a distant fourth is the use of contaminated blood products via transfusion. All of these routes of transmission are actually behaviors. Most importantly, they are behaviors that, for the most part, are closely intertwined with deeply rooted moral, cultural, and socioeconomic issues, all interacting at the same time. Understandings about sexual behavior, for example, are at the center of the moral-religious systems of virtually every society and culture. Yet sexual behavior is also closely tied to *gender definitions and relationships* across cultures, and it is inescapably tied to issues of poverty and wealth. Therefore, to understand sexual transmission of HIV in a particular place, you will need to look at all of these factors, at a minimum! And this doesn't even touch on HIV risks that people take because they simply don't know that they are taking a risk.

The patterns by which HIV/AIDS is spread vary from country to country, from society to society, by gender, and by subgroup. Not only that, but these patterns change over time as the epidemic evolves. A few examples:

- In the United States, HIV/AIDS was first identified, and took its earliest toll, among men who had sex with men (MSM). Not long after, it became clear that injecting drug users and their partners were seriously impacted as well, along with other specific high-risk populations (e.g., sex workers, runaway and homeless youth, incarcerated populations). Although the discovery of multiple anti-retroviral therapies in the mid-1990s reduced HIV/AIDS mortality because of increased survival rates, new infections continue. More recently, the epidemic has centered on women of color (heterosexual transmission) and has returned among MSM.[119,‡]

- In Sub-Saharan Africa, where the pandemic is currently most severe, heterosexual transmission has been, and remains, the primary path of transmission.[120] This is generally due to a number of factors, including patterns of migrant work, traditional gender roles in which men have multiple female partners, and lack of access to prevention and treatment. It is also exacerbated because prolonged ethnic conflict and civil war, like such conflicts everywhere, often involve rape and abuse of women.

- In Southeast Asia, Thailand was an early epicenter of HIV/AIDS, largely due to the sex trade but also because of high rates of injection drug use.[121] Because of an intense, government-led program of condom distribution and prevention, the spread of HIV/AIDS was slowed. However, it then began to increase rapidly in Vietnam, due to injection drug use and the sex trade, and Cambodia (due to the sex trade, heterosexual transmission, and largely associated with a rapid move towards economic development following the cessation of civil war in the 1990s, which involved migrant labor in big cities such as the capital Phnom Penh), as well as in Myanmar (Burma).[120,122,123]

- In Eastern Europe and Russia, the epidemic is more recent, and is primarily associated with injection drug use and its concomitant spread to sexual partners of injecting drug users.[123] However, according to UNAIDS, it is rapidly expanding.[120] Eastern Europe and Central Asia have the fastest growing epidemics in the world, rising from about 30,000 people living with AIDS in 1994 to an estimated 1.3 million in 2003. The economic changes after the early 1990s may have a lot to do with the epidemic in the region, resulting in a dramatic increase in trade—both legal and illegal—and a scramble for ways to make money.

- According to World Bank estimates, well over 5 million people in India are living with AIDS.[125] The behavioral risk factors include unsafe sex, such that 84% of cases result from sexual transmission, with prevalence rates very high among sex workers and related to lack of condom use. Other risk factors include migration and mobility, where a significant number of migrant workers are away from family and community for extended periods of time and likely to have sex with sex workers; men who have sex with

men (MSM), for which data, although limited, show that some men having sex with men concurrently have heterosexual partners, becoming a "bridge" population for HIV transmission; injection drug use (IDU)—for example, in the northeastern states of India the HIV/AIDS epidemic is expanding among injection drug users, through sharing of injection equipment; low status of women, contributing to the spread of the epidemic due to unequal relationships and therefore increased vulnerability of women to infection; and stigma against those who are infected,

Gender Roles and HIV Risk Among the Roma (Gypsies)[128]

The Roma (Gypsies), the largest ethnic minority group in Central and Eastern Europe, have cultures that are traditional, often closed, and autonomous of majority populations. Roma communities are characterized by pervasive social health problems, widespread poverty, limited educational opportunities, and discrimination. Although some evidence suggests high levels of HIV sexual risk behavior among Roma, little is known about the cultural and social context in which risk behavior occurs. In this study, in-depth interviews were used to elicit detailed information about types of sexual partnerships and associated sexual risk behaviors, as well as the use and perception of protection, knowledge and beliefs about AIDS and STDs, and sexual communication patterns in a sample of 42 men and women aged 18–52 living in Roma community settlements in Bulgaria and Hungary. Based on the interview data, men appeared to have significantly more latitude with respect to sexual behavior before and during marriage, engaging in unprotected sex with primary and multiple outside partners, with considerably more relationship power and control than women. In contrast, women are expected to maintain virginity before marriage and then sexual exclusivity to their husbands. Condom use is not normative and is mainly perceived as a form of contraception. Although awareness of AIDS was common, it was generally not perceived as a personal threat. Misconceptions about how HIV is transmitted are widespread, and women—in particular—had very little knowledge about STDs, HIV transmission, and protective steps. The study suggested an urgent need for the development of HIV prevention programs culturally sensitive to Roma populations in Eastern Europe, where HIV rates are rapidly rising.

---

‡ Also see the entire issue of *American Journal of Public Health*, June 2003, volume 93.

resulting in marginalization and higher concentrations of risk.

- In China, the HIV/AIDS epidemic was limited until the mid-1990s, when it began to grow dramatically.[126] This initial growth was focused among injection drug users and people using donated blood. Currently, there is an estimated 650,000 people living with AIDS in China, according to a joint World Health Organization and UNAIDS estimate.[127] Primary risk behaviors involved in the spread of the epidemic include injection drug use, contamination of blood and blood products, commercial sex workers (lack of knowledge about HIV risk and condom use), men who have sex with men, and migrant workers (a risk factor for casual sexual relationships).

Addressing HIV/AIDS-related risk behaviors is clearly complex. For each of the major routes of transmission, there are many behaviors involved, and a great deal of variation across cultures and circumstances. Just to take on sexual transmission as a topic area of research interest, here are only a few of the kinds of behavioral issues you would need to think about:

- What is the range of sexual practices and in what contexts do they occur? Heterosexual? Same-sex? With migrant workers?

- Which are riskiest for HIV transmission, multiple or single partners?

- What types of partners are there and are risk situations different by type of partner?

- Are there situations where sex is forced, or necessary for survival?

- What are the gender rules and relationships that are involved? Can one partner, for example, easily communicate to the other about HIV risk and prevention? Or will this be difficult?

Or, for example, to take on injection drug use and the sharing of needles:

- Who are the users (e.g., young, old, male, female, poor, middle class)?

- Do people inject in a public setting (like a park, alley, or house), with others, or by themselves?

- Is sharing of equipment common or necessary? How is this done (for example, do people actually share needles, or do they share water used for rinsing)?

- Do injection drug users know about HIV risks? Are they able to take precautions, or does addiction override such attempts?

- What are the treatment and prevention options? Are there, for example, needle exchange programs? Drug treatment programs?

BEHAVIORS, THEORIES, AND INTERVENTIONS

The three examples provided in the three previous sections show the complex link among behavior, social and environmental factors, and a health problem. The kinds of theories and frameworks I will discuss in the book are meant to be *tools* that will help guide you through the thick web often associated with health behavior. Trying to figure out what to do is made at least a little easier through the process of *identifying* what you think is going on (in terms of behavior and ecological influences), *choosing appropriate theories* or *frameworks* that best address what you think is going on, and using them to help you design programs.

Chapter Questions

1. What are some key links between the environment and behavior in terms of the problem of obesity?

2. Would it be fair to say that obesity is a problem resulting just from individual choice in terms of behavior?

3. What kinds of factors may influence youth to engage in violence?

4. What are consistent patterns of behavioral risk for HIV/AIDS around the globe? How do you think these patterns are influenced by the larger social or economic context?

5. Where would you focus your efforts to address behaviors related to obesity? Youth violence? HIV/AIDS?

REFERENCES

1. Flegal K, Carroll M, Ogden C, Johnson C. Prevalence and trends in obesity among U.S. adults 1999–2000. *JAMA.* 2002;288(14):1723–1727.

2. World Health Organization (WHO). Diet, nutrition and the prevention of chronic diseases. Report of a joint WHO/FAO expert consultation. *WHO Technical Report Series* No. 916. Geneva, Switzerland.

3. Mokdad A, Marks J, Stroup D, Gerberding J. Actual causes of death in the United States, 2000. *JAMA.* 2004;291(10):1238–1245.

4. National Heart, Lung and Blood Institute (NHLBI). *Clinical Guidelines on the Identification, Evaluation, and Treatment of Overweight and Obesity in Adults: The Evidence Report.* NIH Publication No. 98–4083. Rockville, MD: National Institutes of Health.

5. Jeffery RW, Utter J. The changing environment and population obesity in the United States. *Obesity Res.* 2003;11(Suppl):12S–22S.

6. French SA, Story M, Hannan P, et al. Cognitive and demographic correlates of lowfat vending snack choices among adolescents and adults. *J Am Diet Assoc.* 1999;99(4):471–476.

7. Jeffery RW. Community approaches to obesity treatment and prevention: the Minnesota experience. *Prog Obes Res.* 1999;8:837–843.

8. Bandura A. *Social Foundations of Thought and Action: Social Cognitive Theory.* NJ: Prentice-Hall; 1986.

10. Green LW, Kreuter MW. *Health Promotion Planning: An Educational and Ecological Approach.* New York: McGraw Hill; 1999.

11. Stokols D. Establishing and maintaining healthy environments: toward a social ecology of health promotion. *Am Psychol.* 1992;47(1):6–22.

12. Glanz K, Basil M, Maibach E, Goldberg J, Snyder D. Why Americans eat what they do: taste, nutrition, cost, convenience, and weight control concerns as influences on food consumption. *J Am Diet Assoc.* 1998;98:1464–1467.

13. Story M, Neumark-Sztainer D, French SA. Individual and environmental influences on adolescent eating behaviors. *J Am Diet Assoc.* 2002;102(3):S40–S51.

14. Weinberg Z. No place to shop: food access lacking in the inner city. *Race, Poverty Environ.* 2000;7(2):22–24.

15. Morland K, Wing S, Diez Roux A, Poole C. Neighborhood characteristics associated with the location of food stores and food service places. *Am J Prev Health.* ;22(1):23–29.

16. Counihan C, Van Esterik P, eds. *Food and Culture: A Reader.* London: Routledge; 1997.

17. Messer E. Anthropological perspectives on diet. *Ann Rev Anthropol.* 1984;13:205–249.

18. Pollock N. *These Roots Remain: Food Habits in Islands of the Central and Eastern Pacific Since Western Contact.* Honolulu, HI: University of Hawaii Press; 1992.

19. Weismantel M. *Food, Gender, and Poverty in the Ecuadorian Andes.* Prospect Heights, IL: Waveland Press; 1988.

21. Douglas M. Deciphering a meal. In: Counihan C, Van Esterik P, eds. *Food and Culture: A Reader.* London: Routledge; 1997:36–54.

22. Bindon J. Taro or rice, plantation or market: dietary choice in American Samoa. *Food Foodways.* 1988;3:59–78.

23. Flinn J. Tradition in the face of change: food choices among Pulapese in Truk State. *Food Foodways.* 1988;3:19–39.

24. Kahn M. Men are taro (they cannot be rice): political aspects of food choices in Wamira, Papua New Guinea. *Food Foodways.* 1988;3:41–57.

25. Manderson L, ed. *Shared Wealth and Symbol: Food, Culture, and Society in Oceania and Southeast Asia.* Cambridge, England: Cambridge University Press; 1986.

26. Kahn M. *Always Hungry, Never Greedy: Food and the Expression of Gender in a Melanesian Society.* Cambridge, England: Cambridge University Press; 1986.

27. Nichter M. Modes of food classification and the diet-health contingency: a South Indian case study. In: Khare R, Rao MSA, eds. *Food, Society and Culture: Aspects in South Asian Food Systems.* Durham, NC: Carolina Academic Press; 1986:185–221.

28. Young M. *Fighting with Food: Leadership, Values, and Social Control in a Massim Society.* Cambridge, England: Cambridge University Press; 1971.

29. Messer E. Methods for determinants of food intake. In: Pelto G, Pelto P, Messer E, eds. *Research Methods in Nutritional Anthropology.* Tokyo: United Nations University; 1989.

30. Brown P, Konner M. An anthropological perspective on obesity. *Ann N Y Acad Sci.* 1987;499:29–46.

31. Cassidy C. The good body: when big is better. *Med Anthropol.* 1991;13:181–213.

32. deGarine I, Pollock N, eds. *Social Aspects of Obesity.* Luxembourg: Gordon and Breach; 1995.

33. Nichter M, Nichter M. Hype and weight. *Med Anthropol.* 1991;13:249–284.

34. Ritenbaugh C. Obesity as a culture-bound syndrome. *Culture Med Psychiatry.* 1982;6:347–361.

35. Sobo E. The sweetness of fat: health, procreation, and sociability in rural Jamaica. In: Counihan C, Van Esterik P, eds. *Food and Culture: A Reader.* New York: Routledge; 1997:256–271.

36. Cohn S. Being told what to eat: conversations in a diabetes day centre. In Caplan P, ed. *Food, Health, and Identity.* London: Routledge; 1999:193–212.

37. Massara E. Que gordita. In Counihan C, Van Esterik P, eds. *Food and Culture: A Reader.* New York: Routledge; 1997:251–255.

38. Amos A, Gray D, Currie C, Elton R. Healthy or druggy? Self image, ideal image, and smoking behavior among young people. *Soc Sci Med.* 1997;45(6):847–858.

39. Douglas M, Wildavsky A. *Risk and Culture: An Essay on the Selection of Technological and Environmental Dangers.* Berkeley, CA: University of California Press; 1982.

40. Nations M. Epidemiological research on infectious disease: quantitative rigor or rigormortis? Insights from ethnomedicine. In: Janes C, Stall R, Gifford S, eds. *Anthropology and Epidemiology: Interdisciplinary Approaches to the Study of Health and Disease.* Dordrecht: Routledge and Kegan Paul; 1986:97–123.

41. Rose G. *The Strategy of Preventive Medicine.* Oxford, England: Oxford University Press; 1992.

42. Bourgois P, Lettiere M, Quesada J. Social misery and the sanctions of substance abuse: confronting HIV risk among homeless heroin addicts in San Francisco. *Soc Prob.* 1997;44(2):155–174.

43. O'Nell TD, Mitchell CM. Alcohol use among American Indian adolescents: the role of culture in pathological drinking. *Soc Sci Med.* 1996;42:565–678.

44. Wikipedia, http://en.wikipedia.org/wiki/Built_environment.

45. Saelens BE, Sallis JF, Black J, Chen D. (2003). Neighborhood-based differences in physical activity: An environment scale evaluation. American Journal of Public Health, 93, 1552–1558.

46. Centers for Disease Control. 2005. *The Guide to Community Preventive Services: What Works to Promote Health.* Oxford: Oxford University Press.

47. Colditz GA, Samplin-Salgado M, Ryan CT, Dart H, Fisher L, Tokuda A, Rockhill B. "Harvard Report on Cancer Prevention, Volume 5: Fulfilling the potential for cancer prevention: policy approaches." *Cancer Causes Control,* 13:199–212 (2002).

48. Andersen RE, Wadden TA, Bartlett SJ, Zemel BS, Verde TJ, Franckowiak SC. Effects of lifestyle activity vs structured aerobic exercise in obese women: a randomized trial. *JAMA* 281:335–340, 1999.

49. Vuori IM, Oja P, Paronen O. (1994). Physically active commuting to work—testing its potential for exercise promotion. Medicine and Science in Sports and Exercise, 26, 844–850.

50. Brownson RC, Housmann RA, Brown DR, et al. (2000). Promoting physical activity in rural communities. Walking trail access, use and effects. American Journal of Preventive Medicine 18:235–41.

51. Anderson RN, Smith BL. Deaths: leading causes for 2001. *Nat Vital Stat Rep.* 2003;52(9):1–86.

52. Centers for Disease Control and Prevention (CDC). May 24, 2004. Web-based injury statistics query and reporting system (WISQARS). Available at: www.cdc.gov/ncipc/wisqars. Accessed

53. Foshee VA, Linder GF, Bauman KE, et al. The safe dates project: theoretical basis, evaluation design, and selected baseline findings. *Am J Prev Med* 1996;12(5 Suppl):39–47.

54. U.S. Department of Health and Human Services. *Youth Violence: A Report of the Surgeon General.* Rockville, Md.: U.S. Department of Health and Human Services, Centers for Disease Control and Prevention, National Center for Injury Prevention and Control, Substance Abuse and Mental Health Services Administration, Center for Mental Health Services, and National Institutes of Health, National Institute of Mental Health; 2001.

55. Huizinga D, Loeber R, Thornberry TP. *Recent Findings from the Program of Research on Causes and Correlates of Delinquency.* (U.S. Department of Justice, Office of Justice Programs, Office of Juvenile Justice and Delinquency Prevention, NCJ 159042). Washington, DC: U.S. Government Printing Office; 1995.

56. Thornberry TP, Huizinga D, Loeber R. The prevention of serious delinquency and violence: implications from the program of research on causes and correlates of delinquency. In Howell JC, Krisberg B, Hawkins JD, Wilson J, eds. *Sourcebook on Serious, Violent and Chronic Juvenile Offenders* Thousand Oaks, CA: Sage; 1995:213–237.

57. Elliott DS. Serious violent offenders: onset, developmental course, and termination. The American Society of Criminology 1993 Presidential Address. *Criminol.* 1994;32:1–21.

58. Catalano RF, Hawkins JD. *Risk Focused Prevention: Using the Social Development Strategy.* Seattle, WA: Developmental Research and Programs; 1995.

59. Hawkins JD, Catalano RF, Miller JY. Risk and protective factors for alcohol and other drug problems in adolescence and early adulthood: implications for substance abuse prevention. *Psychol Bull.* 1992;112:64–105.

60. Bell CC, Jenkins EJ. Community violence and children on Chicago's Southside. *Psychiatry.* 1993;56:46–54.

61. Dryfoos JG. *Adolescents at Risk: Prevalence and Prevention.* New York: Oxford University Press; 1990.

62. Tolan P, Guerra N. What works in reducing adolescent violence: an empirical review of the field. In: *Report to The Center for the Study and Prevention of Violence.* Chicago: University of Illinois at Chicago; 1994.

63. Garmezy N. Resiliency and vulnerability to adverse developmental outcomes associated with poverty. *Am Behav Sci.* 1991;34(4):416–430.

64. Pransky J. *Prevention: The Critical Need.* Springfield, MO: Burrell Foundation and Paradigm Press; 1991.

65. Benson P, Galbraith J, Espeland P. *What Kids Need to Succeed.* Search Institute and Free Spirit Publishing; 1994.

66. Search Institute. 1998. Developmental assets: an investment in youth. Available at: http://www.search-institute.org/assets/index.htm. Accessed January 4, 1999.

67. Benard B. *Fostering Resiliency in Kids: Protective Factors in the Family, School, and Community.* Unpublished paper; 1991.

68. Brofenbrenner U. 1979. *The Ecology of Human Development.* Cambridge, MA: Harvard University Press.

69. Green LW, Kreuter MW (Eds). 1999. *Health Promotion Planning: An Educational and Environmental Approach.* Third Edition. Mountain View, CA: Mayfield Publishing Co.

70. Jessor R, Jessor SL. *Problem Behavior and Psychosocial Development: A Longitudinal Study of Youth.* New York: Academic Press; 1977.

71. Jessor R, Donovan J, Costa FM. *Beyond Adolescence: Problem Behavior and Young Adult Development.* New York: Cambridge University Press; 1991.

70. Donovan JE, Jessor R. The structure of problem behavior in adolescence and young adulthood. *J Consult Clin Psychol.* 1985;53:890–904.

72. Donovan JE, Jessor R, Costa FM. Syndrome of problem behavior in adolescence: a replication. *J Consult Clin Psychol.* 1988;56(5):762–765.

73. Elliott DS, Huizinga D, Menard S. *Multiple Problem Youth: Delinquency, Substance Use, and Mental Health Problems.* New York: Springer-Verlag; 1989.

74. Oetting ER, Beauvais F. Peer cluster theory, socialization characteristics and adolescent drug use: a path analysis. *J Counsel Psychol.* 1987;34(2):205–220.

76. Elliott DS, Huizinga D, Ageton S. *Explaining Delinquency and Drug Abuse.* Beverly Hills, CA: Sage; 1985.

77. Hawkins JD, Weis JG. The social development model: an integrated approach to delinquency prevention. *J Primary Prev.* 1985;6:73–97.

78. Markus H, Wurf E. The dynamic self-concept: a social-psychological perspective. *Ann Rev Psychol.* 1987;38:299–337.

79. Oyserman D, Markus H. Possible selves and delinquency. *J Personality Soc Psychol.* 1990;59(1):112–125.

81. Hirschi T. *Causes of Delinquency.* Berkeley, CA: University of California Press; 1969.

82. Sutherland EH, Cressey DR. *Criminology,* 10th ed. Philadelphia: Lippincott; 1978.

83. Oyserman D, Packer MJ. Social cognition and self-concept: a socially contextualized model of identity. In: Nye JL, Brower AM, eds. *What's Social About Social Cognition? Research on Socially Shared Cognition in Small Groups.* Thousand Oaks, CA: Sage; 1996.

84. Ogbu JU. Minority coping responses and school experience. *J Psychohistory.* 1991;18:433–456.

86. Bourdieu P. 1990. The Logic of Practice. (Trans. R. Nice.) Cambridge, England: Polity (originally published 1980).

87. Bourdieu P. 1977. *Outline of a Theory of Practice.* Cambridge: Cambridge University Press.

88. Baumrind D. Familial antecedents of adolescent drug use: a developmental perspective. In: Jones CL, Battjes RJ, eds. *Etiology of Drug Abuse: Implications for Prevention.* Rockville, MD: National Institute on Drug Abuse; 1985:13–44.

89. Kaplan HB, Martin SS, Johnson RJ, Robbins C. Escalation of marijuana use: application of a general theory of deviant behavior. *J Health Soc Behav.* 1986;27:44–61.

90. Simcha-Fagan O, Gersten JC, Langer TS. Early precursors and concurrent correlates of patterns of illicit drug use in adolescents. *J Drug Issues.* 1986;16:7–28.

91. Herrenkhol TL, Maguin E, Hill KG, Hawkins JD, Abbott RD, Catalano RF. 2000. "Developmental Risk Factors for Youth Violence." *Journal of Adolescent Health* 26:176–186.

92. Blumstein A. 1995. "Youth Violence, Guns and the Illicit-Drug Industry." *Journal of Criminal Law and Criminology* 86:10–36.

93. Spunt BJ, Goldstein PJ, Bellucci PA, Miller T. Race/ethnicity and gender differences in the drugs-violence relationship. *J Psychoactive Drugs.* 1990;22(3):291–303.

94. Goldstein P. The drugs/violence nexus: a tripartite conceptual framework. *J Drug Issues.* 1985;493–506.

95. Wilson WJ. *The Truly Disadvantaged: The Inner City, the Underclass, and Public Policy.* Chicago: University of Chicago Press; 1987.

96. Bourgois P. *In Search of Respect: Selling Crack in El Barrio.* Cambridge, England: Cambridge University Press; 1996.

97. Bourgois P. In search of Horatio Alger: culture and ideology in the crack economy. *Contemp Drug Prob.* 1989;16(4):619–650.

98. Anderson E. The story of John Turner. In: Harrell AV, Peterson GE, eds. *Drugs, Crime and Social Isolation.* Washington, DC: Urban Institute Press; 1992.

99. Anderson E. *Streetwise: Race, Class and Change in an Urban Community.* Chicago: University of Chicago Press; 1990.

100. Fagan J. Drug selling and licit income in distressed neighborhoods: the economic lives of street-level drug users and dealers. In: Harrell AV, Peterson GE, eds. *Drugs, Crime and Social Isolation.* Washington, DC: Urban Institute Press; 1992.

101. Fagan J, Wilkinson DL. 1998. "Guns, Youth Violence and Social Identity in Inner Cities." In M. Tonry and M. H. Moore (eds), *Youth Violence*. Chicago: University of Chicago Press.

102. Edberg M. AIDS risk behavior among runaway youth in the Washington, DC-Baltimore area. In: *Report of Multi-Site Runaway Risk Behavior Study*. Rockville, MD: National Institute on Drug Abuse; 1992.

103. Cook PJ, Laub JH. August 2001. *After the Epidemic: Recent Trends in Youth Violence in the United States*. Working Paper SAN01–22, Terry Sanford Institute of Public Policy. Durham, NC: Duke University.

104. Blumstein A. 1995. "Youth Violence, Guns and the Illicit-Drug Industry." *Journal of Criminal Law and Criminology* 86:10–36.

105. Blumstein A. 2001. "Why is Crime Falling?—Or Is It?" *Perspectives on Crime and Justice Lecture Series*. Washington, DC: National Institute of Justice.

106. Blumstein A, Wallman J (Eds.). 2000. *The Crime Drop in America*. New York: Cambridge University Press.

107. Spiegel I. 1995. *The Youth Gang Problem: A Community Approach*. New York: Oxford University Press.

108. Crick NR, Dodge KA. A review and reformulation of social information-processing mechanisms in children's social adjustment. *Psychol Bull.* 1994;115:74–101.

109. Crick NR, Dodge KA. Social information processing mechanisms in reactive and proactive aggression. *Child Dev.* 1996;67:993–1002.

110. Cole J, Dodge KA. (1998). Aggression and antisocial behavior. In W. Damon (Editor in Chief) and N. Eisenberg (Vol. Ed.), Handbook of child psychology, 5th edition. Volume 3. Social, emotional, and personality development. NY: John Wiley & Sons.

111. Huesmann LR, Guerra NG. Children's normative beliefs about aggression and aggressive behavior. *J Personality Soc Psychol.* 1997;72:408–419.

112. Farrington DP. The psychosocial milieu of the offender. In: Gunn J, Taylor PJ, eds. *Forensic Psychiatry: Clinical, Legal and Ethical Issues.* Oxford: Butterworth-Heinemann; 1995:252–285.

113. Lochman JE, Dodge KA. Social-cognitive processes of severely violent, moderately aggressive and non-aggressive boys. *J Consult Clin Psychol.* 1994;62:366–374.

114. Slaby RG, Guerra NG. Cognitive mediators of aggression in adolescent offenders: 1. Assessment. *Dev Psychol.* 1988;24:580–588.

115. Colder CR, Mott J, Levy S. 2000. "The Relation of Perceived Neighborhood Danger to Childhood Aggression." *American Journal of Community Psychology* 28(1):83–103.

116. UNAIDS. *2004 Report on the Global AIDS Epidemic*. Geneva, Switzerland: UNAIDS; 2004.

117. Piot P, Bartos M, Ghys PD, Walker N, Schwartlander B. The global impact of HIV/AIDS. *Nature.* 2001;410:968–973.

118. Auerbach JD, Wypijewska C, Brodie HKH. *AIDS and Behavior: An Integrated Approach*. Washington, DC: National Academy Press; 1994.

119. Centers for Disease Control and Prevention. *HIV/AIDS Surveillance Report, 2003*, Vol. 15. Atlanta, GA: U.S. Department of Health and Human Services, Centers for Disease Control and Prevention; 2004.

120. UNAIDS. *2006 Report on the Global AIDS Epidemic*. Geneva, Switzerland: UNAIDS; 2006.

121. Beyrer C, Jittiwootikarn J, Teokul W, et al. Drug use, increasing incarceration rates, and prison-associated HIV risks in Thailand. *AIDS Behav.* 2003;7(2):153; citing Ministry of Public Health, Thailand, *HIV/AIDS Sentinel Surveillance Report*. Bangkok; 2000.

122. UNAIDS Joint United Nations Programme on HIV/AIDS. *AIDS Epidemic Update: December 2003*. Geneva, Switzerland: UNAIDS; 2003.

123. Dehne KL, Pokrovskiy V, Kobyshcha Y, Scwartlander B. Update on the epidemics of AIDS and other sexually transmitted infections in the newly independent states of the former Soviet Union. *AIDS.* 2000;14(Suppl): S75–S84.

124. UNAIDS/WHO. *Epidemiological Fact Sheets on HIV/AIDS and Sexually Transmitted Infections, 2004 Update*. Geneva, Switzerland: UNAIDS; 2004.

125. World Bank, www.worldbank.org.

126. Chinese Bureau of Hygiene and Tropical Diseases. *AIDS Newsletter*. Beijing: Chinese Bureau of Hygiene and Tropical Diseases; 1996.

127. Chinese Ministry of Health, UNAIDS, and WHO. *2005 Update on the HIV Epidemic and Response in China*. Beijing: Chinese Ministry of Health; 2006.

128. Kelly JA, Amirkhanian YA, Kabakchieva E, et al. Gender roles and HIV sexual risk vulnerability of Roma (gypsies) men and women in Bulgaria and Hungary: an ethnographic study. *AIDS Care.* 2004;16(2):231–245.

SECTION II

On the Roots of Behavior—
A Multidisciplinary Survey

Social/Behavioral Theory and Its Roots

"We vivisect the nightingale
To probe the secret of his note"

—T.B. ALDRICH (1836–1907), AMERICAN WRITER

"No theory is good except on condition that one uses it to go beyond."

—ANDRE GIDE (1869–1951)

"It is difficult, if not impossible, for most people to think otherwise than in the fashion of their own period."

—GEORGE BERNARD SHAW (1856–1950)

THINKING ABOUT THEORY

You've heard this discussion before, perhaps in a science class or a philosophy class. Still, before we proceed to talk about theory we need to make sure we are proceeding with the same understandings about what it is we are talking about.

First of all, the idea of theory is most associated with its use in the context of the *scientific method*. Let's examine that, because its association with science gives the term a specific kind of meaning. Here, for example, is one definition of theory, specifically oriented to the way in which theory is put into practice in social science:

> [Theory is …] A set of interrelated constructs (concepts), definitions, and propositions that present a systematic view of phenomena by specifying relations among variables, with the purpose of explaining and predicting phenomena."[1]

The philosopher of science Karl Popper framed theory in the manner most commonly used today in scientific inquiry.[2] For Popper, a theory is a proposed explanatory solution to a problem. Most important, though, a theory's validity is not determined by proving the theory true, because that is easy to do (i.e., it is easy to come up with cases that confirm a theory). The true test is in *falsifying* a theory. Therefore, theory is an explanatory proposition that can be tested, and tested by falsification. If over time it is not falsified—assuming that it is tested in situations relevant to what the theory claims—then it remains part of the ongoing body of scientific knowledge. If it is falsified, then it can be either reworked or discarded. Either way, science is advanced.

Before going any further, however, let's take a look at what theory is in a more basic sense. Definitions of theory, boiled down to their essence, refer to a kind of *story* (I will use the broader term *account*). So, we can think of theory as an account that is said to explain something, and to posit connections between phenomena. For example:

"It is theorized that apples, and other physical objects, fall from trees because of a force called gravity which exerts that effect."

"It is theorized that certain substances, called carcinogens, cause cells in the human body to mutate and grow abnormally, out of control (in other words they are cancerous)."

From theories, you can derive more specific applications such as hypotheses, principles, and constructs. We are going to spend a little more time on these applications later in this chapter. But first let's focus on the general idea of theory as a story or account. It could be said that a key characteristic of modern humans from prehistoric times has been the creation of tales, myths, and stories that, for example, describe an entire cosmological system, explain the creation of society, explain how men and women came to be what they are, and so on. These are all theories in the broad sense, for they present a coherent account from which more specific judgments and conclusions can be drawn. So, if a theory says that men were created from fire and women from water, one could hypothesize, for example, that:

- Men are highly emotional and prone to conflict (fire), while women are better at solving or stopping conflicts (water on fire).
- Men are destructive, while women nourish.
- Men provide what is necessary to survive in adverse conditions (fire, warmth), while women provide the sustenance (water) necessary all the time.

Michel Foucault (1926-1984):

Basically, Foucault argued, in his many writings, that: 1) discourse—which refers to a broader category of the various modes of expression, including language, and how they are actually used—is the product of a historical period and its dominant social-economic institutions; and that 2) the discourse of a particular historical period incorporates a kind of system of rules for how to think about the world (what is true and false, normal or not normal, and so on). In the Modernist era of the Industrial Revolution and science, for example, the type of discourse associated with science *predisposes* us to think in terms of truth or falsity based on rational or empirical criteria.

Now we might hear this theory of the origin of men and women, and the various derivative hypotheses, and pass them off as mere "folk tales." But why? By what standards would we make such a judgment? We would say, most likely, that there is no proof for such things, and that they contradict known facts about the origins of gender.

Who is right?

The problem here is that evaluating the validity of a theory or specific proposition is, of necessity, based on some set of standards or rules by which to make such a judgment. In this sense, theories can be seen as "language games" like those described by philosopher Ludwig Wittgenstein,[3] or a type of statement that is part of the tautological *discourse* of science described by recent French philosopher Michel Foucault.[4-7]

They are propositions that have meaning, validity, and truth (or falsity) within a specific context, such as a historical context, a social context, or a cultural context. Within their contexts, they are commonly held to be meaningful. Thus, to understand why a particular theory is meaningful, or to evaluate its validity, you need to understand the contextual ground rules, so to speak. Understanding those ground rules is one of the most important tools you can have in making a good assessment of theories about human behavior and in deciding when and where those theories will be useful to you in a practical sense.

What, then, is the context in which we use theory? What are the ground rules?

THE CONTEXT OF THEORY IN THE WESTERN TRADITION

Let's start right out by stating that the term *theory* as it is commonly used derives its meaning from a context of Western philosophy and science—that is, the tradition originating with the Greek philosophers and carried through in various forms, largely in Europe and North America. To say so is not to privilege this understanding of theory, but simply to understand where it comes from so that its use can be *situated*—that is, placed in a social and historical context. Now of course, over the years this tradition has been influenced, amplified, and paralleled by currents of thought from outside its Euro-American mainstream, for example, by Islamic scholars Avicenna (ibn-Sina) and Averroes (ibn-Roshd), and Chinese philosophers Confucius (Figure 3-1), Chuang Tzu, and others. But for the most part, we are going to be talking about the concept of theory as a Western philosophical product.

Confucius's teachings are thought to have laid the groundwork for the "ideal man" including how man (and woman) should live and interact with others, and how man (and woman) should participate in society. *Source:* http://plato.stanford.edu/entries/confucius/

What does "the Western tradition" mean? Again, let's boil it down. Here are several key elements of the tradition that are relevant to understanding our use of theory.

Order and Regularity

It would be silly to suggest that the idea of *order* is unique to Western thought. All cultures have at their root ideas about the "natural order of things." This is truly a fundamental human characteristic. And some of the most important non-Western philosophies and systems of society, including Confucianism, Taoism, and Navajo cosmology, include highly elaborated concepts of natural order.

However, in Western society the idea of order took a specific turn that fed directly into the development of science. The progressive discovery of an assumed order underlying nature, combined with the *practical application of that knowledge to human ends*, has been the focus of Western philosophy and science at least since the early Greeks. Somewhere around the 4th century BCE, Democritus began to conceptualize the world as being composed of what he called "atoms," discrete bits of matter that have size, shape, and solidity. Aristotle, in a series of astounding works, analyzed the logic of language, and, among other intellectual feats, explicated a scheme for categorizing and understanding natural phenomena based on concepts of matter and form, motion, space, and time.[8] In contrast to other seminal Greek philosophers such as Plato, however, Aristotle emphasized ordering (classification) systems that would have *practical* application. Other early Greeks were involved in the search for order as well, including a number of mathematicians such as Pythagoras and Euclid.

In the Middle Ages, roughly the period from the fall of the Roman Empire in the 5th century ACE to the 15th century ACE, inquiry into the order of nature was treated as synonymous with understanding divine order. This is not surprising, because a key characteristic of the Middle Ages was a monopoly of knowledge and scholarship by the church. Thus, Thomas Aquinas (in *Summa Theologica*, transcribed in the 13th century) argues for the coexistence of philosophy, created by human reason, and theology, revealed knowledge that exceeds human reason and must be accepted on faith. His proof of the existence of God, for example, includes the argument that the order inherent in the natural world presupposes a being that created the order.

The explosion of scientific discovery in the period known as the Enlightenment (in general, the 17th–18th cen-

FIGURE 3-1 Confucius (551–479 BCE)

Source: Picture downloaded from: http://en.wikipedia.org/wiki/Confucius

turies) represented a fundamental break from church control over knowledge and theory. This came about for a number of reasons: the invention of the printing press in the 15th century and the resulting spread of literacy; exploration of new lands bringing evidence of human and geographic diversity; discoveries in astronomy that revealed other planets and suggested that the earth was not the center of the universe (e.g., Galileo); the rise of natural philosophers like Locke, Voltaire, Rousseau, and others; and new directions in art during the Renaissance. During the Enlightenment, the locus of explanation for natural phenomena shifted from the divine to the secular—to what was viewed as the primacy of reason and worldly evidence. Importantly, the rise in secular and rationalistic explanations also coincided with the beginnings of the Industrial Revolution, and the shift in power from the church and monarchy to those who exploited science and technology for the production of goods.

Yet the focus on order and regularity remained; the universe could be viewed through the metaphor of a mechanical clock whose gears clicked and turned inexorably, in autonomous, infinite repetition. Scientific inquiry abounded with the discovery of new laws; Newton and the law of gravity is a classic example. As scientific discovery grew, domains of inquiry that were once unified as natural philosophy or natural science began to diverge into discrete "fields"—biology, physics, astronomy, and later sociology, anthropology, and psychology. The latter three fields, focusing more on the study of human beings and society, sought to (and still do) develop as sciences in the same way as the physical sciences. Foreshadowed by Francis Bacon and later Voltaire, Auguste Comte and others in the 19th century pushed for a science of humanity that would discover and use laws of human behavior—order and regularity—for the development of society. This general view was called *positivism*.

> *Positivism:* The philosophical tradition asserting that knowledge is based on natural phenomena and their properties and relations as verified by the empirical sciences.

Not all scientists or thinkers agreed with this trend, and in a debate that continues to resonate today, the human sciences were and remain split by controversies about whether they should conceptualize themselves in the same way as the physical sciences, or as something different in important ways (see the work of Schiller, Dilthey, Husserl, as well more recent postmodern thinkers such as Foucault and others). In any case, *the idea of theory today is inseparable from the idea of order.*

Predictability

In a sense, predictability is the child of order and regularity, for if nature is ordered, and we discover the details and rules of this order, then we can, theoretically, *predict* what will happen. By now, this idea is so ingrained in our common sense knowledge that few people actually stop to think that it is itself an idea. But every night, when we listen to the weather report, we have an expectation that someone is using science to make accurate (more or less) *predictions* about the weather tomorrow or over the next week. When we go to the doctor and get a prescription, we assume that the doctor has diagnosed the trouble and, based on science, is predicting that a 10-day course of the prescribed medication will alleviate or cure the problem.

It was Auguste Comte (1798–1857) who really institutionalized this as a goal for the social or human sciences. He argued that human beings had gone through three stages of thought on the road to modern science: the theological, attributing events and phenomena to the supernatural; the metaphysical, attributing phenomena to fundamental

energies or ideas; and the positive, where phenomena are explained by observation, hypothesis, and experimentation.[9] In Comte's view, the orderly application of a positivistic approach would eventually lead to an ability to predict and thus shape society.

Empirical Data

Here is where we have to bring in an important word—*epistemology*. Basically, epistemology refers to ideas about how we know what we know. For example: Do we know something to be true because we see it and can touch it? Do we know something is true because the thought exists in our mind? Do we know it is true because somewhere in a sacred text it is said to be true? These three questions actually represent three major trends in thought about how we know what we know—the first corresponds to *empiricism*, the second corresponds to *rationalism*, and the third corresponds to a *theologic* or *deist* orientation.

The scientific tradition in which the concept of theory developed is rooted in the *empiricist* tradition of John Locke and David Hume, both British empiricists. The epistemology underlying empiricism is encapsulated by the idea that *what we know comes to us from our senses*. We perceive an objective reality that is "out there" to be perceived, and our ideas about existence stem from those perceptions. This is in contrast to the *rationalist* tradition (from Descartes) in which *reality is based in our mind (not an objective world "out there")*, or the *phenomenological* tradition (e.g., William Dilthey, Edmund Husserl), which argues that because it is individuals who do the perceiving, and individual perception is necessarily influenced by both biology and one's own life experiences, culture, and history, that perception is never objective, but subjective; therefore, what we know of reality can never extend beyond our experience of it. Reality is then not objective, but an *experienced* reality.

Science in the empiricist tradition has thus relied on the collection of observable, tangible data as evidence for statements about reality. In keeping with the ideas of order and predictability, then, a theory in this tradition is supposed to say something about the *observable, tangible* relationships between phenomena—relationships that are evidence-based. In later chapters, we will see how this "standard of evidence" is embedded in almost all the theoretical approaches we will study, and we will also ask if that is always enough.

Progress and Perfectability

Progress in some form or another is part of many cultural traditions of thought. In Buddhist or Hindu cultures, for example, progress entails the recycling of one's soul, one's karma, through reincarnation, until the soul reaches a state of enlightenment or nirvana. In Western culture, the idea of progress has some roots that sound very similar. In Plato's seminal philosophical work, the *Republic*, there is the famous allegory of the cave, in which the path to true knowledge is represented by a journey from the depths of a cave where all is shadow and image (not the "real thing"), to the final stage of emergence out into the light, where it is possible to see the true essence (the "Form") of things.

Francis Bacon, philosopher, one-time Lord Chancellor in England, and grand intellectual reformer of the late 16th and early 17th centuries, proposed (in several treatises on the advancement of learning) to replace the entire existing intellectual framework, which consisted of unchallenged superstition, philosophy, and style over substance, with a new paradigm emphasizing empiricism, progress, and the practical use of knowledge.[10-12]

Almost every major scientific and social thinker from the Enlightenment onward has incorporated the assumption of progress as an essential part of their theories. You can certainly say this about, for example, Charles Darwin and evolutionary theory; Herbert Spencer and Social Darwinism; G.W. Friedrich Hegel and the historical progression of spirit; social theorists Karl Marx, Max Weber, and Emile Durkheim and their respective ideas about the stages through which societies evolve; and psychologists such as Sigmund Freud and Erik Erikson and the stages of psychological development. For all these thinkers, time does not stand still.

In short, the assumption of progress is an integral part of our way of thinking. For the endeavor we call science, and the meaning of theory, it is impossible to separate progress out. "Doing science" by definition involves a continuous accumulation of knowledge, leading towards a more and more expansive understanding of our world. Proposing and testing theory is an essential part of this process, where theory is the "tactic" used to generate scientific investigation, and to build knowledge.

From this description, can you see how theory, in this context, incorporates concepts of order, predictability, empirical data, and progress?

ANTECEDENTS

Let's now review a range of more specific theoretical antecedents to current behavioral theory as it is employed in public health. The primary fields from which public health behavioral theory have been derived are psychology and social psychology, so we will begin with these, then proceed briefly to several other fields, including ecology, sociology, anthropology, and others that have made important contributions.

A Sample of Thinkers in the Western Tradition

- *Plato and Aristotle:* Classical Greek philosophers, focusing on wide-ranging themes from ethics to the nature of social organization, the composition of matter, the classification of knowledge, and much more.
- *Rene Descartes:* French philosopher and progenitor of the *rationalist* tradition.
- *John Locke and David Hume:* English philosophers and representatives of the *empiricist* tradition.
- *Auguste Comte:* Originator of the idea of a "science of society."
- *Edmund Husserl and William Dilthey:* Proponents of the tradition of *phenomenology*.
- *Charles Darwin:* Key founder (with others) of evolutionary theory and natural selection.
- *Emile Durkheim (sociology), Franz Boas (anthropology), Sigmund Freud (psychology):* Influential social theorists of the early 20th century.
- *Karl Popper:* Philosopher of science and champion of the scientific method.
- *Michel Foucault:* French philosopher of the mid-20th century who elucidated the connections among language, power, and thought.

Psychology/Social Psychology

As in any discipline today, there are numerous subfields and subdisciplines. This is also true for psychology, but certain subfields have had the most impact on behavioral theory in public health. *Freudian psychology*, for example, has not left much of a mark in this respect. But *behavioral, cognitive, ecological,* and *humanistic* psychological theory have all made significant contributions, as has *social psychology*.

Behaviorist Psychology

This is an early school of psychology dating from the late 19th century in which behavior is said to be learned or conditioned through the action of stimulus-response mechanisms. Little importance is placed on the thinking process itself, or such things as emotion, because human beings are treated as organisms and the most important process is considered to be the impact of an environment on what were viewed as the brain's *reflexive* responses. Internal mental processes are thus treated as a kind of "black box," where a stimulus is applied and a behavior results. The first behaviorists were Russian, including the seminal researcher Ivan Pavlov (1849–1936). Pavlov designed an experiment using an approach that has come to be called *classical conditioning*. He rang a bell at the same time that he placed meat powder on a dog's tongue (which caused the dog to salivate). After repeating this a number of times, he tried ringing the bell alone, with no meat powder. The dog salivated anyway, demonstrating the effect of the *conditioned stimulus* of the bell, which had become associated with the meat powder. In the United States, Edward Thorndike and John Watson were well-known early behaviorists.

B.F. Skinner (1904–1990) developed the modern approach to conditioning, known as *operant conditioning*.[13] Still based on the same basic assumptions about the reflexive responses that connect behavior to environment, this form of conditioning involves a number of steps and processes: A specific behavior is conditioned through the application of positive and negative reinforcers associated with the behavior. Reinforcers, however, can be provided at various intervals or *schedules* that have different effects in terms of maintaining the behavior, and a behavior can be learned through *shaping*—by reinforcing approximations of the behavior that keep getting closer and closer to the actual behavior. Behaviors can also be *deconditioned*. The approach as a whole is referred to as *behavior modification*.

Behaviorist approaches are currently used as therapy in smoking cessation and other addiction treatments. Importantly, for our purposes, the basic assumptions about learning behavior through positive and negative reinforcement appear in a number of health behavior theories.

Cognitive Psychology

As its name suggests, cognitive psychology focuses on the thinking process itself as the source of behavior. So, in contrast to behaviorism which views internal mental processes as insignificant, the inside of the black box is of interest this time. The thinking process as addressed in cognitive psychology includes perception, memory, decision making, interpretation, reasoning, and judgment, among other faculties.

According to Jean Piaget, one of the most influential thinkers in this school, there are two key ways in which we process information: *assimilation*, fitting new information into existing categories of knowledge, and *accommodation*, changing/adapting existing beliefs to incorporate new information.[14-17] Piaget is also famous for his theory on the stages of cognitive development: sensorimotor, preoperational, concrete operational, and formal operational.

Cognitive psychology is an important part of such behavioral theories as the Health Belief Model, Theory of Planned Behavior, and Social-Cognitive Theory (among others), all of which assume that internal processes, to one degree or another, determine behavior. This includes calculations of risk and benefit, expectations related to outcome, and so on.

Humanistic Psychology

In part a reaction to what some perceived as the mechanistic and determinist character of behaviorism, cognitive psychology, and Freudian psychology, the development of humanistic psychology drew on a philosophical tradition that emphasizes individual *agency*, the capacity of people to make choices and determine their future. The basic belief or assumption underlying humanistic psychology is that human beings ultimately desire to grow and attain their potential. However, as Abraham Maslow articulated in his famous *hierarchy of needs*,[18] before people can pursue this kind of higher-level growth, they must first be able to satisfy a set of needs, from basic physiological to emotional and social.

Although the ties between this approach and a specific public health theory are not always direct, it is clearly a general influence on the "philosophy" of public health, commonly expressed in definitions of public health or health promotion as the goal of improving *quality of life* for the general public, or goals related to the promotion of *healthy lifestyles* and *healthy choices*. Thus health promotion, in part, involves the promotion of conditions, including the satisfaction of basic needs such as housing, employment, and access to health care, which allow people to live healthier (higher quality) lives.

Social Psychology

Although the discipline of psychology as a whole is concerned with the mental processes and behaviors of individuals, the branch known as social psychology is concerned about how individuals (and their mental processes) interact with their social surroundings—groups, relationships, and other social units. This may include inquiries regarding issues of group dynamics, authority and legitimacy, emotion and its expression, aggression, self and identity, motivation, gender, group prejudices (the process of "othering"), norms, attitudes, and other related topics. Health behavior, as we saw in the first chapter, is often complex and motivated by social factors, so the subject matter of social psychology is clearly related to a number of behavioral theories and approaches in public health.

Like everything else we have been discussing, we can't possibly cover the whole of social psychology, so we will have to pick out a few individuals or approaches for illustrative purposes. One important issue is the nature of social influence on individual behavior; for example, the famous experiments on authority and obedience conducted by psychologist Stanley Milgram[19,20] in which he tested the willingness of individuals to administer a harmful electric shock to other individuals if instructed to do so by persons who were presented as "authorities." The results of this study were widely publicized and raised considerable questions about people's willingness to set aside their own moral judgments in order to obey or conform to authority. Other studies have looked at the effect of belonging to groups on conformity of behavior and thought. Irving Janis,[21,22] for example, investigated the phenomenon of "groupthink" in government decision making; Crandall[23] investigated the same phenomenon in terms of its effect on eating disorders within a sorority.

Another area of focus has to do with attitudes and behavior. Attitudes are complex connections of belief, identity, and social relations. Social psychologists have been interested for a considerable period of time in the relationships between attitudes and behavior and the consistency of attitudes. Two early positions included the idea that when behaviors contradict attitudes (*dissonance*), people tend to rationalize or adjust their attitudes in order to address the dissonance between attitudes and behavior.[24] Another view held that people infer their attitudes over time from experiences about how they behave in similar situations.[25] Very much related to specific health behavior theories we will be discussing in later chapters, psychologists Martin Fishbein and Icek Ajzen proposed *intentions* as an intermediate factor between attitudes and behavior, where attitudes are one of several factors (including perceived norms/opinions of significant others) that act on intentions.[26,27]

Social Sciences: Sociology, Cultural Anthropology

Sociology and anthropology have some similarities in that both fields focus on the social, societal, or cultural aspects of behavior in contrast to the more individual focus of psychology. Neither are clinical disciplines; thus, research and theory rely on different methods and approaches than are found in psychology, but from there they differ. Sociology has generally focused more on domestic social phenomena, whereas cultural anthropology has addressed both global and domestic themes, often in a comparative manner. Sociologists are more interested in social groups, social hierarchies, social structures, and the nature of social interaction. Cultural anthropologists are interested more in the role of culture in human behavior, in the ways in which life patterns are organized, in systems of knowledge and belief, and in the language, symbols, and other ways we "represent" life and its meaning.

Influences from sociology on public health include:

- *The influence and role of social structure and class on the paths available to individuals:* Karl Marx, Friedrich Engels, Max Weber, and many others have written about the ways in which societies are divided by class; more recently, theorists like Pierre Bourdieu[28] have looked at the way in which class/social position becomes part of one's practical understanding about what to expect in terms of day-to-day life (including health). This has also played a role in concepts about social *ecologies* and their role in health.
- *The influence of the group on behavior:* Group *norms* and conformity. There is overlap here with social psychology; however, these issues are very important to later developments in health behavior theory. Emile Durkheim,[29] among others, had a tremendous early influence on the discussion of social conformity.
- *Social capital:* The social networks and resources one has, and how these influence access to education, jobs, health care, and other social benefits.[30-32]
- *Social organization:* Durkheim,[29] Weber,[33,34] and others contributed significantly to theory and analysis of the ways in which society is structured, the ways in which labor is divided, and the nature of and motivation for social action.

Anthropology has, since early in the history of the discipline, addressed issues related to public health.[*] In the early 20th century, Franz Boas laid the groundwork in his fight to counter racist stereotypes and to help the public understand varieties of cultural patterns on their own terms. Margaret Mead, perhaps the most public of anthropologists, utilized her research on childrearing, adolescence, and gender issues to influence the debate here in the United States about how to understand and work with adolescents (among other issues).

A number of anthropologists in the mid-20th century, including Ruth Benedict, Margaret Mead, Abram Kardiner, Cora DuBois, John and Beatrice Whiting, Irving Hallowell, and Anthony F.C. Wallace, focused their work on the connections between culture and personality, and its expression as behavior. This line of inquiry continued with cognitive and psychological anthropologists such as Ward Goodenough, Roy D'Andrade, Melford Spiro, Claudia Strauss, Dorothy

---

[*] Anthropology as a whole encompasses four subfields: sociocultural anthropology, archaeology, physical (biological) anthropology, and anthropological linguistics. Cultural anthropology and physical anthropology have had the most interaction with issues of public health.

Holland, and Naomi Quinn, who have looked, for example, at *cultural models* people refer to in patterning their behavior. Other directions in anthropology, for example the *materialist* tradition exemplified by the work of Marvin Harris, have focused more on the relationship between human behavior and systems of production.

Influences of cultural anthropology on public health theory and practice include:

- *The holistic approach to health (and other) behavior reflected in what is known as the ecological model.*[35] This refers to the idea that human behavior can never properly be understood outside of the social, cultural, and situational context in which it occurs, as we saw in our introductory chapter.

- *The idea of cultural competency* or *culturally appropriate (health) programs and care:* Health, concepts of what is healthy or not healthy, classifications of disease and/or illness and the causes of diseases and illnesses, what kinds of treatments are appropriate and who are the health providers, and how to interact with someone who is ill are heavily influenced by culture. Given the diversity of patient populations, understanding what kinds of health beliefs and practices a patient brings and how to interact with diverse populations is a very important part of the development of health promotion and treatment programs.

- *The relationship of specific cultural settings and practices to health problems:* Anthropologists like Merrill Singer[36] and Paul Farmer[37,38] have been deeply involved in research underscoring the link between conditions of poverty and oppression and the spread of HIV/AIDS. Mark Nichter is well known for his work on culture and adolescent smoking,[39] among

other issues. Arthur Kleinman has been a pioneer in exploring and presenting the sociocultural nature of disease and illness, and how these are experienced and treated across cultures.[40]

Ecology and Biological Systems

In a different vein, the fields of ecology and human ecology have influenced the way in which health behavior is currently conceptualized as an outcome of a complex system of influences from several domains (e.g., policy and regulation, sociocultural factors, the physical environment, and individual factors). This is known as the *ecological model,*[35,41,42] and it is the prevalent general framework in public health for understanding health behavior. (Remember? We referred to it in Chapter 1.)

Ecology is the study, within the general field of biology, of the ways in which living organisms function within systems. The food chain is an obvious example: Many different organisms depend on other organisms and a specific physical environment for their existence. When there is a disruption in the system, say, if one organism becomes extinct or a crucial body of water dries up, the entire system and its organisms are affected. Human ecology applies the same focus to the ways in which humans function as a part of a biophysical and social environment. In other words, human existence cannot be conceptualized as separate from the environment in which we live. From both fields, the general principle is the same: *Life, and the behavior of living organisms, exists within interdependent systems.*

The idea of ecology should help you tie together all the kinds of theories and approaches we will cover in this book, in the sense that each theory is useful in describing or understanding a piece of the puzzle. Yet it is the way that the pieces work together that is the key.

Chapter Questions

1. Define *theory*. Why is a theory like a story?

2. The term *theory* as we know it takes its meaning from a Western tradition of philosophy and science that has four main tenets. What are they?

3. What are the "schools of thought" in psychology that contributed to modern behavioral theory?

4. What are some contributions from the social sciences—sociology and anthropology—on modern behavioral theory?

5. Why, as public health practitioners, is it important for us to understand the concepts of social psychology? Anthropology?

6. How has the study of natural systems contributed an important concept to modern behavioral theory in public health?

7. Why is it important to develop health promotion programs within the context of an ecological model?

REFERENCES

1. Kerlinger, FN. (1986). *Foundations of behavioral research* (3rd ed.). New York: Holt, Rinehart and Winston.

2. Popper K. *Conjectures and Refutations.* London: Routledge and Kegan Paul; 1963.

3. Wittgenstein L. *Philosophical Investigations.* New York: Macmillan; 1965.

4. Foucault M. *The Archaeology of Knowledge.* Sheridan Smith AM, trans. New York: Harper Colophon; 1972.

5. Foucault M. *The Birth of the Clinic: An Archaeology of Medical Perception.* Sheridan Smith AM, trans. New York: Vintage/Random House; 1976.

6. Foucault M. *Discipline and Punish: The Birth of the Prison.* Sheridan A, trans. New York: Vintage/Random House; 1979.

7. Foucault M. *Power/Knowledge: Selected Interviews & Other Writings, 1972–1977.* Gordon C, ed. Gordon C, Marshall L, Mepham L, Soper K, trans. New York: Pantheon Books; 1980.

8. Aristotle. *The Complete Works of Aristotle: The Revised Oxford Translation.* Barnes J, ed. Princeton University Press; 1984.

9. *The Columbia Encyclopedia,* 6th ed. Comte, Auguste. New York: Columbia University Press; 2001.

10. Gaukroger S. *Francis Bacon and the Transformation of Early-Modern Philosophy.* New York: Cambridge University Press; 2001.

11. Vickers B. ed. *Francis Bacon.* New York: Oxford University Press; 1996.

12. Whitney C. *Francis Bacon and Modernity.* New Haven, CT: Yale University Press; 1986.

13. Skinner BF. *Walden II.* New York: Macmillan; 1948.

14. Piaget J. *The Child's Conception of the World.* New York: Harcourt, Brace Jovanovich; 1929.

15. Piaget J. *The Moral Judgment of the Child.* New York: Harcourt, Brace Jovanovich; 1932.

16. Piaget J. *The Mechanisms of Perception.* London: Rutledge & Kegan Paul; 1969.

17. Piaget J. *The Science of Education and the Psychology of the Child.* New York: Grossman; 1970.

18. Maslow A. *Motivation and Personality,* 3rd ed. New York: Harper; 1987.

19. Milgram S. Behavioral study of obedience. *J Abnorm Soc Psychol.* 1963;67:371–378.

20. Milgram S. *Obedience to Authority.* New York: Harper & Row; 1974.

21. Janis IL. *Victims of Groupthink.* Boston, MA: Houghton Mifflin; 1972.

22. Janis IL. *Groupthink: Psychological Studies of Policy Decisions and Fiascoes,* 2nd ed. Boston, MA: Houghton Mifflin; 1982.

23. Crandall CS. Social contagion and binge eating. *J Pers Soc Psychol.* 1988;55:588–598.

24. Festinger L, Carlsmith JM. Cognitive consequences of food compliance. *J Abnorm Soc Psychol.* 1959;58:203–210.

25. Bem D. An experimental analysis of self-persuasion. *J Exp Soc Psychol.* 1965;1:199–218.

26. Fishbein M, Azjen I. Attitudes towards objects as a predictor of single and multiple behavioral criteria. *Psychol Rev.* 1974;81:59–74.

27. Fishbein M, Azjen I. *Belief, Attitude, Intention, Behavior: An Introduction to Theory and Research.* Reading, MA: Addison Wesley; 1975.

28. Bourdieu P. *Outline of a Theory of Practice.* Cambridge: Cambridge University Press; 1977.

29. Durkheim E. *The Division of Labor in Society.* New York: Free Press; 1893/1997.

30. Bourdieu P. The forms of capital. In: Richardson J, ed., *Handbook of Theory and Research for the Sociology of Education.* New York: Macmillan; 1986:

31. Coleman JS. Social capital in the creation of human capital. *Am J Sociol.* 1988;94(Suppl):S95–S120.

32. Putnam R. *Bowling Alone: The Collapse and Revival of American Community.* New York: Simon and Schuster; 2000.

33. Weber M. *Economy and Society.* Roth G, Wittich C, trans/eds. New York: Bedminster Press; 1968.

34. Weber M. *Essays in Sociology.* Gerth HH, Mills CW, eds. New York: Oxford University Press; 1958.

35. Green LW, Kreuter MW, eds. *Health Promotion Planning: An Educational and Environmental Approach,* 3rd ed. Mountain View, CA: Mayfield; 1999.

36. Singer M. AIDS and the health crisis of the urban poor: The perspective of critical medical anthropology. *Soc Sci Med.* 1994;39(7):931–948.

37. Farmer P. *Infections and Inequalities.* Berkeley: University of California Press; 1998.

38. Farmer P. *Pathologies of Power.* Berkeley: University of California Press; 2003.

39. Nichter M. Smoking: what's culture got to do with it? *Addiction.* 2003;98(Suppl 1):139–145.

40. Kleinman A. *Patients and Healers in the Context of Culture: An Exploration of the Borderland Between Anthropology, Medicine and Psychiatry.* Berkeley: University of California Press; 1981.

41. Bronfenbrenner U. *The Ecology of Human Development.* Cambridge, Mass.: Harvard University Press; 1979.

42. Lewin K. In: Cartwright D, ed. *Field Theory in Social Science: Selected Theoretical Papers.* New York: Harper & Row; 1951.

Individual Health Behavior Theories

LEARNING OBJECTIVES

By the end of this chapter, the reader will be able to:

- Describe key behavioral theories focusing on the individual—the Health Belief Model, Theory of Reasoned Action, Theory of Planned Behavior, Trans-Theoretical Model, and the Precaution Adoption Process Model
- Understand how these individual-oriented theories might be applied
- Understand selected critiques of these theories

"No man* is an island, entire of itself; every man is a piece of the continent, a part of the main."

—JOHN DONNE, *DEVOTIONS UPON EMERGENT OCCASIONS,* **1624**

WHAT ARE WE TALKING ABOUT?

Now that you have a sense for the roots of behavioral theory in public health, we'll start by taking a look at a selection of theories commonly used in public health research and programming that focus on the *individual* as the primary source of behavior. This may seem obvious—*of course* it is individuals who generate their own behavior! We aren't robots!

No we are not. But let's go back to the story of the roommate and his possible motives for brushing his teeth. He was certainly making decisions and acting as an individual, but the information he used to make his decisions, the situation that was motivating him, and aspects of his family upbring-

---

* Or woman, of course. This quote is from the 17th century.

ing that influenced his "toothbrushing habit" all involved complex interconnections with a social world.

So it is for the theories we will be discussing in this chapter. These are theories that focus on the thought processes *individuals* go through before taking a health-related action. Although the focus is on what happens within individuals, it is important to remember the context. The decisions people make to take or not take an action are based on cues, references, and information from their social, physical, and cultural environment. No person, as the poet John Donne said, is an island.

THE HEALTH BELIEF MODEL (HBM)

Origins and Basic Elements

The first of these individual theories we will talk about is called the *Health Belief Model*, or *HBM*.[3-5] We are discussing this one first in part because it is the oldest of the individual behavioral theories used in public health, and also because it is one of the most widely used in public health.

The HBM originated in the 1950s from the work of U.S. Public Health Service (USPHS) social psychologists Godfrey Hochbaum, Irwin Rosenstock, and Stephen Kegels.[6] The theory was developed in response to a very practical question. The USPHS sponsored free tuberculosis screening (via x-ray) in mobile clinics that were placed right in neighborhoods. You would think that a lot of people would come and get screened, because of the free screening and convenient access, right? But very few people did, so Hochbaum conducted research to find out why turnout was so low, given the easy access. In conducting this research, the larger issue that he investigated was motivation—what motivated people

What *Is* an Individual?

Here's a philosophical question for you: Just what is an individual?

You may think this is a no-brainer. An individual, you say, is, like me, an autonomous self that has a distinct physical unity (me, my body, and I), a personality, a way of talking, a way of walking, my own goals, my own motivations, and the ability to plan, initiate, and carry out action. You know, ME.

Okay, but let's just look at that for a second. We can start with that body of yours. Your physical being, as you know, is genetic—it comes from parents and other ancestors. So, yes, it's you, but, it's kind of them too. Now let's go to that personality. Some of that may have genetic influences too. But your personality, your way of talking, walking, dressing, and all that . . . you didn't think all of that up from scratch, did you? You got it from somewhere. Just like the musician who is called a "unique" sax player, you pulled together pieces of "how to be," kind of like those riffs on the sax. You put them together in your own way. But most of those pieces didn't magically appear. They came from the social and cultural world around you, including your family; the examples of "how to be male" or "how to be female" that you saw in your personal life; on television, videos, or film; from the tales, stories, songs, and other narratives about people who were good versus people who were not; what a good life consists of; lessons and advice from family, community, and faith organizations; people you have seen who have a style or a "look" that you like and want to emulate; and so on!

It's not so easy to draw a clear line between yourself and everyone else. Of course you take all these influences and shape them, "inhabit" them as your individual life. Yet this process inexorably connects you to your world, and complicates easy descriptions of individual behavior and motivation. Think about this when we discuss the individual behavior theories in this chapter.*

---

* If you are interested in this issue, there is a lot written about it, and it is worth knowing that there is a great variety across cultures in how the idea of the "individual" is conceptualized. Louis Dumont,[1,2] for example, makes a distinction between societies that are said to be constructed of individuals (where the individual is the key, autonomous unit) versus societies that are the *source* from which individuals come (and where society is thereby viewed as more important than the individual).

to come out and get screened? His initial conclusions were that people were most likely to get an x-ray if: 1) they thought they were at risk, or *susceptible* to tuberculosis; and 2) they believed there was a benefit in early detection of tuberculosis.

This was the nucleus of the theory. In its early formulation, health seeking and other health behavior was thought to be motivated by four factors:

1. Perceived susceptibility
2. Perceived severity
3. Perceived benefits of an action
4. Perceived barriers to taking that action

As more research was conducted about the HBM and its applicability, and as it was used to develop and implement programs across a number of health issues such as patient adherence to medical treatment, prevention behavior, and participation in health screenings, two more components were added to the theory. First was the idea that *cues to action* were needed as direct motivation to act. In 1988, the influence of what was then called Social Learning Theory[7,8] (see the discussion in Chapter 5) led to the addition of the sixth component—a person's belief in his or her ability to take the action, commonly referred to as *self-efficacy*.

The following are the current components of the HBM. When reading these components, think of them as parts of a *theoretical statement*. So, the statement would read: Person X—let's call her Jane—will engage in a given preventive or healthy behavior *if*:

- She thinks she is *susceptible* to the specific health problem the behavior will prevent. In other words, Jane believes she is potentially at risk.
- She thinks the health problem is *severe*; that is, she believes that if she gets it, the consequences will be severe.
- She thinks that taking preventive action will do some good. So, for Jane there are *perceived benefits* in taking the action.
- She thinks that there aren't too many negative consequences if she takes the action, that there is not a lot standing in the way. The *perceived barriers* are low.
- Something happens that gives her a "push" to act—a friend is diagnosed with the disease, she sees a television program about it, and so on. In other words, Jane experiences a *cue to action*.
- She believes she is capable of taking the action—that she has the skills, the will, and whatever else is necessary. She has *self-efficacy* with respect to the action.

Table 4-1 summarizes these components.

Finally, the HBM is known as a *value expectancy* model, which basically refers to the assumption that people will engage in healthy behavior if 1) they *value the outcome* (being healthy) related to the behavior, and 2) they think that the behavior is likely to result in that outcome.

Using the HBM

To use the HBM in a health promotion program, you can think of the six components or constructs as "levers" to employ as influences on behavior. They provide guidance in structuring a program. But they can't be used just as is, without further specification. Here's why: Suppose you were concerned about a group of serious urban blues musicians who were heavy smokers and you wanted to encourage them to quit smoking. You set out to conduct a health promotion campaign using the HBM, and begin developing informational materials straight from the six constructs:

- You develop some brochures and Internet materials that contain very clear information about the *risks* and the *severity* of lung, throat, and other cancers, as well as emphysema, that are caused by smoking. You even throw in a few graphic pictures. Okay, so you've hit on the first two constructs.

- Now to the second two. You put together some flyers, posters, Web ads, and even radio spots advertising a number of quit-smoking programs and products that are relatively inexpensive or covered by insurance, and promise that clients will be smoke-free in a month. You're trying to show that the *costs* of quitting are *low*. Then, in the same flyers, posters, and ads, you include testimonials from people who've quit, and who are ever so happy about their new healthy state of being. You include those because you are trying to show that the *benefits* are *great*. Four constructs down, two to go.

- Now you need a *cue to action*. Hmm . . . what will you use? Luckily, you find out that a famous musician recently died of cancer. You are, somehow, able to get some quotes from his wife saying that "if only he had quit" and so on. You put that information in blues clubs and music stores, figuring that it ought to inspire some action. Now you just have one construct to go.

- For *self-efficacy*, you put together a brief steps-to-quitting booklet entitled "One Two Three Quit," congratulating yourself on the music-related title. Then you send out some trained "quit coaches" to provide a free starter demonstration at local YMCAs and at the meeting of the local musicians union.

TABLE 4-1 Components of the Health Belief Model (HBM)

Behavior is an outcome of ...	
Perceived Susceptibility	The degree to which a person feels at risk for a health problem.
Perceived Severity	The degree to which a person believes the consequences of the health problem will be severe.
Perceived Benefits	The positive outcomes a person believes will result from the action.
Perceived Barriers	The negative outcomes a person believes will result from the action.
Cues to Action	An external event that motivates a person to act.
Self-Efficacy	A person's belief in his or her ability to take action.

Got all the constructs covered, wouldn't you say? Do you think it will work? After all, you took the HBM by the book and plugged it right into your program components.

But suppose you follow up three months later and find out that: 1) not one of the musicians has quit, or even tried; 2) most of your pamphlets, flyers, and other information have been tossed or not used; and 3) barely a handful of people came to the *free* quitting demonstrations. What on earth happened, you ask?

You just succumbed to the "EZ program structure illusion." We're going to be talking about that a lot in this book. Basically, whenever you consider a behavioral theory or framework, remember that when you learn it or read about it, the theory is typically presented in the abstract. The constructs need to be shaped by real-world information before you can even begin to use it or understand whether or not it is effective. Human behavior in reality is complex. The real world won't usually let itself be plugged into a theory so easily.

The key to avoiding the EZ program structure illusion is to do some *research* and to *target your program, and the theory, to the people you are trying to help.* Second, don't think of the theory as the *complete story*. It is *a tool, a guideline, and a framework* to help you develop an effective program. It is your job to use theory as appropriate, and to keep a critical eye on the match between the theory or theories and what you see out there.

All right, let's say you want to give HBM a try again as a framework for structuring your smoking cessation program targeting the blues musicians. In order to make constructs like "costs/benefits to quitting" or "perceived severity" meaningful, you have to get a handle on what exactly would be a cost for these musicians. So, you may do some interviews with blues musicians and find out that: 1) hardly any of them have insurance; and 2) getting a gig, and a regular one, is so precious that losing playing time, even if only a month, to go to some quit-smoking program could set someone back many months in terms of trying to maintain a reputation with the club owners who pay them to play and with the audiences that they need to come hear them. That puts your "EZ" cost/benefit pamphlets and flyers in perspective, doesn't it? Of course the musicians aren't going to pay attention! Remember, you claimed that the quit-smoking programs were relatively inexpensive or covered by insurance, and that many of them require about a month's time. Your target population has neither the insurance coverage nor the time for such things. And, importantly, the *real cost* was seen as *losing gigs*. This may be more of an immediate concern than the long term risk of getting cancer. So instead of showing them the risks of smoking, you've actually shown them the risk of participating in a quit-smoking program.

In addition, say you also learn, from going to a few blues clubs, spending a little time with the musicians, and doing a few more interviews, that smoking is not only prevalent among most of the musicians, but it is kind of a social ritual. It's just part of how fellow musicians talk, play their guitars, and present themselves as part of the musicians' world. So that picture of a healthy, smoke-free musician you used to illustrate benefits just might not seem very relevant to the musicians you are trying to target.

With this little bit of information you could redo your HBM-based health promotion campaign so that it makes more sense for the intended beneficiaries. For example:

- The focus of your "perceived severity" themes shifts from the disease consequences of smoking to the potential cost of losing future gigs and careers. Maybe you have a tagline that says "Got throat cancer? Can't get gigs. Got lung cancer? Can't get gigs." Or "Charles is a blues man. He smoked three packs a day. Now his only audience is a couple of nurses."

- To demonstrate that the costs of quitting are relatively low, this time you focus on quit-smoking modalities that a blues musician could really use, like the nicotine replacement patch, which is easily available at local grocery stores and pharmacies and doesn't take critical time away from performing.

You get the idea.

The following is an example of a specific health promotion program that used the HBM:

Mammography Screening Intervention: In Maryland, outreach initiatives have been unsuccessful in engaging low-income African-American women in mammography screening. This study aimed to identify factors influencing screening rates for low-income African-American women. Based on the Health Belief Model, a culturally targeted intervention was implemented to promote a no-cost mammography-screening program. Data were collected from women 40 years of age and older on their history of mammography use and their knowledge and beliefs about breast cancer. A 50% screening rate was achieved among 119 eligible participants. Significant predictors of screening behaviors were perceived barriers, lack of insurance, and limited knowledge. This culturally targeted intervention resulted in an unprecedented screening rate among low-income African-American women in Baltimore, Maryland.[9]

Things to Think About/Critiques

No theory is without its critique—it wouldn't be a theory then, would it? And the HBM, as the longest running health behavior theory, has its share. Let's look at some of the critiques.

Critique one: The HBM primarily focuses on individual decisions, and does not address social and environmental factors. In large measure, this is true. What HBM assumes is an internal, rational process where individuals assess their degree of risk and make a cost-benefit calculation about whether or not to engage in the preventive or health-oriented behavior. But those "calculations" will vary based on the kinds of information and interpretations being made. The process involves some element of external, social influence, in the sense that external rewards—let's say, for example, looking better or avoiding the cost of medical care through prevention—are certainly a part of a person's calculation of benefits and costs. But there is not a lot of emphasis placed on external context.

Critique two: The HBM assumes that everyone has equal access to, and an equivalent level of, information from which to make the rational calculation. Fair enough. Not everyone has all the information necessary to make the decision the same. The model does not really account for disparities in knowledge, though you could say that it has a potential effect on the disparities just because programs structured on the HBM will by nature attempt to provide information that will influence someone's decisions.

THE THEORY OF PLANNED BEHAVIOR (TPB)/ FORMERLY KNOWN AS THE THEORY OF REASONED ACTION (TRA)

Origins and Basic Elements

This individual-oriented theory comes in two versions—an initial version and a later, revised version. The initial version, called the *Theory of Reasoned Action (TRA)*, was supplanted by a later version, called the *Theory of Planned Behavior (TPB)*. The revision was developed to address certain key critiques of TRA,[10-13] but both are versions of one overall theory.

TRA/TPB is one in a long line of theoretical attempts to pin down the relationship between people's attitudes and their behavior. For a long time, social psychologists, researchers, and theorists have been concerned with this issue. Why? Well, think about the differences between an attitude you have expressed and what you actually do in a particular situation. Are you always exactly true to your attitudes? If you answer a survey about attitudes, and report that you agree with the statement "honesty is the best policy," does this actually reflect whether you will be honest in every circumstance? Probably not. It may reflect what you will do some of the time, or even most of the time. But if you are being robbed, and the robber asks you how much money you have, you may not think it's the best policy to be honest in that situation. Or if you think someone will be hurt by your honesty, you may not think it best in that situation either.

The issue, in the spirit of the general social science project we discussed in Chapter 3, is *predictability*. Do attitudes predict behavior? In what ways are they predictors, and in what ways are they not predictive. This has been the concern, and it is the issue that Fishbein, first in the late 1960s, and then together with Ajzen, sought to address with TRA/TPB.[10-13]

Like the HBM, TRA/TPB focuses on rational, cognitive decision-making processes. There is an assumption of rational, reasoned behavior here (hence the name!)—that people think about what they are going to do before they do it. However, after reviewing previous research, Ajzen and Fishbein concluded that it was necessary to separate the general construct of *attitudes* from what they called *behavioral intentions*.[10-13] In other words, there may not always be a link between attitudes and behavior, but if you look more carefully at the process, people move from attitudes and situations to attitudes about specific behaviors and assessments about how the behavior is viewed by others (what the norms

Social Norms

To be brief, social norms are customary codes of behavior in a group or culture, together with the beliefs about what those codes mean. Suppose there is a norm that holds *you don't steal candy from children*. That is both a guide for how to behave (or not behave), and an affirmation of the meaning behind it—that it is not right to take or steal candy from those who cannot defend against you, or something of that sort. They are *norms* because they are generally adhered to standards among a group about what should be "normal."

are regarding the behavior) before they do something. These various stages culminate in an *intention to do a behavior*. According to the original TRA formulation, a behavioral intention follows from:

- A person's attitude towards a specific behavior
- Their perception of the *subjective norms* associated with that behavior

By *subjective norms,* the theory refers to whether the behavior is likely to be approved or disapproved by the social groups of influence for the person who is deciding whether or not to do the behavior. In this sense, you could say that TRA/TPB does a little better job than HBM of accounting for the social context surrounding someone's behavioral decision making.

Together, these two factors lead to a behavioral intention, which, according to Ajzen and Fishbein, is much more predictive of actual behavior.[10-13] So, to use one example adapted from Montano and Kasprzyk[14(p68)]: Our friend Jane may have a fearful attitude about breast cancer as a disease. This is an attitude about breast cancer, but it is not necessarily predictive of what she will do to prevent getting breast cancer—say, getting a mammogram. For that, the theory holds that you have to look more closely at a person's attitude about *getting a mammogram,* and about her assessment of certain social consequences of getting one. So Jane may fear breast cancer, but also feel reluctant to get a mammogram because she is personally skeptical about the overuse of expensive medical testing *and* she believes that she might be ostracized by her equally skeptical friends or social group if she got one. This translates into a *low behavioral intention to get a mammogram*, despite Jane's concern about breast cancer.

Now it gets more complicated. Ajzen and Fishbein break up attitude toward a behavior and subjective norm into several parts each, like this[12]:

- *Attitude towards a behavior* results from: 1) a person's belief about *what* will happen if they do it (expected outcome), combined with 2) their assessment of whether the outcome is good or bad.
- *Subjective norm* results from: 1) a person's beliefs about what other people in his or her social group will think about the behavior, combined with 2) their motivation to conform to these social norms. (For example, if a person feels pretty confident about his or her acceptance by the social group, he or she may not feel a powerful need or desire to take the group's norms into consideration in deciding whether or not to do some particular behavior.)

The Reformulation as TPB

Not long after TRA was formulated and tested as a framework for programs that sought to change people's health behavior, a significant flaw was revealed. It's all fine and good to picture the decision-making process as described in TRA, where individuals go through these fairly complex cognitive assessments before making decisions, and then, in a rational manner, move from assessments to behavior. Clean and neat. The problem, however, is that in the real world, someone could go through this process of assessment, and *have a behavioral intention, but still not be able to do the behavior.* Why? Because other factors may prevent them—factors outside their internal cognitive process, and outside their control. Using the mammogram example, suppose, as we said, Jane was concerned about breast cancer, she had a *favorable* attitude about getting a mammogram, and she was not going to be swayed by the skepticism of her social group. At the same time, she worked on a small farm, and the nearest place to get a mammogram was hours away by bus, because her car wasn't running. Not only that, but she was very concerned that if she left her work on the farm even for a few hours, certain very important tasks would not get done, potentially affecting whether her shipment of milk got to market.

What is she to do? She has an *intent* to get a mammogram, but she *doesn't feel that she can, given the other circumstances.* Getting a mammogram is *not a behavior over which she has complete control,* because of her circumstances. So in Jane's case, and others where circumstances get in the way of intent, *behavioral intention alone* is not a sufficient predictor of behavior.

To address situations like this, a new element was added to the TRA—*perceived behavioral control*.[13] Basically, this refers to the degree to which someone believes they have control over whether they can take the action and the strength of that belief. For analytical purposes, the construct *perceived behavioral control* is separated into two parts:

- *Control beliefs:* A person's beliefs about factors that will make it easy or difficult to do the behavior. For example, in Jane's case, if she thought it would be easy to get a ride to the mammogram screening facility (even though her car wasn't working), that would be a *facilitating control belief.* If she didn't think she could get a ride, it would be a *constraining* belief.[14]
- *Perceived power:* This refers to power of the control beliefs. In Jane's case, if she felt that getting a ride was the only possible way she could get to the screening facility, that would have a lot to do with how much of a determining factor her facilitating or constraining control belief was in predicting her behavior.

All these labels and terms are undoubtedly confusing. This does happen, sometimes, when we attempt to parse human behavior into discrete analytic variables or parts. So try to think about this in common sense terms. The addition of perceived behavioral control really means the following with respect to the TRA/TPB theory as a whole:

If Jane has a positive attitude towards getting a mammogram . . .

If *either* her friends or social group think it's a good idea *or* she doesn't care that much what they think in this case . . .

And if she thinks she can probably get a ride to the mammogram facility, or if not, ride a bike or take the bus (meaning that she has a reasonably high level of perceived behavioral control) . . .

Then the likelihood is high that she'll go get the mammogram!

Table 4-2 summarizes the various components of TRA/TPB.

Using the TRA/TPB

To use the TRA/TPB (let's just call it TPB now) in a health promotion program, again, as for the HBM, think of the theoretical constructs as levers or "pieces of the puzzle" that need to be in place in order to promote a certain behavior (e.g., getting a mammogram). Also like HBM and practically every other theory we will discuss, they provide guidance but aren't sufficient in themselves to structure a program. All those terms and variables need to be specified for a particular group of people who are the focus of an intervention.

Let's try using the TPB with those blues musicians and smoking again. You have three basic constructs to work with: attitude to the behavior (in this case, quitting smok-

TABLE 4-2 Components of the Theory of Reasoned Action/Theory of Planned Behavior (TRA/TPB)

Theory of Reasoned Action	Theory of Planned Behavior
Attitude	
• A person's beliefs about what will happen if he or she performs the behavior	*Perceived Behavioral Control*
• A person's judgment of whether the expected outcome is good or bad	• *Control beliefs:* A person's beliefs about factors that will make it easy or difficult to perform the behavior
Subjective Norms	
• A person's beliefs about what other people in his or her social group will think about the behavior	• *Perceived power:* The amount of power a person believes he or she has over performing the behavior
• A person's motivation to conform to these perceived norms	
Behavioral Intention	
• A person's intention to perform a behavior	
• Influenced by attitude, subjective norms, and perceived behavioral control, behavioral intention is most predictive of actual behavior	

ing), subjective norms, and perceived behavioral control. You set out to conduct a health promotion campaign using the TPB, and begin developing program components and informational materials straight from the three constructs. Beware, though, of falling into the "EZ program structure illusion." Quickly, you find out that you are shooting in the dark, so to speak, because you have no idea what the possible social norms are that may influence a blues musician's intention to quit smoking, or even what social group is most important in terms of their norms (and what are those norms?). Is it, for example, fellow blues musicians? Or is it family members? Or both? Finally, you have no idea what the possible facilitating and constraining factors are that would go into a blues musician's perception of control over the behavior of quitting smoking.

If you took the preliminary "research information" about blues musicians that was discussed earlier, at least you would have a start, and your promotion program might look like this:

• You try to develop brochures/Internet materials that you think will feed positive beliefs about the behavior of participating in a quit-smoking program. The materials focus on the positive outcomes to be expected—better health, and the relationship of better health to, say, a better singing voice or the ability to withstand the rigors of being on the road. That's construct number one.

• Next, you do some group educational sessions, right near the blues clubs, on the benefits of quit-smoking programs, including benefits to their health and voice. What you're trying to do with this component is improve group attitudes and norms about quit-smoking programs—fellow musicians being the key social group in this case. If you are successful, musicians who are considering quitting will be able to factor these positive social norms into their intention to quit, according to the theory.

• Finally, you do your best to minimize the things that might be viewed as constraining factors by a musician contemplating quitting: You work with the local musician's union or association to expand available insurance coverage (and you make sure that musicians learn about this change), and you form a group of club owners who promise they will never drop a performer who takes a short amount of time off for a quit-smoking program. For this, you agree to place free advertisements about their club in promotional materials about nightlife in the city. And, you make sure that this new policy is communicated clearly to performers. What you are trying to do here is *influence blues musicians' beliefs about how much they can control the behavior of quitting.*

Who knows? You might have some success with this one.

Now here is an example of a specific health promotion program that used the TPB:

TPB and Exercise Study: The Theory of Planned Behavior provides a useful framework to study attitudes toward participation in physical activity. The objective of the study was to test the effectiveness of an intervention in manipulating the variables of the Theory of Planned Behavior and exercise habits with 366 high school students. The students were divided into intervention and control groups. A questionnaire to measure components of the theory, and the Baecke Questionnaire of Habitual Activity measuring exercise habits, were administered. The intervention lasted 12 weeks and included posters and lectures promoting participation in physical activity. Analyses showed the intervention was effective in improving attitudes towards physical activity, perceived behavioral control, intention, and self-reported actual behavior, but less effective in other respects. The results provide useful information for physical education teachers interested in promoting students' positive attitudes towards physical activity.[15]

Things to Think About/Critiques

There are a number of critiques to think about regarding the TRA and TPB. Let's look at a few of them:

Critique one: Like the HBM, TRA/TPB assumes that behavior is the output of rational, linear decision-making processes. By this critique, "rational" does not imply "correct" according to some objective standard.[14(p73)] But it does imply a certain kind of thinking process. Do people actually go through such processes, and do they do it in the kind of mechanistic order that is implied by this theory? What about "gut instincts" or emotion as decision motivators? What about habit? What about gender—are there factors that are different for men and women? What about culture, education level, income, or other demographic characteristics? Presumably, some of these latter factors could be subsumed under the general notion of "attitudes" toward a behavior, in what social groups to consider when identifying relevant norms, or in perceived control factors that may differ by gender and demographics. But if so, what does the theory really tell us except some very general ways to think about the decision-making process, because everything of importance essentially has to be "filled in"?

Critique two: The construct "perceived behavioral control" is very unclear, and so is its relationship to the actual control a person might have over his or her behavior. What

exactly is the relevance of *perceived* behavioral control? We know that this construct was added to address situations where people had less than full control over whether they would perform a behavior (regardless of their intent). Because this is a theory about attitudes and intentions, not social conditions per se, the construct is framed in terms of perception. So what it refers to may or may not have much to do with a person's ability to exercise control, just their beliefs about it. Okay, that makes sense. But so many things go into a person's beliefs about control (again, the difference between this construct and self-efficacy, which we will discuss more in the next chapter, is hard to define), that it appears difficult to really assess this construct. What if someone just has low self-esteem and regardless of the actual social or physical factors that may inhibit behavior, they will discount their "control" over what they do? Does this count? What if they come from a culture or social group in which fatalistic attitudes are common—if our friend Jane, for example, simply felt that she was not the determining factor in whether she got a mammogram, but that "fate" or some outside force was.

Critique three: Time between intent and action is not considered. What if someone has an intent and perceived control. How long is this "good for" in terms of its ability to predict behavior? Let's say we interview Jane on a Monday about all the factors related to behavioral intention and perceived control, and she has a high degree of both, but her mammogram is scheduled for three weeks from that Monday. Will the likelihood of her going to the appointment then be the same as if she had a same-day appointment?

TWO MODELS OF BEHAVIOR CHANGE IN STAGES: THE TRANSTHEORETICAL MODEL (TTM) AND PRECAUTION ADOPTION PROCESS MODEL (PAPM)

Origins and Basic Elements

We are going to discuss these two models together because they really represent one basic theoretical approach (change occurring in stages, over time), and they are similar in many ways. You could say that the other individual theories we have discussed so far are "point in time" theories; that is, they focus on the attitudes, beliefs, and decisions about behavior that occur as a single process, related to a particular behavior. Will Jane get a mammogram? If she feels susceptible, if she feels the risk is severe, if the barriers are low, and so on. The result is, she does it or she doesn't, based on her decision-making process.

A number of researchers and theorists began to question the "point in time" structure. Prochaska and DiClemente[16,17] conducted research on change processes among people who were quitting smoking, and found that a very important dimension of behavior change was not included under other theories—the idea that change takes place in *stages*, over time. In other words, people don't necessarily go through one process of making a decision, but many processes. Each one is different, because each of these "little decisions" is related to one part of a continuum of change. We can see how this works with, say, buying a new car. It usually isn't just one decision, but many, as illustrated in the following scenario:

Monday: Jane goes out to her car, which, as you remember from our earlier example, wasn't working well. She looks at it and thinks "OK, what am I going to do about this? I have to find out what's wrong." She then goes back inside, gets on the phone, and calls several car repair places. They tell her things like "It sounds like your auto-flywheel-rotator-cuff manifold adjuster is down. Yeah, we can fix it. It'll be about 800 bucks." She sighs, but sets up an appointment.

Tuesday: She goes out to her car in the morning, because she has an appointment to get it fixed. She looks at her forlorn vehicle, paint faded, fabric torn on the passenger seat, and asks, "How am I going to get this thing to the garage?" Then she calls a tow truck, and the driver says "That'll be about $150 to tow it." She sighs, and says "Let me call you back." She sits at the table, has a bite to eat, and puts her head in her hands. As she looks down, she sees last Saturday's newspaper on the floor. Staring right at her is a bright ad. "CLEARANCE SALE! MUST SELL 100 NEW CARS THIS WEEK! FINANCING AVAILABLE! COME TO JOE'S AUTO MART, 51 CENTRAL STREET, DOWNTOWN." "Hmm," she thinks. "A new car? Hadn't thought of it, but . . . you know. . . ." She doesn't call the tow truck driver back.

Friday: (Having skipped her Tuesday car repair appointment) After thinking about it for a few days, and looking at her savings, she calls up Joe's Auto Mart and asks what kinds of cars they have, and what the prices are. "Oh, you have two SuperCar wagons left? At 50% off? Well, can you hold onto them? I'll be there tomorrow morning for a look." Then she calls her friend Ben Jones, who says he'll give her a ride in the morning.

Saturday: (At Joe's Auto Mart) Jane is looking at the two wagons. One is a forest green, the other a kind of dusky, metallic gray. She opens and shuts the door. It makes a nice, dense click when it closes, not like the hollow rattling she has gotten used to with her old Ford. "Wanna test drive it?" says the beady-eyed salesman, chewing a toothpick. Though she looks at him with distaste, she agrees. He hops in the passenger side and gives her the keys. She picks the metallic gray one—a little racier. The seats are firm, and smell fresh. The dash is a tautly organized, flat panel that makes her feel, well, efficient. She puts it in gear, and it moves from a stop with a crisp surge. "Wow!" She says to herself. "This is great. I feel so sharp, like a toned animal."

Saturday noon: Jane signs a whole lot of papers, and she has herself a new car. The first one in years.

Her decision, as you can see, was not just one process. There was the initial stage, where she tried to get her car fixed, and then came to appreciate the magnitude of the problem if she tried to make the old car run. Then there was the stage where she first entertained the novel idea of buying a new car. Then there was kind of a preparation process, where she looked into her finances and investigated the options. Then she began to move towards buying, by calling the dealer and setting up a ride to see the cars for sale. Then she went and tried out the new car (the "new behavior"). The experience was good, very good. Finally, she bought it.

It is important to note that neither the TTM nor PAPM are *theories*, per se. They are complex descriptions of a process that *incorporate* various theories as explanations for movement through the process. In this sense, they are *models*.

Transtheoretical Model

Prochaska and DiClemente figured that changing behavior was often just like the car scenario described above. Not only that, but for each step or stage in the continuum of change, something different is going on, such that different behavioral theories are applicable by stage. So describing change means that many theories are necessary, each relevant to stages in the process. In one stage, it may be that someone is aware of a problem and is making a decision about taking action; in that stage, HBM or TPB may be applicable. But in another stage, a person may not even be aware that there is a problem, so they are not at the place where they can make such decisions. They are not ready for change. First, the problem has to "get on their agenda." So, other theories may better describe the process of "becoming aware."

Because of the framework of change in stages, and the necessity of multiple change theories by stage, the Prochaska and DiClemente model was called the Transtheoretical Model or TTM (sometimes referred to as "stages of change" for short). The other model, called the Precaution Adoption Process Model, is based on a similar understanding about change.

According to the TTM, the following stages describe the overall process of behavior change, from A to Z, so to speak.[18(pp100-104)] A person may enter this continuum at any stage, not necessarily at the beginning:

- *Stage One: Precontemplation:* A person does not intend to take action. This may be because they simply don't know that there is a problem with whatever they're doing (say, eating high fat food and not exercising), or because they are not interested or motivated to change for other reasons.
- *Stage Two: Contemplation:* A person is thinking about changing some time in the future (say, six months), and is weighing the *pros and cons* of doing so. This can take some time. In this stage, people are not yet ready to take action. That process of weighing the pros and cons is known under this theory as the *decisional balance.* It is the process that determines whether a person will continue moving towards change.
- *Stage Three: Preparation:* A person is ready to do something. They *intend* (remember that construct from TRA/TPB?) to act soon, and have some kind of plan or idea about what they want to do. For people in this stage, programs that provide action steps (e.g., a weight loss program, a fitness program, a stress reduction program) are appropriate.
- *Stage Four: Action:* You can guess this one. A person has taken action, and recently, towards change. But not every action counts—only those actions that are known to be steps to prevent or reduce the risks for the health problem being addressed.
- *Stage Five: Maintenance:* A person has made a significant change in their behavior in terms of health risk, and is now focused on keeping that behavior change going, not slipping back into old habits. This often requires serious work. Think, for example, of smokers who have actually quit. For a good long while, the hardest task for them is to avoid, or withstand the strong temptation to have a smoke again.
- *Stage Six: Termination:* A person in this stage has truly completed the process of behavior change. This is the smoker who has finally gotten past any further temptation to smoke. It is no longer part of that person's behavior at all, just as if they never smoked in the first place. However, getting to this stage is not typical. Most people who have made a health behavior change stay somewhere in the maintenance stage.

A key construct in this stage is *self-efficacy.* We've mentioned it before—a person's confidence that they can change a specific behavior. In the maintenance stage, you could say people are developing their self-efficacy (with respect to a specific health behavior change). When they reach the termination stage, they "have" self-efficacy.

Through all six stages, the TTM model also holds that there are a number of change processes that can contribute to moving from one stage to another. These change processes serve as guides for interventions intended to move people across stages. Because the list is a long one, it will not be presented here in its entirety. Here are a few examples:

- *Environmental re-evaluation:* This process includes when a person thinks about how something they do affects others in their social environment. A good example is a mother who smokes, and upon hearing about the effects of second-hand smoke, she starts thinking about the effect of her smoking on her children. This may help motivate change. (This is a *cognitive* process.)
- *Counter-conditioning:* This process includes when a person learns something to do that *substitutes* for the behavior they want to change and can be called on to counter the impulses to engage in the less desirable behavior. An example is developing the habit of exercising instead of smoking. (This is a learned *stimulus-response* process.)

The Precaution Adoption Process Model (PAPM)

The PAPM takes the same basic idea that led to the TTM and applies it to a general category of behavior—taking a *precaution* against something, like putting smoke detectors in your home. PAPM was developed by Weinstein and Sandman specifically to help understand people's willingness/unwillingness to conduct home radon testing.[19] The motivation for its development was similar to TTM—its authors believed that existing theories of behavior change were not adequate to represent how people react to hazards. So, drawing from TTM, Weinstein and Sandman framed the PAPM, which is somewhat different in the way stages are defined. PAPM stages are as follows:

- *Stage One: Unaware of the Issue:* It isn't likely that people will change a particular habit or health behavior if they have never heard that there is any problem associated with it. After all, "If it ain't broke, don't fix it." That's what the first PAPM stage refers to—simple lack of knowledge or awareness.

- *Stage Two: Unengaged by Issue:* Here the PAPM makes a distinction between categories of people who, in the TTM, are lumped together in the precontemplation stage. Under PAPM, there is a significant difference between those who don't know about a behavior-related risk (Stage One) and those who may know, but are not engaged enough to do anything about it (Stage Two). This second category of people are in the "unengaged" stage, and are considered to be at a different place in the change process, requiring a different type of intervention.
- *Stage Three: Deciding About Acting:* This is an intermediate stage where people who are aware of (and engaged in) a health behavior problem begin to make some decision as to whether they intend to do something about it. Notice the similarity to the construct *behavioral intention* in TRA/TPB, except in this case, the model also accounts for people who decide they are not going to act.
- *Stage Four: Deciding Not to Act:* In the PAPM, deciding not to act is accounted for as a stage. What it means speaks for itself: After thinking about it, people decide they are not going to do anything. So this stage actually takes people "out of the loop" of the behavior change. There is no such stage included in TTM.
- *Stage Five: Deciding to Act:* No mystery here. After thinking about it, some people decide they will do

something. Remember, though, that according to the PAPM this stage is *not the same as actually taking action.* It's just the decision to do so.
- *Stage Six: Acting:* Taking the action, but not yet maintaining it. Taking it for the first time.
- *Stage Seven: Maintenance:* This stage was adopted from the same stage in the TTM model. It refers to continuation of the behavior, but, interestingly does not separate the *continued effort* to keep up a behavior from the "post-temptation" termination stage in TTM where effort is no longer needed.

As for TTM, there are many specific processes involved in moving from one stage to the next. Some of these processes involve decisions based on beliefs about benefits (of taking action) vs. costs, perceptions of social norms, confidence or skills needed to make the change, and so on—processes addressed by many of the nonstage individual theories of behavior change. And, as noted by Weinstein and Sandman,[20] variables and factors important at one stage are not necessarily the same as those that come into play in another stage.

In addition, the PAPM explicitly states that the proposed stages occur *in order.* This is, perhaps, a stronger statement about the importance of the order of stages than is present in TTM, although order is inherent to the latter approach.

Table 4-3 summarizes the components of both TTM and PAPM, showing similarities and differences.

TABLE 4-3 Components of the Transtheoretical Model (TTM) and the Precaution Adoption Process Model (PAPM)

Transtheoretical Model	Precaution Adoption Process Model
Stage One: Precontemplation	Stage One: Unaware of the Issue
	Stage Two: Unengaged by the Issue
Stage Two: Contemplation	Stage Three: Deciding About Acting
Stage Three: Preparation	Stage Four: Deciding Not to Act
	Stage Five: Deciding to Act
Stage Four: Action	Stage Six: Acting
Stage Five: Maintenance	Stage Seven: Maintenance
Stage Six: Termination	

Using Stage Models: TTM or PAPM

Using stage models can be a little complex, for a number of reasons. First of all, what you are trying to do in using these models for a health promotion intervention is to move your target group or population from one stage to another. For this, you need to:

- Assess what stage your target group is in. To do this, you must use an appropriate way to measure stage *in relation to the health problem and behavior(s) you intend to address.* The particulars of stages related to smoking cessation will be different than those of the stages involved in an effort to change diet and increase exercise. Also, people within your target group may differ in terms of stage. What do you do then? There may be more than one intervention necessary, or you will just focus on a subset of the group that, for example, is at highest risk.
- Based on the stage(s) your group is in, make sure your intervention draws on the *change processes* that are relevant to moving from that stage. For example, if most people are unaware, then an educational effort ("consciousness raising") focusing on the problem itself is appropriate.
- Have some assessment criteria for determining whether your target group has moved to the next stage or stages.

As for the other theories and models, research or some existing information is necessary to connect the abstract models to actual circumstances and people.

Let's go back to the blues musicians, just one more time, and try one of the stage models. The PAPM might be useful here because it distinguishes between being unaware and being unengaged, an important distinction, based on what we already know about these musicians. Let's say we do more research (surveys, interviews) and find out that about half the musicians are aware of cancer risks from smoking—from ad campaigns and such—but are unengaged, for many of the reasons already mentioned. The other half are in the "deciding about acting" stage, somewhere between the contemplation and preparation stages of the TTM. Looks like you're going to need two separate interventions.

For the first group, the key is going to be engaging them in the issue, making it *matter.* We already learned about some of the issues that were highest on their priority list, and that smoking cessation programs were perceived as conflicting with some of those issues. So the challenge is to raise the profile, and to put cancer risk higher up on the agenda so that the musicians will be more engaged. This is related to what

we discussed earlier about increasing the musicians' sense of *susceptibility* and *severity*, and to *reducing perceived barriers* that otherwise might contribute to an attitude of "I can't do anything about it anyway." You could focus on:

- Increasing the relevance of the risk, by tying cancer directly to its impact on singing, on longevity of music careers, and on "getting an audience"
- Reducing the perceived barriers to participating in smoking cessation, by working with musicians' unions, club owners, etc. (as discussed earlier)
- Increasing the presence of smoking/cancer risk and prevention materials in places where blues musicians congregate

Then you would measure their "engagement" before your intervention and after, to see if what you did made any difference in moving them closer to the engaged stage.

The second group is already engaged and thinking of doing something about it. So, the task here is to position the next stage—action—as easy. This could include increasing the accessibility of cessation programs so that quit-smoking groups are provided, say, at music stores. It could also include the formation of quit groups among musicians so that the barrier of social habit or social pressure is minimized and the groups reinforce behavior change. And it could include the dissemination of information about quit-smoking programs, again, in places where blues musicians congregate. Then, you would conduct an assessment to see if these efforts moved members of this second group to the action stage.

Here are a few examples of specific health promotion programs that have used the TTM and/or PAPM:

Stages of Change (TTM) for Exercise: This study examined the use of the stages of change model to design an exercise intervention for community volunteers. The "Imagine Action" campaign was a community-wide event incorporating the involvement of local worksites and community agencies. Community members registering for the campaign were enrolled in a six-week intervention program designed to encourage participation in physical activity. The campaign was promoted throughout community worksites, area schools, organizations, and local media channels. One question designed to assess current stage of exercise adoption was included on the campaign registration form. The intervention included written materials designed to encourage participants to initiate or increase physical activity, a resource manual describing activity options in the community, and weekly "fun walks" and "activity nights." *Results:* Subjects were significantly more active after the six-week intervention. Sixty-two percent of participants in Contemplation became more active while 61% in Preparation became more active. *Conclusions:* Most participants increased their stage of exercise adoption during the six-week intervention. This study provides preliminary support for use of the stages of change model in designing exercise interventions.[21]

PAPM for Home Radon Testing: Hypotheses generated by the Precaution Adoption Process Model, a stage model of health behavior, were tested in the context of home radon testing. The specific idea tested was that the barriers impeding progress toward protective action change from stage to stage. An intervention describing a high risk of radon problems in study area homes was designed to encourage homeowners in the PAPM model's undecided stage to decide to test, and a low-effort, how-to-test intervention was designed to encourage homeowners in the decided-to-act stage to order test kits. Both movement to a stage closer to testing and purchase of radon test kits were assessed. As predicted, the risk treatment was relatively more effective in getting undecided people to decide to test than in getting decided-to-act people to order a test. Also supporting predictions, the low-effort intervention proved relatively more effective in getting decided-to-act people to order tests than in getting undecided people to decide to test.[22]

Things to Think About/Critiques

There are a number of critiques to think about regarding the TRA and TPB. Let's look at a few of them:

Critique one: People don't always go through a fixed set of stages, in a straight line, as both the TTM and PAPM propose. Instead, people often go in circles, moving from one stage to the next, then doubling back and reentering the process. Say, for example, someone named Fred begins smoking after breaking up with his girlfriend. After a year, Fred decides that he wants to quit, because of the stench and the health risks. So, he is in TTM's preparation stage. Fred goes to a quit-smoking program, and in fact stops (action stage). This keeps up for a few weeks (maintenance), but then, when going out to the movies one night, Fred sees his old partner! With somebody else! It's like a small earthquake. Flustered, he pops into a Quickie-Mart and buys a pack of smokes. Uh-oh, back a few stages. But after a few days, Fred recovers, and slowly begins to cut back on his smoking, returning to a quit stage in another two weeks. You can see that this is a cyclical process, and when he reenters the "behavior change" path he is not where he started before.

Critique two: How do you measure what stage people are in? To do so, you have to develop an arbitrary set of criteria to measure stage. That's not terribly hard for some stages. If, for example, you want to know whether people are in an unengaged or unaware stage, you can ask questions like: "Have you ever heard of (HEALTH PROBLEM)? Is (HEALTH PROBLEM) important to you?" But when you get to other stages, like *contemplation* vs. *preparation,* or *maintenance* vs. *termination,* or *deciding about acting* vs. *deciding to act,* it gets a little trickier. It is easy at that point to engage in arbitrary hair-splitting about what stage someone is in, and thus what sort of intervention they should get.

Chapter Questions

1. Why have we called the theories in this chapter *individual* theories? What do they assume about behavior?

2. According to the Health Belief Model, what is the decision-making process a person goes through before taking a health-related action?

3. The Theory of Planned Behavior evolved because it didn't account for what kind of factor that could influence behavior?

4. What is it about the Transtheoretical Model that is "transtheoretical"?

5. What are the key stages in TTM and PAPM? How are they similar or different?

REFERENCES

1. Dumont L. *Homo Hierarchicus: The Caste System and its Implications*, rev ed. Chicago: University of Chicago Press; 1980.

2. Dumont L. *Essays on Individualism: Modern Ideology in Anthropological Perspective*. Chicago: University of Chicago Press; 1986.

3. Becker MH, ed. The health belief model and personal health behavior. *Health Educ Monogr*. 1974;2:Entire issue.

4. Janz NK, Becker MH. The health belief model: a decade later. *Health Educ Q*. 1984;11(1):1–47.

5. Hochbaum GM. *Public Participation in Medical Screening Programs: A Sociopsychological Study*. Public Health Service publication No. 572. Washington, DC: Government Printing Office; 1958.

6. Rosenstock IM. Historical origins of the health belief model. *Health Educ Monogr*. 1974;2:328–335.

7. Bandura A. *Social Learning Theory*. Englewood Cliffs, NJ: Prentice Hall; 1977.

8. Bandura A. *Social Foundations of Thought and Action*. Englewood Cliffs, NJ: Prentice Hall; 1986.

9. Garza MA, Luan J, Blinka M, et al. A culturally targeted intervention to promote breast cancer screening among low-income women in East Baltimore, MD. *Cancer Control*. 2005;12(Suppl 2):34–41.

10. Fishbein M, ed. *Readings in Attitude Theory and Measurement*. New York: John Wiley & Sons; 1967.

11. Fishbein M, Ajzen I. *Belief, Attitude, Intention, and Behavior: An Introduction to Theory and Research*. Reading, MA: Addison-Wesley; 1975.

12. Ajzen I, Fishbein M. *Understanding Attitudes and Predicting Social Behavior*. Englewood Cliffs, NJ: Prentice Hall; 1980.

13. Ajzen I. The theory of planned behavior. *Organ Behav Human Dec Processes*. 1991;50:179–211.

14. Montano DE, Kasprzyk D. The theory of reasoned action and the theory of planned behavior. In: Glanz K, Rimer BK, Lewis FM, eds. *Health Behavior and Health Education: Theory, Research and Practice*, 3rd ed. San Francisco, CA: Jossey-Bass; 2002:.

15. Tsorbatzoudis H. Evaluation of a school-based intervention programme to promote physical activity: an application of the theory of planned behavior. *Perception Motor Skills*. 2005;101(3):787–802.

16. DiClemente CC, Prochaska JO. Self-change and therapy change of smoking behavior: a comparison of processes of change in cessation and maintenance. *Addict Behav*. 1982;7:133–142.

17. Prochaska JO, DiClemente CC. Stages and processes of self-change of smoking: toward an integrative model of change. *J Consult Clin Psychol*. 1983;51:390–395.

18. Prochaska JO, Redding CA, Evers KE. The transtheoretical model and stages of change. In: Glanz K, Rimer BK, Lewis FM, eds. *Health Behavior and Health Education*, 3rd ed. San Francisco, CA: John Wiley & Sons; 2002:.

19. Weinstein ND, Lyon JE, Sandman PM, Cuite CL. Experimental evidence for stages of health behavior change: the precaution adoption process model applied to home radon testing. *Health Psychol*. 1998;17(5):445–453.

20. Weinstein ND, Sandman PM. A model of the precaution adoption process: evidence from home radon testing. *Health Psychol*. 1992;11:170–180.

21. Marcus BH, Banspach SW, Lefebvre RC, Rossi JS, Carleton RA, Abrams DB. Using the stages of change model to increase the adoption of physical activity among community participants. *Am J Health Promotion*. 1992;6(6):424–429.

22. Weinstein ND. The precaution adoption process. *Health Psychol*. 1988;7:355–386.

CHAPTER 5

Social, Cultural, and Environmental Theories (Part I)

"Man* is a social animal."

—BENEDICT (BARUCH) SPINOZA, *ETHICS*, 1677

WHAT ARE WE TALKING ABOUT?

We just finished discussing theories that focus on the *individual*. In talking about these theories, remember that we addressed the blurred line between what we think of as an individual and his or her social/environmental context. In this chapter (Part I) and the next (Chapter 6: Part II), we are going to review a selection of theories that focus primarily on that social/environmental context, and the way it interacts with individuals. So, in a sense, we are talking about the same

thing, but from a different vantage point. Another way of looking at it is to view the individual theories as addressing *internal* factors, whereas the social/environmental theories address *external* factors. Given our discussion of blurred lines, however, this is clearly not an adequate way to characterize the differences. The fact is, there is no definitive way to make the separation, and so we make do with arbitrary terms like internal/external or individual/social so that we can at least position our thinking.

Not surprisingly, talking about social/environmental context raises a lot of questions. What *counts* as a meaningful definition of context? How far out from the individual do we go to understand the factors that influence individuals? This one question alone has probably taken up more writing space than 100 sets of encyclopedias. Political economists would argue, for example, that the choices of behavior individuals have are constrained by their position within an economic and political system that defines "spaces" within which people can act. Social network theorists and proponents of social-cognitive theory would likely focus on closer social networks and groups. Cultural anthropologists would point to systems of meaning and living patterns shared across one or more societies or peoples.

SOCIAL COGNITIVE THEORY (SCT)/FORMERLY KNOWN AS SOCIAL LEARNING THEORY

Origins and Basic Elements

In discussing social/environmental theories, we're going to start somewhat close to the individual and work outwards, so to speak. *Social Cognitive Theory (SCT)*[2,3] has become perhaps the most well known and productive of these kinds of

---

* Again, we would now say man or woman, or just people; the quote is from the 17th century.

What *Is* a Social/Environmental Context?

Think about it this way. You are born into a family that lives in a certain setting (e.g., suburban, rural, urban, well-off, not so well-off, ethnically homogenous or ethnically diverse, and so on). As you grow up, you learn *habits of life* and *meanings*; that is, in addition to learning routines (like brushing your teeth), patterns, and skills, you learn what is good and bad, what kind of life you should (or you can) lead, what morals and values you believe in, what the codes of behavior are in different situations, and much more. Some of this you learn from family. Some you learn from what you hear and see in the movies, on the Web, or on television. Some of this is woven into the very language you speak and the way you talk.

At least part of this socialization process is unique to your situation and your environment, whereas some is shared across culture(s) and society as a whole.

Over time, you also develop friends and social networks. You may go to school with some of them, some of whom may become lifelong friends. You go to work and develop social networks there. Perhaps then you get married and all of a sudden have a new family, a new network.

At the same time, you also live in a physical space. Maybe you live in the Southwest (United States), where it can get very hot in the summer. Your daily routine is affected by the location where you live. Maybe you live in northern Minnesota, where winter lasts a long time and you don't have large population centers or mass transit. Maybe you live downwind of several chemical processing plants, and the pollutants from those plants have long lent a brownish tinge to the sky at sunset. Or, perhaps you live in a coastal area prone to flooding and hurricanes.

Finally, you live in a political-economic space, a space that is governed by a specific political system, with its rules, values, procedures, and allocations of power, and where the available employment, the types of industries and businesses that exist, and the products that are available are all related to a general system. Part of this system includes the regulations and laws that exist affecting health.

And in addition to being influenced by all these things, you also learn from your own personal experience interacting with the environment you live in.

All of these pieces and more form your social/environmental context. All have an influence on what you do, your *behavior*. Psychologist Urie Bronfenbrenner referred to this as a person's ecology, something like layers of an onion,[1] because what an individual thinks and does cannot help but involve an ongoing interaction with the kinds of social/environmental factors just mentioned.

If you are trying to understand what influences behavior, how on earth do you untangle all of this, much less do something about it?

That, as they say, is the question.

theories, at least in public health, because of its specific focus on the interaction between individuals and their immediate environment, which differentiates it from the individual-oriented theories discussed in Chapter 4.

To understand SCT, though, it is useful to know something about its evolution, because the theory as a whole integrates several constructs that have been added since its introduction. SCT began as a theoretical offshoot of behaviorism (see Chapter 3), which, if you remember, is a theory about how people learn that posits individual behavior as a response to conditioning. In the 1960s, Albert Bandura and others proposed that the behaviorist principle of *operant conditioning*—in which a person learns behavior through negative and positive reinforcement—also worked when the reinforcement was directed towards other people.[4] In short, Johnny can learn not to touch a hot stove when he sees that

his sister Mary experiences pain and a burn when she does. Or, Johnny can learn to raise his hand in class when he sees that the teacher rewards others who do that. The rewards or punishments don't specifically have to happen to Johnny.

This original formulation of the theory was called *Social Learning Theory (SLT)*, and the key principle was learning by observation or *vicarious learning*. But not long after, Bandura expanded his approach to behavioral learning by introducing the concept of *self-efficacy*,[5] which, as we have already seen in the previous chapter, has been adopted by a number of other behavioral theories. The idea of self-efficacy as a key element in how people change behavior moves beyond the mechanistic conditioning process of behaviorism, and gives individuals a role in their own processes of change. Having this role is also referred to as *agency*. Around the same time, the idea of *reciprocal determinism* was added—where behavior is part of a continuous interactive cycle that includes individuals and their social and physical environment.[6,7] This interactive process is why we have included SCT in this chapter instead of Chapter 4. In the mid-1980s,[2] Bandura renamed the theory Social Cognitive Theory to move it once and for all away from its behaviorist roots and to position it as a theory that addresses individuals *consciously* operating within an environment. In recent years, Bandura and others who have utilized SCT in applied research have come to focus even more on the importance of the self-efficacy construct.

At this point, it may not be exactly clear how these constructs relate together as a *theory* that explains behavior change. Let's cluster them with other elements of the theory we haven't mentioned yet in a way that will, hopefully, begin to clarify what Bandura and other SCT proponents think happens. According to SCT, changing a behavior is a function of the following factors:

- *Individual ("internal") characteristics:* A person's sense of *self-efficacy* about the new behavior, their confidence that they can do it and overcome obstacles (barriers) to doing it. The person's *behavioral capability*, their level of knowledge and skill as these relate to the new behavior. The person's *expectations* and *expectancies* about what will happen if they make the change and if that expected outcome is good or likely to be rewarded. Their level of *self-control* in terms of making the change. Their *emotional coping* ability, to deal with the emotions involved in the behavior change.

- *Environmental ("external") factors:* The social/physical environment surrounding individuals. The behavior of others ("modeling") and the consequences of that behavior, which results in *vicarious learning*. The *situation* in which the behavior takes place, and perceptions of that situation by individuals. *Reinforcements* (negative or positive) that are given to individuals in response to behavior.

- The interactive process of *reciprocal determinism*, where a person acts based on individual factors and social/environmental cues, receives a response from that environment, adjusts behavior, acts again, and so on.

How does each of these factors weigh in during the process of "behaving"? Well, it's not clear in the sense of precise science—the nature of many of these relationships is being investigated as we speak, and the role of some of these factors (e.g., self-efficacy, observational learning) is better understood than other factors. Let's consider a situation that is adapted from an actual case I encountered while doing research on health risk behavior among runaway youth.

What Is Self-Efficacy?

Think of *self-efficacy* in this way: When a child first learns to ride a bike, it's likely that he or she will not feel very confident right away. After all, look at a bike the way a child would: It's riding on two wheels and you have to balance it to keep it from falling over! It doesn't look that promising at first. A child who has a lot of *self-efficacy* with respect to physical activity may very well feel the same concern at the start, but past experience mastering other seemingly difficult physical tasks gives him or her just the extra push needed to get on the bike and give it a try, even if a few falls are involved. That sense of self-efficacy will help the child pedal that bike and gain enough speed to keep it balanced.

By contrast, a child with low self-efficacy regarding physical tasks may feel more hesitation, and when he or she actually gets on the bike, he or she may be reluctant to pedal it for fear of falling over. That, of course, means that it is more likely to fall over. So it may take this child more time—and more help may be needed—to gain the experience of pedaling it fast enough to keep it up. But once the child gets it, self-efficacy is gained, and this sense of self-efficacy may help the child master future physical tasks.

Bandura applies this basic idea to any behavior, where self-efficacy is one of the keys to change.

A 16-year-old girl (we'll call her Theresa) comes from an immigrant family that is very strict in both the social and religious sense. She goes to a private religious school until she is about 12 years old, when she transfers to a public middle school. She is very shy, and feels like she doesn't know how to behave around the kids in the public school. As a result, she comes to feel like an outsider. By the time she reaches high school, she decides she is going to make a change.

Let's stop the action right there for a moment. She is moving from one social *environment* to another. She has certain *perceptions* about the situation she is in. So far, her behavior has not earned her much in the way of positive reinforcement. At this point, she doesn't feel like she has the *behavioral capability* to win peer approval, and is a little short on *self-efficacy* with respect to how to act so as to gain that approval.

By the time she reaches high school, she has done a lot of *vicarious learning*. She sees what kinds of behaviors she thinks make other girls popular (behaviors that result in positive reinforcement). Although she gets good grades, that does not appear to be enough in her mind to gain approval; in other words, the behaviors she has engaged in within this environment have not resulted in the desired effect. Because, as an individual, she has *agency*, she formulates something of a plan, based on her vicarious learning experience. She decides that she is going to be "bad," and to "get a reputation." In order to achieve this, she believes that she has to change her behavior in a serious way. She needs to drink—and not just drink, but get known for her capacity to drink. And she has to engage in risky sex, and get known for this as well. At this point, she isn't giving much thought to the consequences of excessive drinking or risky sex, such as HIV/AIDS, early pregnancy, alcoholism, liver and other diseases, and drunk driving accidents, to name a few.

As she starts doing this, she comes into conflict with an important part of her environment—her family. But because peer approval is so compelling a need for her at this point, she can't resolve that *situation*, and in fact perceives it as a barrier to the social world she wants to enter. So, she runs away. (When I interviewed her, she was living part of the time with people she met at pool halls where she hung out. She spent a good deal of the interview trying to describe how "bad" she was, to the point, she said, where "all the local cops knew her." As the interview proceeded, I began to see that she exaggerated much of what she did so that her behavior would match the reputation she was trying to create.)

So, what she was doing—her behavior—was formulated (a cognitive process) as part of an interaction among her personal characteristics and perceptions, her behavior, and the environment she was in (including the social response she got for her behavior).

The following table (Table 5-1) summarizes these components.

Using SCT

If we take the example of Theresa described above, we can put together an intervention based on SCT aimed at reducing her drug abuse (in this case alcohol) and risky sex. To do this, we will emphasize a few key constructs from SCT, including self-efficacy, behavioral capability, and vicarious learning. The intervention might include the following components:

- Social skills training in a group setting where Theresa (and girls like her) can gain *behavioral capability* with respect to non-risky behaviors that help establish good relationships with peers and contribute to the goal of popularity that was so important to Theresa. These skills might include communication, self-presentation, and leadership. The group format will enable participants to gain peer feedback and reinforcement. As girls in the group learn some of these skills and are rewarded for it, they may gain in *self-efficacy* as well.

TABLE 5-1 Social Cognitive Theory

Individual Characteristics	
Self-Efficacy	A person's confidence that he or she can perform a behavior.
Behavioral Capability	A person's level of knowledge and skill in relation to a behavior.
Expectations	What a person thinks will happen if he or she makes a behavior change.
Expectancies	Whether a person thinks the expected outcome is good or likely to be rewarded.
Self-Control	How much control a person has over making a change.
Emotional Coping	A person's ability to deal with emotions involved in a behavior change.
Environmental Factors	
Vicarious Learning	A person learns by observing the behavior of others and the consequences of that behavior.
Situation	The social/physical environment in which the behavior takes place, and a person's perception of those factors.
Reinforcement	Positive or negative responses to a person's behavior.
Reciprocal Determinism	The iterative process where a person makes a change based on individual characteristics and social/environmental cues, receives a response, makes adjustments to his or her behavior, and so on.

- To boost self-efficacy, each girl in the group may be assigned a task or project for which she will be the leader. The task may be to put on a small event, or raise money to help a youth-serving organization.
- An education component concerning the risks and outcomes of the kinds of behavior Theresa and other group members were involved in. The goal would be to affect participants' *perceptions* about these risk-related situations.
- Working with the principle of *vicarious learning*, each of the girls could be assigned a mentor who is relatively young—college age, for example—and who can involve their "mentee" in an activity they themselves are doing successfully; for example, theater. The mentor in this case takes on the role of social "model."

General SCT-based goals for such an intervention would include the idea that skill and self-efficacy building as described above would give the participants tools to achieve the same social goal (popularity, peer approval) that motivated their risky behavior, but in less damaging directions; the idea that spending time with a mentor who is successfully engaged in various activities would provide learning opportunities and behavioral examples the participants could draw upon; and that learning about the negative consequences of their previous risky behavior, in the context of the other program activities, might affect their perceptions about the value of that behavior.

Now here are examples of specific health promotion programs that used elements of SCT:

Adolescent Mothers HIV Risk Reduction Program: The purpose of this intervention and study was to determine whether adolescent mothers in a tailored HIV/AIDS prevention program (using SCT and other theories) had significantly greater perceived self-efficacy and perceived behavioral control to use condoms, and more favorable outcome expectancies and subjective norms regarding condom use than those who just received health education (control group). *Results:* Women in the tailored intervention showed more improvement than those in the education-only group. Among other results, women in the tailored intervention had improved self-efficacy and subjective norms supporting protected sex and fewer partners. *Conclusions:* These results supported a relationship among several constructs from social cognitive theory and the theory of reasoned action, and subsequent sexual risk behaviors. HIV prevention programs for adolescent mothers should be designed to include

these theoretical constructs and to address contextual factors influencing their lives.[8]

Internet-Based Obesity Prevention Using SCT: A major focus of Healthy People 2010 is promoting weight management and physical activity because overweight, obesity, and a sedentary lifestyle are strongly associated with risk for heart disease and stroke, diabetes, cancers, and premature death. Research points to the long-term weight gain prevention in normal weight (21–25 BMI), overweight (25–29 BMI), and even moderate obese (30–34 BMI) people as one alternative to prioritizing weight loss in health behavior interventions. This is because on a population basis annual weight gain is small (approximately 0.8 kg/year) and preventing weight gain appears to require only a small level of activity either through a modest increase in physical activity and/or consuming slightly less calories to maintain an energy balance. A more dynamic use of Social Cognitive Theory (SCT) for developing programs to maintain health behavior changes is emerging with some evidence of long-term maintenance. The high use of the Internet provides a vehicle to reach different population segments with readily accessible, SCT-tailored long-term programs. Research studies using the Internet with tailored SCT interventions have shown changes in nutrition practices, physical activity, and weight loss for up to a year. *Conclusions:* One promising approach to weight gain prevention in population segments is the development and widespread use of longer-term Internet programs using specific principles and procedures from SCT.[9]

Things to Think About/Critiques

As usual, there are critiques:

Critique One: This critique is possibly the most obvious one: SCT is very complex, and because it includes so many constructs that are said to be related to behavior it can be viewed as less of a theory than a generally related "grab-bag." After all, if you were trying to state SCT as a hypothesis, of the form "Person A is likely to engage in Behavior B if _____," how exactly would you do it? No such clarity is possible, and there are no relative weights given to different factors or any clear statement about the role of each factor or when that factor comes into play.

Critique Two: Related to the first critique, SCT has gone through a number of evolutions, as we have noted. As it evolved, the emphasis moved from a behaviorist variant to its current focus on self-efficacy, yet all the components ever included in the theory are still "hanging around." It's a little like saving old clothes. You wore them once, but do they define you now, even though you still have them in your closet?

SOCIAL NETWORK THEORY

Origins and Basic Elements

Social Network Theory (SNT) is a broad area of theory whose implications range from sociological and health-related applications to communications, political opinion, esoteric mathematical and systems theory applications, and others. It first surfaced in theoretical form among sociologists in the 1950s, related to a study of Norwegian villages,[10] and has since expanded in numerous directions.[11-15] The key to social network theory as an explanation of behavior is this: Although specific or unique characteristics of individuals (e.g., attitudes, beliefs, gender, etc.) are not so important to the theory, *relationships* between and among individuals are important, as is how the nature of those relationships influences beliefs and behavior. By relationships, SNT refers to sets of relationships that an individual participates in, for example, family/kin networks, work networks, and any other social groups of which the individual is a member. These are usually depicted graphically in a social network diagram or *sociogram*, that looks like Figure 5-1.

Specifically concerning health, these networks can play an important role in whether someone acts in a way that is either risky (e.g., smoking, no exercise) or good for their health (e.g., eating healthy, exercise), what information someone is exposed to about health, and what kinds of social support a person has available to them for help concerning such issues as adhering to a treatment, coping with a difficult health condition, or quitting smoking.

In order to be used, SNT requires research on the social networks of interest (related to a health issue). This research seeks to identify people in the network (actors), and the kinds of linkages or ties that exist between those people. For example, if you were interested in the way social networks impact on exercise behavior at a worksite, you would want to know:

- The people in the network—in this case, employees at the worksite.
- The frequency of interactions between people in the network.

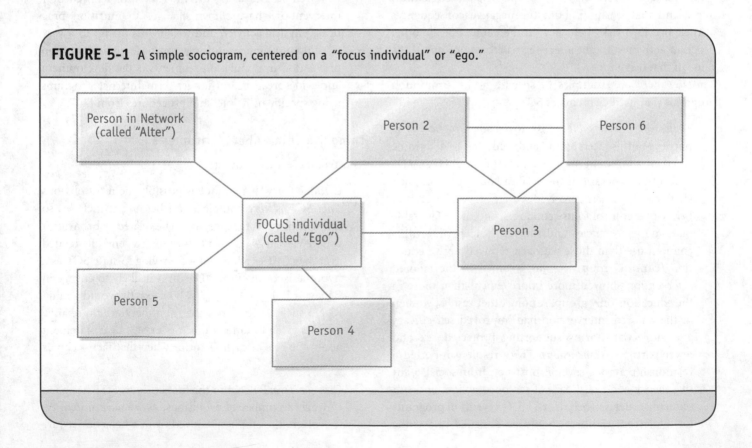

FIGURE 5-1 A simple sociogram, centered on a "focus individual" or "ego."

- The types of interactions between people in the network; in other words, are all interactions solely related to work matters, during the workday, or are there social interactions beyond that and interactions that involve exercise, such as a group of employees who regularly jog or play basketball at lunch?
- Differences in relational roles: Are there individuals who are key members of the network in the sense of being a part of several kinds of interactions, being the organizer of exercise or social activities, and so on?
- Are there groups or *cliques* in the larger work network? What is the nature of these cliques?

This information would tell you a lot about social influences on whether or not people exercise, and it would also tell you something about channels of communication and channels of influence if you were trying to increase exercising at that worksite. For example, suppose there was a person named Ed who was an important member of the subgroup of employees who jogged at lunch, and Ed was also a member of several of the subgroups that got together for social activities outside of work. Ed is then a real gold mine in terms of influence. If you worked with Ed and asked him to help increase the number of people who exercised, he could play a big role in bringing others into the "jogging" network or be instrumental in distributing information about obesity prevention to the networks he is a part of.

There are many different types of networks to think about. The most common in terms of health research and interventions is what is called an *ego-centered network*; that is, a "map" of the social relations surrounding an individual, typically called "ego" in SNT jargon. (The others in a network are called "alters," so an ego-centered network includes an ego and alters.) This version of a network is based on the perspective of the ego. A *full relational network*, on the other hand, includes reciprocal information from other members of the network.[16] The following list is a sample of the kinds of network qualities that you might look for in assessing the role of a network on the health behavior of individuals who were part of that network:

- *Centrality vs. marginality of individuals in the network:* The degree to which a given individual has interactions with many people in the network, and plays an important role in network activities.
- *Reciprocity of relationships:* Are relations one-way or two-way? For example, if Jane's relationship with fellow employee Bill involves no more than receiving her mail when he drops it off, it is largely a one-way relationship. If, on the other hand, Jane gets her mail from Bill, but processes paperwork that Bill gives her, and goes jogging with Bill at lunch, then the relationship is two-way and more complex.
- *Complexity or intensity of relationships in the network:* Is it a network mostly composed of one-way relations? Or is it primarily multiplex relationships? Do all the people in the network have relations with several alters, making a very complex or dense pattern of interaction?
- *Homogeneity or diversity of people in the network:* Are all members family? Are all members male? Or female? Or is there a diversity of types of members?
- *Subgroups, cliques, and linkages:* Are there concentrations of interaction among some members of the group? What is the nature of these? Are any members linked to other social networks?
- *Communication patterns in the network:* How does information circulate through the network? Is it viewed equally coming from anyone in the network, or do some members have more credibility?

Then there are key questions about the role of the network related to health behavior. You can look at a network with respect to *health risks*, or look at it in terms of the *supportive* role it plays in promoting healthy behaviors among its members. The first type might include, for example, a group of injection drug users who, by virtue of sharing needles and other interactions, create a shared situation of high risk for HIV/AIDS, hepatitis, and tuberculosis, among other health problems. The second type of network might include, for example, a smoking cessation support group that meets regularly and engages in social activities together. The latter network functions to increase individuals' positive health behavior.

The following summarizes the various components of Social Network Theory:

Relationships between and among individuals are important, as is how the nature of those relationships influences beliefs and behavior.

Relationship characteristics:

- Centrality vs. marginality of individuals in the network
- Reciprocity of relationships
- Complexity or intensity of relationships in the network
- Homogeneity or diversity of people in the network
- Subgroups, cliques, and linkages
- Communication patterns in the network

Using Social Network Theory

SNT is most useful in health promotion as a strategy to use, not surprisingly, for relatively limited or defined groups of people. It isn't a mass or large population intervention. To use it, there are basically two steps involved (not including evaluation):

1. *Research to identify the important characteristics of the network.*[16] For an ego-centered network, this will typically involve identifying one or more individuals with respect to some activity where you believe a network is involved, interviewing them about their interactions with others, and developing a map with relationship data. For a full relational network it is more difficult, because you have to interview all or a significant number of people in the network.

2. *Development of an intervention that specifically works with the network as a facilitator.* This could mean using the network to distribute information. Let's revisit the earlier example in Chapter 4 targeting blues musicians. The musicians appeared to be a social network, and smoking prevention information might be best and most credibly disseminated through someone in that network. Or, in combination with the social modeling aspect of Social Cognitive Theory, you could try to work with individuals in the network, preferably those with influence, to introduce risk-reducing behavior by modeling it to the other musicians. In the workplace network referred to previously, this might mean that individuals in a social activities network who began jogging at lunch start recruiting others in the network to do so as well.

Here are a couple examples of specific health promotion programs that have used Social Network Theory:

The Multicultural AIDS Prevention Project (MAPP): Dr. Robert Trotter II and colleagues at Northern Arizona University first identified networks of injection drug users in semirural Flagstaff, Arizona. By uncovering the highest risk relationship patterns in these networks, the team was able to direct targeted educational and other interventions to those "relational subsets."[16,17]

Natural Helper Interventions: There are often people in communities or social groups who have ongoing roles as "natural helpers." These individuals can play an important role in a health promotion intervention. In one example, the Black Churches Project identified such helpers in church congregations, who were then trained as health promoters.[18,19] The presence of these health promoters within an existing social network provided an important, accessible, and effective source of health information and support for these networks. </ul>

Things to Think About/Critiques

A few critiques to consider:

Critique one: SNT is a limited theory and approach. It is primarily useful for small or defined group interventions. If the idea is to promote health behavior change in a larger population, it is not feasible to use SNT other than as, for example, one of several approaches to disseminating information.

Critique two: Using SNT is labor-intensive and can be difficult. Identifying networks and conducting interviews is time consuming, and if you are looking for full relational data—that is, information from all or a significant number of network members—confidentiality concerns can be a barrier.

SOCIAL PROCESS THEORIES AND APPROACHES: DIFFUSION OF INNOVATIONS (DOI) AND SOCIAL MARKETING

Origins and Basic Elements

Diffusion of innovations (DOI) and social marketing are going to be reviewed together because they are examples of approaches that are less theory driven and more of a description of a process for how behavior tends to change in groups of people or communities.

Diffusion of Innovations

DOI approaches in health promotion have roots in rural sociology—studies, for example, on the diffusion of new agricultural technologies, such as a hybrid crop strain.[20,21] Descriptive research on the diffusion of cultural practices was also a major feature of American anthropology in the 1920s and 1930s. The general theory that came to be known as diffusion of innovations was set out by Everett M. Rogers in 1962 in a book that has been revised through four editions and continues to be a classic.[22] The approach has been used to address diffusion of technologies, communication, medical/health technologies and behaviors, and a wide range of other items. The primary concern of DOI is *the process by which a behavior or technology makes its way into a population and is (or is not) adopted.* According to Rogers, "*Diffusion* is the process by which an innovation is communicated through certain channels over time among members of a social system,"[22(p35)] with a goal of maximizing exposure and reach. The *innovation* is the behavior or technology that is perceived by the target population as *new*.

In the process of diffusion as described by DOI, you may notice similarities to stages-of-change models we discussed in the previous chapter. This is, in part, because DOI theory does posit a *process* of dissemination, which can't help but include a chronological element. Consider the following key processes in the dissemination of an innovation to a social group,[23] as conceptualized in DOI theory:

1. *Innovation development:* This refers to the development of the innovation itself—planning, formative research, and testing. Remember that an innovation can be a technology (such as oral rehydration packets intended to alleviate dehydration in children with diarrhea) or a behavior (such as exercise, HIV testing, etc.).

2. *Dissemination:* This has been defined as "active knowledge transfer from the resource system to the user system,"[24] and it involves the identification of communication channels and dissemination channels.

3. *Adoption:* Here is where we see a number of parallels to the Transtheoretical Model (TTM) and Precaution Adoption Process Model (PAPM). Adoption refers to the "uptake" of the behavior or technology by the intended audience. According to DOI, this requires movement through the following stages: knowledge of the innovation, persuasion or attitude development (about adopting), decision (to adopt), implementation, and confirmation. (Do you see the stages of change parallels?) The decision to adopt is said to be influenced by three types of knowledge: awareness knowledge (innovation exists), procedural knowledge (how to use), and principles knowledge (understanding how the innovation works).

4. *Implementation:* This refers to *initial* use of the practice or technology. Program focus is often on improving the self-efficacy and skills of those who have adopted the behavior or technology. A *linkage agent* (e.g., outreach educator) can help facilitate this process.

5. *Maintenance:* After individuals (in a population or group) begin to engage in a new behavior or use a technology the first time, the next step is to keep that pattern going. The focus is on *sustainability*. This could also refer to *institutionalization* of a behavior or technology.

There are a number of other constructs and concepts included in DOI theory—it is, after all, an extensively used and documented approach. One of these additional concepts is the idea that innovations are adopted in a staged process by different *categories of adopters*: early adopters, early majority

adopters, late majority adopters, and laggards. Identifying these groups within a target population can help in planning different dissemination strategies for each. If, for example, you are trying to get restaurant chefs to adopt and introduce new, low-fat foods at fine restaurants, the *early adopters* might be up-and-coming chefs who are trying to break away from the pack and make a name for themselves. If your preliminary research suggests this, your dissemination strategy might very well target those chefs first, with the idea that adoption of some of these new food offerings, accompanied by publicity, would spur adoption by other chefs.

Another concept is the idea that there is a *diffusion context*. This refers to the complex of factors related to the social group targeted by the program and the program of innovation dissemination itself that may facilitate or hinder diffusion. So, for example, in a country with strict centralized control, one aspect of the diffusion context is that the "flow" of dissemination would have to be channeled initially through one gateway or portal. Or, in a local community in the United States, there may be political or social structures in a community that inhibit diffusion of a new behavior.

Then, there is a whole list of "product attributes" that are said to be important determinants of the speed and extent of diffusion. These include the following:[23(Table 14.2)]

- *Relative advantage:* Is innovation better than what it will replace?
- *Compatibility:* Does innovation fit with the intended audience?
- *Complexibility:* Is the innovation easy to use?
- *Trialability:* Can the innovation be tried before making the decision to adopt?
- *Observability:* Are the results of the innovation observable and easily measurable?
- *Impact on social relations:* Does the innovation have a disruptive effect on the social environment?
- *Reversibility:* Can the innovation be reversed or discontinued easily?
- *Communicability:* Can the innovation be understood clearly and easily?
- *Time:* Can the innovation be adopted with a minimal investment of time?
- *Risk and uncertainty level:* Can the innovation be adopted with minimal risk and uncertainty?
- *Commitment:* Can the innovation be used effectively with only modest commitment?
- *Modifiability:* Can the innovation be modified and updated over time?

As you can see, many of these attributes are really related to the extent of barriers to adoption.

Social Marketing

This is a specific kind of approach to health communications and behavior change in groups or populations that incorporates principles of *marketing* to achieve health aims. In short, it is a way of treating behavior change as a "product" that you (as a health promotion professional) are essentially trying to market. Potential consumers, the target population, are understood as thinking about health behavior change in the same way they would about other product choices. The health promotion goal is to have people *voluntarily* adopt the health behavior or health technology, because they come to view the behavior as in their interest. So the term *marketing* may be a bit misleading. It is the voluntary choice aspect that is similar,[25] and in order to promote voluntary adoption, the choice of behavior being "offered" has to be presented as attractive in the sense of its costs and benefits. You may notice similarities in this basic goal to constructs discussed as part of the diffusion of innovations theory and even to individual behavior theories such as the Health Belief Model.

The social marketing approach was first introduced in the late 1960s/early 1970s by Kotler and Zaltman,[26,27] though others took up the approach soon after.[28,29] It has since been used widely in health behavior change efforts in the United States and internationally, the latter particularly with respect to reproductive health and HIV/AIDS programs.

CLASS EXERCISE

1. The class divides into a *diffusion team* (five students) and an *audience*.
2. Take a simple object like colored pens. The audience does not know in advance what the objects are. The diffusion team has to develop and carry out a brief strategy for diffusing the pens (or other items) to the audience—getting the audience to use them—based on an assessment of diffusion context, by emphasizing product attributes, and by seeking early adopters/change agents.
3. The audience is divided up into early adopters, majority adopters, and "laggards."

The principles of a social marketing approach are typically summarized as the "four Ps"—product, price, place, and promotion. More specifically:

- *Product:* What is the behavior or technology you are offering? What are its benefits? For example, let's say you are trying to promote smoking cessation among pregnant women. The *product* includes several elements; one is the actual behavior of not smoking or quitting smoking, which may include a specific program or product (like the patch or nicotine gum). Another is the idea of a healthy baby. Another might be the idea that the mother will live longer to see her child grow up. A key formative research task is to identify the most important benefits of the "product" among the target population.

- *Price:* For the target population, what are the costs involved in adopting a behavior/using a technology? Using the smoking intervention example, smoking may have other key benefits, such as the glue for social interactions or friendship activities or maybe the perceived costs of quitting are high. Understanding the costs as perceived by a specific target population is a research task.

- *Place:* How do you distribute or make the behavior or technology easily available to the target population? This has to do with issues of *access* and *availability*. Using our example: Smoking cessation programs would have to be made easily available (possibly even in-home), or located within other institutions where an expectant mother would go, such as her prenatal care clinic. With respect to condoms (as another example), this might mean placing them where they would be available for last minute use.

- *Promotion:* How do you promote or make the target population aware of the previous three elements? Using our example: The social marketing campaign would have to make expectant mothers aware of the great benefits of quitting, that the price is not so bad, and that programs are easily available and even attractively located.

Usually, as in regular marketing, multiple channels and repeated or sequenced messages are most effective. In other words, the research team needs to come up with a slogan or way to phrase the message and a dissemination plan to get the message out through various media, as well as interpersonal methods (e.g., community presentations), and via print materials that accompany something of importance.

There are a number of other important social marketing constructs. *Market segmentation*, for example, is a term common in marketing parlance. It refers to the segmentation of a target population into meaningful subgroups so that messages and campaigns can be appropriately channeled. Thinking again of our example, research may show that the types of messages and channels for expectant teen mothers will be significantly different than those for adult expectant mothers. Another general term is *targeting*. This is the process of developing campaigns that are closely tailored to the needs, attitudes, beliefs, and behaviors of specific market segments. Both social marketing and general health communication efforts incorporate much of the behavioral theories and constructs we have already discussed, including self-efficacy, vicarious learning, perceived costs/benefits, and so on.

Table 5-2 summarizes the components of social marketing approaches.

Using DOI and Social Marketing

Let's say that you wanted to engage in an effort to increase helmet use among "bikers," the general social group of serious Harley-Davidson motorcycle riders (not counting many of those who have taken it up more recently as a fad). Generally speaking, helmet use is not looked on with favor by bikers, and in fact *not* wearing a helmet is a more common norm. There are several reasons, from the viewpoint of the biker community:

- Required use of helmets impinges on the freedom of bikers to ride the way they want to ride, and, after all, being a biker *means* freedom. Being a biker is "one of the last free ways of life left in this country."
- Bikers are skilled riders; they don't need protection.
- Wearing a helmet gets in the way of your senses and feel of the road—you can't hear or see as well.

So, you face something of a challenge.

Using a DOI approach, you would be thinking of helmets as a kind of *innovation* to be adopted. You might have to start by redesigning a helmet that would fit the biker image a little better. Maybe it would be black, with biker decals and emblems. Maybe Harley-Davidson could endorse it. Developing the innovation is similar in this case to the idea of a *product* in social marketing. Both approaches, in that sense, include a deep concern with promoting the *benefits* of the object to be disseminated or marketed. One of the potential categories of benefit is *price*. So, perhaps you could seek a government subsidy to help reduce the comparative cost of buying a helmet. (Do you have any other ideas?) It might be useful to see if a well-known biker would endorse

helmet use and use one himself, and in doing so become an *early adopter*. Information about these biker helmets would be disseminated through *channels* that are credible and useful to bikers, for example, through bike repair shops, dealers, and biker events. This is also part of *promotion* in social marketing, one of the "four P's."

Now here are some examples of specific health promotion programs that have used DOI or social marketing:

Diffusion of Innovations and Doctor's Use of the Internet: Family physicians must be aware of the latest and best evidence for a broad range of clinical and public health topics. The Internet is an important source of this information, but not all family physicians use the Internet. This project and study used diffusion of innovations theory to identify strategies for increasing Internet use among family physicians. Using pre- and post-test surveys to learn about physician information sources, project staff developed a DOI strategy that focused on their use when not constrained by heavy patient volume (a barrier). When physicians used it at these times, they gained confidence in its utility and became more skilled in its use, thereby increasing their usage. *Conclusions:* Identifying barriers and using that information to find ways to increase adoption was effective, and suggested other Internet approaches (online medical education) that would further enhance their use.[30]

A Social Marketing Intervention—The 5 A Day Campaign: The National Cancer Institute, together with the Produce for Better Health Foundation, developed and implemented the "5 A Day for Better Health" national social marketing campaign. The simple message—"eat five or more servings of vegetables and fruit daily for better

TABLE 5-2 Social Marketing: The Four "Ps"	
Product	The behavior or technology you are offering; its benefits
Price	For the target population, the costs involved in adopting a behavior/using a technology
Place	How you distribute or make the behavior/technology easily available to the target population; issues of *access* and *availability*
Promotion	How you promote or make the target population aware of the previous three elements

health"—was repeated using an integrated strategy and many, many channels and materials, including:

- Produce bags
- In-store displays and signs
- Packaging labels
- Recipe cards
- Brochures
- Magazine articles
- News stories
- Internet
- Radio and television
- Billboards
- School communications
- Health fairs
- Cookbooks
- And many more

The program increased knowledge (promotion) of the product and how it could easily be integrated into daily life.[31]

Things to Think About/Critiques

Critique one: The critique mentioned for communications theory in the next chapter has some relevance to social marketing, though less so. Assessing the impact of a social marketing campaign may be difficult because, if a behavior change is the goal, tracking exposure to the campaign for those exposed and assessing the degree to which behaviors, or at least attitudes, have changed is not always easy. However, some social marketing campaigns (and most diffusion efforts) seek to introduce a technology as the behavior change; for example, the use of condoms for HIV/AIDS and STI prevention, or the use of oral rehydration therapy packets for child survival. That is easier to track, simply because it is more tangible and observable.

Chapter Questions

1. What is the interaction between *social* and *cognitive* in Social Cognitive Theory?

2. What does Bandura mean by "reciprocal determinism"?

3. What is a basic difference between the explanation for behavior in Social Network Theory and the explanations in theories such as the Health Belief Model?

4. What do social marketing and diffusion of innovations approaches have in common with marketing in a business context? What is different?

5. What are some of the key factors that determine speed of adoption in diffusion of innovations theory?

REFERENCES

1. Bronfenbrenner U. *The Ecology of Human Development.* Cambridge, MA: Harvard University Press; 1979.

2. Bandura A. *Social Foundations of Thought and Action.* Englewood Cliffs, NJ: Prentice Hall; 1986.

3. Bandura A. Social cognitive theory: an agentic perspective. *Ann Rev Psychol.* 2001;52:1–26.

4. Bandura A. *Principles of Behavior Modification.* New York: Holt, Rinehart & Winston; 1969.

5. Bandura A. *Social Learning Theory.* Englewood Cliffs, NJ: Prentice Hall; 1977.

6. Bandura A. The self system in reciprocal determinism. *Am Psychol.* 1978;33:344–358.

7. Baranowski T, Perry CL, Parcel GS. How individuals, environments, and health behavior interact: social cognitive theory. In: Glanz K, Rimer BK, Lewis FM, eds. *Health Behavior and Health Education: Theory, Research and Practice,* 3rd ed. San Francisco, CA: Jossey-Bass; 2002.

8. Koniak-Griffin D, Stein JA. Predictors of sexual risk behaviors among adolescent mothers in a human immunodeficiency virus prevention program. *J Adolesc Health.* 2006;38(3):297.e1–e11.

9. Winett RA, Tate DF, Anderson ES, Wojcik JR, Winett SG. Long-term weight gain prevention: a theoretically based Internet approach. *Prev Med.* 2005;41(2):629–641.

10. Barnes JA. Class and communities in a Norwegian island parish. *Human Relations.* 1954;7:39–58.

11. Wasserman S, Faust K. *Social Network Analysis.* Cambridge: Cambridge University Press; 1994.

12. Scott J. *Social Network Analysis: A Handbook,* 2nd ed. London: Sage; 2000.

13. Monge PR, Contractor NS. *Theories of Communication Networks.* New York: Oxford University Press; 2003.

14. Rogers EM, Kincaid DL. *Communication Networks: Toward a New Paradigm for Research.* New York: Free Press; 1981.

15. Pescosolido BA, Levy JA, eds. *Social Networks and Health,* 8th ed. Elsevier, Inc.; 2002.

16. Trotter RT II. Friends, relatives, and relevant others: conducting ethnographic network studies. In: Schensul JJ, LeCompte MD, Trotter RT II, Cromley EK, Singer M, eds. *Mapping Social Networks, Spatial Data, and Hidden Populations: Ethnographer's Toolkit,* 4th ed. Walnut Creek, CA: Altamira Press; 1999:.

17. Trotter RT II. Drug use, AIDS and ethnography: advanced ethnographic research methods exploring the HIV epidemic. In *Qualitative Methods in Drug Abuse and HIV Research.* NIDA Research Monograph 157. Rockville, MD: National Institute on Drug Abuse; 1995.

18. Eng E, Hatch JW. Networking between agencies and black churches: the lay health advisor model. *Prev Human Serv.* 1991;10:123–146.

19. Heaney CA, Israel BA. Social networks and social support. In: Glanz K, Rimer BK, Lewis FM, eds. *Health Behavior and Health Education: Theory, Research and Practice,* 3rd ed. San Francisco, CA: Jossey-Bass; 2002.

20. Ryan B, Gross NC. The diffusion of hybrid seed corn in two Iowa communities. *Rural Sociol.* 1943;8:15–24.

21. Rogers EM. Categorizing the adopters of agricultural practices. *Rural Sociol.* 1958;23(4):346–354.

22. Rogers EM. *Diffusion of Innovations,* 4th ed. New York: Free Press; 1995.

23. Oldenburg B, Parcel GS. Diffusion of innovations. In Glanz K, Rimer BK, Lewis FM, eds. *Health Behavior and Health Education: Theory, Research and Practice,* 3rd ed. San Francisco, CA: Jossey-Bass; 2002:.

24. Quote citation.

25. Kotler P, Roberto EL. *Social Marketing Strategies for Changing Public Behavior.* New York: Free Press; 1989.

26. Kotler P, Zaltman G. Social marketing: an approach to planned social change. *J Market.* 1971;35:3–12.

27. Kotler P. *Marketing for Non-Profit Organizations.* Englewood Cliffs, NJ: Prentice-Hall; 1975.

28. Fine SH. *The Marketing of Ideas and Social Issues.* New York: Praeger; 1981.

29. Manoff RK. *Social Marketing.* New York: Praeger; 1985.

30. Chew F, Grant W, Tote R. Doctors on-line: using diffusion of innovations theory to understand Internet use. *Fam Med.* 2004;36(8):645–650.

31. Kotler P, Roberto N, Lee N. *Social Marketing: Improving the Quality of Life.* Thousand Oaks, CA: Sage; 2002.

CHAPTER 6

Social, Cultural, and Environmental Theories (Part II)

LEARNING OBJECTIVES

By the end of this chapter, the reader will be able to:

- Describe a selection of key behavioral theories focusing on the influence and nature of broader social contexts – communications theory, community and organizational mobilization, political economy, and culture theory

- Understand how these social/cultural/environmental theories might be applied

- Understand selected critiques of these theories

"It seems clear to me that God designed us to live in society—just as He has given the bees the honey . . ."

—FRANCOIS VOLTAIRE, *LETTERS TO FREDERICK THE GREAT,* LATE **18**TH CENTURY

In this second chapter on social, cultural, and environmental theories, we move a little farther out into society and explore a broader context for behavior.

COMMUNICATIONS THEORY
Origins and Basic Elements

We can't begin to address the whole of communications theory in this small section. So before we begin a selected discussion, understand that this is an entire field we are referring to, and a complex one at that. Think of all the issues related to how communication occurs! Still, a limited discussion is useful because you will be able to see how this area of theory relates to health behavior change and the larger issue of how people change what they do.

First, communication is an essential function of any organism. Cells communicate information. Genes communicate information about the structure and function of your body. Birds communicate information, as do dogs and cats. Communication is a process of transmitting, receiving, and processing information important for behavior. But human communication is almost unique among all organisms in that it is *symbolic.* (I say almost unique because some higher order primates, for example, have symbolic communication capabilities.) We don't just bark when threatened or aggressive, or squeak when recognizing food. We can assemble sentences (or any unit of text or symbol) made up of various components of meaning, switch those components around, substitute one thing for another, utter the sentence with humor, say it with pictures for effect, chop it into an abbreviated Internet (e-mail, instant message) format, and structure the sentence in an endless variety of ways to alter its *meaning* and *context.*

For purposes of health promotion, the most typical forms of communication used are interpersonal and mass communication. Each of these has its own complexity. Still, there are some basic areas of inquiry that cut across much of the territory of communications theory. First, there are the mechanical basics, and for that we can refer to a famous quote from communications theorist Harold Lasswell, in which he defined communication as "who says what in which channel to whom and with what effects."[1] This quote introduces us to the basic layout of a communications process initially described by a Bell Laboratories mathematician named Claude Shannon, called the Shannon-Weaver model,[2] where:

1. A sender *encodes* a *message*. The message is the content, the information. Encoding means to package the message in text or symbols of some kind.
2. The sender transmits the message through a *channel* or *medium*, like the telephone, e-mail, or speech.
3. During the transmission, the message may encounter *noise*, which essentially means any interference.
4. The message then goes to a *receiver*, who interprets or *decodes* the information so that it can be used.
5. The receiver may transmit *feedback* or a reaction to the sender.

This is a very "technical" description of communication, and does not take into account many, many factors involved in how information is communicated, such as:

- The context or setting of the communication (e.g., Is it formal or informal?)
- Relationships between sender and receiver (e.g., Does one of the parties have authority over the other? Is there a gender difference?)
- The meaning attached to the channel (e.g., Does sending a message by letter have a different meaning than the same message communicated by telephone?)
- The process of encoding and decoding itself, which is a meaning-making act (*Semiotics* is a branch of communications theory that deals with meaning-making, the use of signs and symbols.)

William McGuire added the factors of attention, comprehension, liking, action, and others to the Lasswell or Shannon-Weaver schema[3]; since its introduction, the basic technical model has been modified by others as well. Can you see how there are many elements to consider in the act of communication? If you look, for example, at a transcript of a conversation between people who are long-time friends, you often see many gaps and unfinished sentences. Why? Because there is a substantial *shared body of knowledge*, or *shared world*, such that the "receivers" can fill in the gaps. Everything does not need to be said. The phenomenon of shared understanding between communicants has been addressed from many angles. In social linguistics there is, for example, the concept of the "speech community,"[4] commonly understood as a social configuration or setting in which speech styles and underlying knowledge are shared enough to sustain distinct communication patterns. William Labov, John Gumperz, and Dell Hymes, among others, have researched and illustrated the close connection between social structure and speech usage.[4-7] From a more poststructuralist or postmodern perspective, theorists like Michel Foucault[8] have pointed out the role of prevailing *discursive practices* in setting the ground rules for communication. The idea of prevailing discursive practices refers to the way acts of communication (discourse) are evaluated (e.g., as credible, not credible, meaningful or not), and how language categorizes or values elements of the social world are determined by rules and assumptions about knowledge and truth at a given historical point in time. There are also the institutions and technologies of communication. According to George Gerbner,[9,10] for example, television has become the dominant medium for *stories* and learning among children. Yet television and its programs are *products*, meant to generate income. This is a significant change from a time when stories and life-learning came from parents and the community, and it has profound effects on the content of these stories.

Let's take a brief look at some of what is involved in the process of communication, thinking about its relevance with respect to public health communication. First, we will focus on the idea of "encoding," and communication as a kind of "code." When you as a speaker send a message to another person or a group of people, what do you do? Do you simply utter a string of information? No, you put the information into a "code" that will make sense to the intended recipient in the way you want it to make sense. For example:

- When people engage in gossip, who is typically the intended recipient? Most likely, it is someone who is *not* the direct recipient of the information. But the whole enterprise of encoding something as gossip aims to utilize the medium of a peer group or community to send part of the message. So, if a *sender* instigates gossip about a certain Mr. Smith so that people say "Listen . . . did you hear about Smith? I hear that he goes to the dog racing tracks. Can you believe that?" Eventually, Smith is going to "get the message" that other people know this information about him and have (for example) a negative opinion of him because of it. So the sender has disseminated some information intended for Smith, but *encoded* in the form of gossip, which, by virtue of what gossip is, communicates the real message to Mr. Smith—that many people (especially his peers) will think he is lowly if he goes to the dog tracks, so he should shape up and act the way the social group thinks is appropriate.
- Advertisers are expert at encoding information; just think of any of a million commercials. What does a Cadillac commercial with Jimi Hendrix music in the

background really encode? What if you see an ad for an SUV that displays the words "Do what we say," "Fall in line," and "Stay on the sidewalk" all over one entire magazine page, and on the facing page stands a picture of the SUV with a tag line saying "Just say no" or "Break out." What does *that* encode?

- Just the mere fact of using specific vocabularies (slang vs. more polite diction), or preceding your communication with a formal greeting, encodes something about the message for its intended recipient.

When a message gets to a recipient, the recipient *decodes* it to interpret its meaning(s). You can see from Figure 6-1 that the encoding and decoding process depends upon many factors. One factor is that the sender and receiver need to have a shared understanding of what the symbols, text, graphics, and other elements of the code mean. If a shared understanding does not exist, the receiver may interpret the message very differently from what the sender really meant. Or, if the receiver is known to have a different communicative or cultural background from the sender, the sender will need to encode the message in a way that the receiver will interpret it as intended. This requires research or other knowledge of the recipient's interpretive patterns. The process is often referred to as *message design.*[11]

What is a communications *channel*? It is the medium through which you transmit information. General examples of channels include newspapers, TV, video, the Internet, interpersonal communication, and rallies. Channels can also be more specific, like Hispanic newspapers, or college radio, or through churches. Selection of channels is important in health communications because, as we have noted, the channel itself is relevant to the meaning of the message and because some channels are better than others for reaching a particular group. For instance, if you are trying to reach men, you are most likely not going to do so through a magazine that targets women (though that might not always be the case!). And if you are trying to reach men who are highly educated, you probably don't want to use a tabloid magazine—that is, if you want your message to be credible.

Finally, yet another issue related to communications theory is the role your selection of messages and channels has in *setting the agenda*, because in order to get people to pay attention to your information, they have to view it as important and relevant. Just like in political campaigns, the use of media and communications in public health aims to *impact the agenda* of what people are concerned about, in order to set the stage for or prompt action. There are many issues and concerns out there and the task is to present specific issues as "high on the agenda." It is a competition of sorts where you have to compete with other issues for public attention, and you will have to find the hook that will raise the agenda level. An initial step doing this is to understand where your health issue fits in the current public agenda or the public agenda of issues for your target population. This is, yet again, a research task.

Figure 6-2 summarizes a few key elements of communications theory, expanding on the "technical model" discussed earlier.

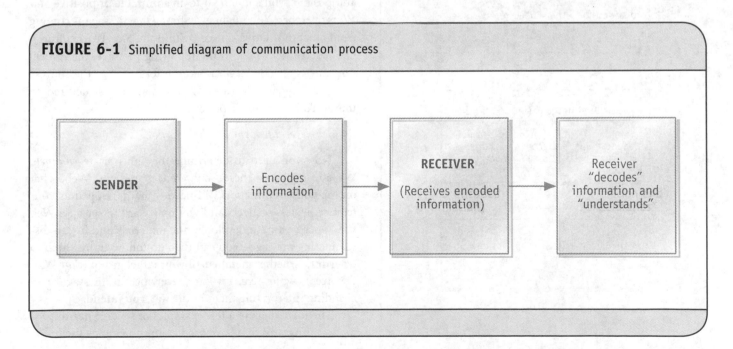

FIGURE 6-1 Simplified diagram of communication process

SENDER → Encodes information → **RECEIVER** (Receives encoded information) → Receiver "decodes" information and "understands"

FIGURE 6-2 The communication process.

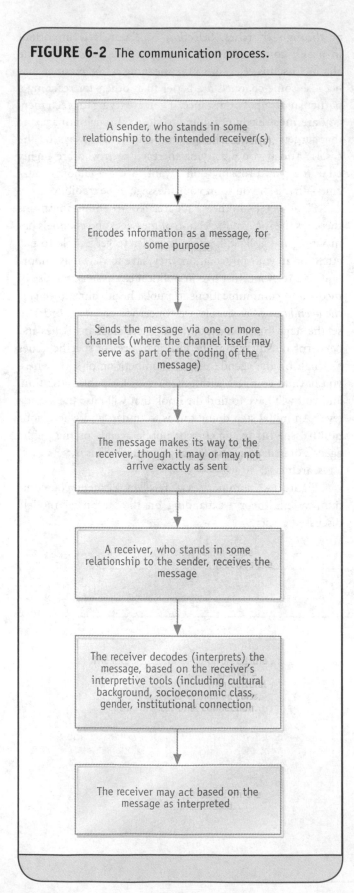

A sender, who stands in some relationship to the intended receiver(s)

Encodes information as a message, for some purpose

Sends the message via one or more channels (where the channel itself may serve as part of the coding of the message)

The message makes its way to the receiver, though it may or may not arrive exactly as sent

A receiver, who stands in some relationship to the sender, receives the message

The receiver decodes (interprets) the message, based on the receiver's interpretive tools (including cultural background, socioeconomic class, gender, institutional connection

The receiver may act based on the message as interpreted

Using Communications Theory

Suppose you wanted to communicate some important health information about smoking to young people who were highly involved in a subculture, such as the devotees of *Star Trek* or *Star Wars*, and whose interactions occurred mostly through two media—the Web and at big conferences. To conduct formative research with respect to the latter group, you went to a few *Star Wars* conferences to record the language used and to conduct interviews, and it was clear that people used many references to *Star Wars* characters in ordinary conversation, as *metaphors* or *similes*. You might hear, for example, sentences like the following:

> "Oh, Janey is acting like a real Princess Leia about the party. She is on a mission, and definitely thinks she is the center of attention."

> "Fred? Oh he's the guy with Chewbacca hair over there."

You would also likely find that participants' e-mail or instant message addresses reflected some *Star Wars* theme, like Alduron, or DeathStar, or Droid.

How would you use communications theory to get a message across? First, you need to determine the content and *encode* it, remember? How will you do that? You already have some clues about codes used by your "target population" that rely heavily on *Star Wars* references. So if you wanted the health behavior (smoking cessation) message you were trying to communicate to be understood as something relevant and positive, you could tie it to an admirable or positive *Star Wars* reference. You might even frame the message as coming from an authoritative source (within the *Star Wars* culture), like Jedi Master Yoda. In the following message, the *content* not only is encoded with reference to Yoda (as the source) and Jedi knights, but also is grammatically structured to mimic Yoda's linguistic pattern:

> *Never a Jedi smokes, he does not.*

Now you need to determine the appropriate *channels*. We already know these—conferences and the Web. That means your information will need to be developed as conference posters or flyers and you may want to set up a Web site. Once you have developed the materials and begun disseminating messages, you can then do follow-up research to determine whether members of your target group (*Star Wars* devotees)—your *receivers*—are receiving the messages and decoding/interpreting them in the way you intend.

The following are a few examples of specific health promotion programs that have used communications theory:

Partnership for a Drug-Free America Media Campaign: The Partnership for a Drug-Free America is a nonprofit coalition of communication, health, medical, and educational professionals and groups that, together with advertising/public affairs organizations, has developed and disseminated national media messages related to the prevention of drug use. The partnership's research-based, educational campaigns are disseminated through all forms of media, including TV, radio, and print advertisements and over the Internet. Campaign information is designed to reach those at risk for drug use (e.g., youth), and those who influence them (e.g., parents, doctors), and to employ messages that are developed through research with "intended audiences." Many collaborations are involved: In its 18-year history, the partnership has utilized the pro bono work of the country's best advertising, public relations (PR), and interactive agencies, and the donated time and space of major media.

Texas Tobacco Prevention Media and Community Campaign:[12] This adult media campaign in Texas combined television, radio, newspaper, and billboard advertisements featuring messages and outreach programs to help adults avoid or quit using tobacco products. The ads also promoted quitting assistance programs from the American Cancer Society Smokers' Quitline, a telephone counseling service. The cessation component of the intervention focused on increasing availability of and access to cessation counseling services and pharmacological therapy to reduce nicotine dependence. Both clinical and community-based cessation programs were offered. Areas that had combined cessation activities with high-level media campaigns had a rate of smoking reduction that almost tripled rates in areas that received no services, and almost doubled rates in areas with media campaigns alone. Analyses of data showed greater exposure to television and radio messages in the areas where high-level media was combined with community cessation activities than in the other areas. Results also showed that exposure to media messages was related to processes of change in smoking cessation and that those processes were related to the quitting that was observed in the group receiving the most intensive campaigns.

Things to Think About/Critiques

Critique one: It is sometimes complicated and difficult to assess the impact of a communications effort. Why? Because there are many levels of possible impact. One is simple exposure, or how many of the intended audience (recipients) report exposure to the message(s). Even if many people are exposed, that doesn't necessarily translate into behavior change. The next level is to assess how many of the people who were exposed either thought about or actually made a behavior change. That means you have to track a sample of those exposed for a period of time after the communications campaign—not an easy thing to do.

COMMUNITY AND ORGANIZATIONAL CHANGE
Origins and Basic Elements

For there to be a change in health behavior, in many cases there must first be a change in the community, in systems (e.g., health care systems), or in organizations relevant to the situation. You can't, for example, expect people to suddenly access diabetes screening (a behavior) even if they have all the information and intent needed, when there are no screening facilities they can go to. You can't expect people in a particular community to get HIV tests or engage in HIV preventive behavior if the community, and its various community institutions, exert strong pressures on individuals *not* to discuss or even admit to any risk for the disease. These are examples of another social fact that is often present with respect to health behavior change issues—communities, organizations, and systems can either support or inhibit health behavior change. Thus, one area of theory and practice has to do with change processes in these larger contextual settings.

As for every other theory area we have discussed, theories of community mobilization, and organizational and systems change are each the subject of entire courses and lifetimes of practice. The goal of this section is to give you an idea about what is involved in addressing these broader aspects of behavior change. We will look at community mobilization and organizational/systems change separately in this section, though both are elements of a general community change effort.

Community Mobilization

Public health is by nature activist, and community mobilization is one category of approaches where that is very evident. In order to foster community change, some of the characteristics of political and social *movements* come into play. Why is community change important? Because many of the conditions that are conducive to or a barrier to health are, as we have seen, ecological. They are community-level conditions or situations, and to make any progress, they will have to be addressed. These conditions/situations could include:

- Lack of available health facilities for underserved populations
- Regulations that allow the sale of cigarettes in locations easily accessible to young people
- A toxic waste site or other source of pollution
- Lack of sidewalks and green space in urban areas

Community mobilizing efforts involve collective action by groups and community members to increase awareness about the problem, advocate for policy change, and engage in many other kinds of activities designed to do something about the environmental condition(s). An important result of community action is *empowerment*, where the community takes charge of the issue, defines what the goals are, and takes the necessary action. By doing this, the community gains experience and a sense of efficacy about resolving local problems.

Community mobilizing as a category of health promotion draws from the historical experience of a wide range of social and political movements:

- The labor movement
- The civil rights and women's movements
- Anti-smoking activism
- HIV/AIDS activism
- The anti-abortion movement
- Other community-based movements, such as Mothers Against Drunk Driving

Key figures in the theory and practice of community mobilization include Saul Alinsky, who (in Chicago) pioneered many of the grassroots and advocacy strategies common today;[13] and Paolo Freire, a Brazilian educator who, in working for the liberation of the poor and marginalized in Latin America, founded an entire approach to participatory social change.[14]

Key issues in mobilizing communities include:

- *Defining the community:* How will you do this? Is it a geographic community? A particular subpopulation? (A lot of politics are involved in defining the community!)
- *Assessing, and working with, the community's capacity for mobilizing:* Some communities have experience and even existing organizations, such as task forces or committees, through which action can be organized. Others do not.
- *Understanding the community agenda and selecting the right issue:* A specific health problem may or may not be at the top of the list of priorities for a given community. Knowing community priorities can help, for example, in pairing a health issue with other priority issues to maximize the potential for community action.

Organizational and Systems Change

Addressing organizational and systems change is an important health promotion approach for reasons similar to the importance of community mobilization. Put simply, health promotion, disease prevention, and health care are all accomplished primarily through *organizations* (e.g., agencies, hospitals, programs) and *systems* (e.g., health care systems, linked service systems, policy coordination systems). Any one of these organizations or systems may be a facilitator or barrier to resolving a particular health issue.

For example, in the area of substance abuse prevention and treatment, one of the most enduring problems has been the fact that prevention and treatment are fields that developed independently, and didn't interact much. Treatment is more of a clinical discipline, involving psychologists, physicians, and social workers. Prevention, on the other hand, has focused more on community outreach and programs, information dissemination, community mobilization, and broader behavior change interventions aimed at factors leading to substance abuse—more of a community-based, social science effort. Treatment and prevention tend to be funded by separate agencies. (Within the Substance Abuse and Mental Health Services Administration, for example, there is a Center for Substance Abuse Prevention [CSAP] and a Center for Substance Abuse Treatment [CSAT]); both are ultimately working toward the same goal.) Unfortunately, efforts to improve collaboration have been slow because of entrenched system differences, from the federal government level all the way down to the community level. Efforts to improve system integration would in this case be an important health promotion objective.

There are whole fields of study and practice devoted to organizational and systems change. The field of *organizational development (OD)*, for example, began with a focus on improving business performance and the quality of work life. Psychologist Kurt Lewin was influential in the evolution of OD as an applied discipline, because Lewin's work focused on group dynamics and the interactions of individuals and groups.[15,16] Sociologist Elton Mayo in the 1920s and 1930s, researchers at the Tavistock Institute of Human Relations in London, and humanist psychologist Abraham Maslow were other influences. Essentially, OD is both a philosophy and an approach to organizational change that views organizations as *systems of human beings.* Change in the organization is said to involve the application of behavioral science to support planned development of strategies and processes, and a fostering of shared goals and motivation among members of the organization that will help the change process occur.[17,18]

Another type of approach views organizational change as a staged process, in some ways similar to stages-of-change approaches for individual behavior. Organizations are said to change through various kinds of stages, for example, "unfreezing," movement, and "refreezing,"[16] or from a point of "unsatisfied demand" through determination of alternatives, decisions, adoption, and institutionalization of change.[19,20] These change processes are an integral part of the adoption of different health policies and practices by an organization itself, or a necessary step in moving an organization to advocate for change (in health-related policies, laws, regulations, etc.).

A number of other issues and concepts are considered to be factors in the organizational change process, including, for example, organizational climate, culture, and capacity.[20] Taken together, changing an organization as it relates to health promotion has parallels to change in communities.

Table 6-1 summarizes organizational culture. Table 6-2 summarizes concepts and factors in community and organizational change.

Using Community and Organizational Change Approaches

Suppose you have the following situation: Several hospitals and medical providers in a county in California have experienced an influx of patients who do not speak English, or who do so on a very limited basis. To handle the situation, changes in the way care is provided are going to be necessary. How will you do this? Here are a few possibilities, combining both organizational and community change efforts:

- Enlist community organizations in a public campaign to increase general awareness of the situation and the implications it has for the health and well-being of the community. Part of the campaign message may even be an effort to persuade the county government to create a task force.
- Conduct direct advocacy with key persons/units in the health care system to present the problem and its implications to providers. For example, if a patient becomes seriously ill or worse because he or she couldn't read the dosage instructions on prescribed medication and the doctor never explained it, there may be liability issues for the clinic.
- Offer training to providers on strategies for providing culturally competent care to the immigrant population. Combine this with assistance in the development of specific practices and policies that will help, such as increasing the number of bilingual staff or changing service hours to accommodate farm workers.

TABLE 6-1 Organizational Culture: What Is It?

- The purpose of the organization—its mission, as understood by members of the organization. A kind of corporate "self-image."
- Values and norms about how that mission should be achieved.
- Codes of behavior in the organization: how to act, and how the behavior codes are related to the organization's self-image (e.g., dedicated, hard-working, fun-loving, people-friendly, etc.).
- Other related standards by which activity is measured, such as quality, efficiency, service, productivity, or innovation.

TABLE 6-2 Community Mobilization, Organizational Change

Community Mobilization

Collective action by community members, groups, and organizations to:
- Increase community awareness about a health problem
- Increase community awareness about environmental and other risks contributing to the problem
- Advocate for policy changes, increased access to services, or other needs
- Involve and *empower* the community in the change process
- Proceed through steps: Defining the community, assessing and working with the community's capacity, and collaborating with the community agenda

Organizational Change

Improving the capability of organizations and systems to respond to health issues through a change process that focuses on:
- Assessing and improving group dynamics within the organization/system (the way people work together)
- Encouraging shared goals and missions
- Identifying organizational impediments to change, and "unfreezing" the organization or system to make changes
- Involving the organization or system in identifying and implementing new policies and practices

The following are actual examples of community mobilization and organizational change efforts in health promotion:

Community Intervention for Safe Motherhood in Uttar Pradesh, India:[21] Mothers and their home birth attendants residing in rural Uttar Pradesh, India, were taught to recognize and take action to resolve specific maternal and neonatal life-threatening problems. As an effort to increase organizational capabilities in the health care system, community mobilization efforts were designed to reduce delays in transport to emergency obstetric care referral units and to increase use of family planning. Retention of knowledge and skills for recognition and intervention for maternal bleeding and newborn sepsis was enhanced when pictorial depictions of the problem, a take-action message, or both were used as memory aids.

Promotion of Hepatitis B Vaccine in Vietnamese-American Children:[22] Chronic infection with the hepatitis B virus is endemic in Southeast Asian populations, including Vietnamese. Previous research has documented low rates of hepatitis B vaccine coverage among Vietnamese-American children and adolescents ages 3 to 18. To address this problem, program designers designed and evaluated two public health outreach "catch-up" campaigns for this population. In the Houston, Texas, metropolitan area, a media-led information and education campaign was mounted, and in the Dallas metropolitan area, a community mobilization strategy was implemented. The success of these interventions was evaluated using the Washington, D.C., metropolitan area as a control site. To do so, computer-assisted telephone interviews were conducted before and after the intervention with random samples of approximately 500 Vietnamese-American households in each of the three program sites. The study assessed respondents' awareness and knowledge of hepatitis B and asked for hepatitis B vaccination dates for a randomly selected child in each household. When possible, researchers validated vaccination dates through direct contact with each child's providers. Both the media and community mobilization interventions showed significant improvements compared to the control community (no intervention). Both community mobilization and media campaigns significantly increased the knowledge of Vietnamese-American parents about hepatitis B vaccination, and the receipt of "catch-up" vaccinations among their children.

Things to Think About/Critiques

Critique one: Mobilizing a community, or changing an organization, is a complex process. If a health promotion effort is being conducted to address a pressing health problem, community mobilization or organizational change efforts may best be directed towards more enduring factors related to the health problem, such as policies and regulations, or increasing access to care. Or, such efforts can be combined with health promotion activities that address more immediate issues, although the process of mobilizing a community, even early on, can certainly have a galvanizing effect on other activities. It is also apparent that change in an organization (and in a community) is often affected by factors that can't be controlled, including a sudden change in leadership, a budget crisis, a disaster, or another event.

POLITICAL ECONOMY

Origins and Basic Elements

You might think that this area of theory is better left to a political science or economics course. Not necessarily, because some of the issues addressed under the heading of political economy have an important bearing on why and how people do what they do and, consequently, how people change what they do. It's not as simple as saying "money changes everything" or using any similar aphorism. There will always be a political-economic context that has an effect on what people do and what they can or cannot do, and to fully understand the factors influencing human action this context must be addressed. We are going to briefly touch on this category of theory with a specific reference to how it has been applied to health behavior. Political economy as a general subject area is vast, encompassing a wide range of theory and history about the links between politics and economics, and their functions in society.

The work of medical anthropologist Merrill Singer, following an explanatory approach pioneered by Eric Wolf,[23] Sidney Mintz,[24] and others, is a good example of how the connections between political economy and behavior are applied in addressing the crisis of HIV/AIDS in poor, urban communities.[25] Let's start with the question, "Why has HIV/AIDS had such a disproportionate effect on poor, minority urban communities?" There are all kinds of possible answers. The political-economic approach addresses the question by first trying to rethink HIV/AIDS as something more than just a *health* problem, but as a product of a larger set of social relationships, particularly relationships of socioeconomic structure, class, ethnicity, and gender. Singer links HIV/AIDS with a litany of other health problems (such as tuberculosis, infant mortality, hypertension, diabetes, cirrhosis, and substance abuse) that are disproportionately found in poor urban populations, and together calls the aggregate situation a *syndemic*—several epidemics that exist together *because conditions promote their coexistence.*[25(pp933-934)]

What conditions are referred to? The prevalence of poverty and unemployment in core urban areas, including a lack of access to health care options; the commonality of deteriorated and substandard schools; the prevalence of "economies of the street" in communities with few links to economic resources, where the available "jobs" are more likely to be related to drug trafficking and other illegal activities; the relationships between lack of employment opportunities and stable family structures; and the overall relationships (in society) between minority and majority ethnic groups, to name just a few.

One of the reasons this kind of approach hasn't been funded to the degree other more behavior-focused approaches have is that to carry out the approach ultimately means addressing significant social configurations, which, as you can imagine, is not a short-term project or one without controversy. But many who have worked with health issues that are immersed in the kinds of social conditions described above know that progress in alleviating the health problems is difficult to achieve without some change in the contributing conditions.

For example, one tested strategy in the developing world to address the socioeconomic position of women and the impact of this position on population, reproductive health, and other issues, is called *microcredit*. Originally the idea of Dr. Muhammad Yunus and the Grameen Bank (originally in Bangladesh), the idea includes the following:

1. Provide small loans to women so that they can start an economic enterprise of some kind, such as selling food, repairing clothes, or something else. These women usually do not have any access to credit (a political-economic fact), so the loans are set up so that individuals in the loan recipient's social or community network are involved as *loan guarantors*.

2. The women "sign on" to guarantee repayment of the loan, thus giving the lending banks some assurance. With these small loans and the business they help support, the recipient women have an alternate source of income and status, and many studies have shown that once women have more opportunities, they choose to have fewer children, meaning that more attention and resources (including health resources) are devoted to those they do have. This results in a public health benefit that occurred because poverty is reduced, a political-economic issue.[26]

Table 6-3 summarizes a political-economic approach.

ANTHROPOLOGY AND CULTURAL THEORY: BEHAVIOR AS ADAPTATION; BEHAVIOR AS MEANINGFUL AND SYMBOLIC

Origins and Basic Elements

Anthropology is a very broad field focusing on an in-depth and comparative study of human behavior. One way in which anthropology seeks to understand behavior is by treating it in the same way we typically treat the behavior of any species—as an adaptation that enabled the species to survive or thrive in a particular environment. This is often the domain of biological or physical anthropology. Another way anthropology looks at behavior is to understand the role that *culture* plays in what people, groups, and societies do. This falls under the purview of cultural anthropology, though the concept of culture is a key construct across all branches of anthropology. In recent years many anthropologists have become involved in issues of health, so much so that a subdiscipline of anthropology called *medical anthropology* has evolved. This subdiscipline, as well as the broader field of anthropology, offers another important way to understand and explain behavior in which individuals are not treated as separate from a sociocultural context.

The field in general developed as a separate discipline in the 19th century—the era of Charles Darwin's *Origin of Species* (together with the discovery of prehistoric human remains) and extensive colonial expansion of Western/European countries in Africa, Asia, the Pacific, and the

---

TABLE 6-3 Political Economy and Health

- Start with a health problem, and rethink it as a product of a larger set of social relationships, particularly relationships of socioeconomic structure, class, ethnicity, and gender.
- A health problem, or co-occurring health problems, can be seen as part of a *trajectory of risk* or *trajectory of exposure* that is shaped by the larger social relationships in which it exists.
- Solutions must address, in part, the social relationships (e.g., economic patterns, relationships of ethnicity, etc.) that contribute to the problem.

Americas. These factors alone prompted two essential areas of questioning: 1) How and when did we become human beings as we are today? and 2) Given the diversity of ways of life, what is it that makes us human? What makes us unique? What is common vs. idiosyncratic across human societies?

The biological anthropologists tend to look at behavior today with the first question in mind and so look at behavior as a species adaptation to (or interaction with) an environment. A number of medical anthropologists come from this perspective in understanding health behavior; for example, Peter J. Brown looks at the way culture served as an adaptive strategy to stave off malaria in Sardinia;[27] Ritenbaugh and Goodby examine the idea that some American Indian peoples have an unusually high incidence of diabetes because of an interaction between their genetic makeup and modern Western diets high in carbohydrates and sugar.[28]

Cultural anthropologists, however, begin with an assumption that the answer to the second set of questions above is *culture*—that is what is common and unique. So the primary focus of cultural anthropology is to amass a descriptive inventory of common and unique cultural patterns (including systems of knowledge), and to generally examine the role of culture in human behavior. Whether or not you've had an anthropology class, you have undoubtedly heard the term *culture*. Because it is so common, its meaning can be very fuzzy. Here is a classic definition, from early anthropologist E.B. Tylor in 1871:

> Culture . . . is that complex whole that includes knowledge, belief, art, morals, law, customs, and any other capabilities and habits acquired by man as a member of society.[29]

In that definition are several elements that have, more or less, remained consistent parts of a lot of definitions of culture: 1) That it exists as a kind of whole—that is, as an integrated pattern of some kind, which brings together many facets of society; 2) that it refers to what people *do* and what people *know*, and the relationship between those things; and 3) that it is *acquired*—that is, you are not born with it, but you learn it during the course of life in society.

I'm going to give you another definition of culture. But before I do, let's acknowledge that *all* people are "cultural." Culture refers to the shared and learned aspects of human cognition and behavior that underlie our ability to interpret the world around us and to take meaningful action. So, you can also think of culture as:

> An ongoing collective framework, developed over time by human societies and groups, for integrating meaning with events, actions and ways of life.

This definition focuses more on what a cultural anthropologist would look for in understanding and explaining health behavior, in that a behavior related to health is guided by some understanding about its meaning or results from a pattern of living that is built around meanings, symbols, and values, as these are connected to a larger social structure. In other words, the behavior cannot be separated from its larger *context*. Let's take a look at the issue of obesity. An anthropological take on the behaviors leading to obesity may focus on the following kinds of factors:

- What do people in a culture or social group think are the components of a good meal? Why? (And how does the definition of a "good meal" compare to what public health experts in the United States consider to be healthy meals?)
- What are common expectations about body type, and what values do various body types have? In some cultures, for example, a man with a large body is viewed with higher esteem, because the large body symbolizes "doing well" or being "healthy."
- Are there relationships between gender and eating or exercise patterns, and how might these affect obesity?
- How are eating and exercise patterns shaped by social structure? For example, in high poverty urban neighborhoods there is typically less access to fresh fruit and vegetables.
- Among the specific group or culture at issue, is "preparing food" a task for some people but not others? Who prepares food?

All of these questions reflect an understanding of the behaviors related to obesity as inseparable from the living and meaning systems of which they are a part, including the role of food, status and body image, gender roles, community social structure, and social tasks.

Another important direction taken by anthropological theory towards health behavior is to connect behavior to underlying *epistemologies* (systems of knowing and beliefs about how we know things) of health. Let me translate: Underlying your day-to-day understanding and actions related to health is some set of beliefs that addresses the following kinds of information:

- What does it mean to be healthy? How do we know when someone is healthy vs. not healthy?
- What are the illnesses, diseases, and conditions that constitute being "not healthy"?
- How does someone become unhealthy? What are the causes? This is very important because many cultures,

for example, understand at least some health conditions to be related to spiritual causes. "Western" cultures, on the other hand, typically attribute most diseases/illnesses to biological causes.

- Related to beliefs about causation, how does someone become healthy if they have a disease or illness? Who do you go to for a remedy? What are the remedies?

Answers to these questions, viewed together, form what in medical anthropology is called an *ethnomedical system*.[30,31] This refers to a basic, underlying set of beliefs, in response to the above kinds of questions, shared to one degree or another by most people in a cultural group. These are the beliefs that guide much of what we understand as healthy vs. unhealthy behavior. So, in a cultural group where having a large body is seen as a sign of well-being, the standard prevention messages about body size, eating, and obesity may not make much sense. (Members of this group might ask, "Don't we all *want* to be large? If someone is thin, it means they are poor, and not doing well. Why would I want that?")

The ethnomedical system also tells you something about the *healing* behavior of group members. If members believe a certain condition is *caused* by a particular spiritual factor, they are not likely to go to a medical doctor for a cure. They will go to a religious or spiritual person. If the condition is believed to be caused by a moral failure of the affected individual, or because of misbehavior of some kind, the condition may be *stigmatized* and the affected individual may go into hiding or avoid public contact—including a visit to the doctor or healer. This was, and remains in some places, the situation for HIV/AIDS victims.

Table 6-4 summarizes key components of an anthropological approach.

Using Anthropological Approaches

Let's say that public money was spent to build a series of health clinics in urban, underserved areas. But a year later, utilization is low. You are charged with finding out what is going on and increasing utilization. You conduct some initial research, and you find out that:

- In certain neighborhoods, people over age 30 just did not use the new health services located nearby.
- In certain parts of the neighborhood, the people are primarily recent immigrant families from Country X. Other parts of the neighborhood are also from Country X, but they have been here longer, and their children have largely grown up in the United States.
- You do some interviews with community leaders in the recent immigrant areas about health care beliefs and utilization.

TABLE 6-4 Anthropological Approach

- Biological anthropology focuses on health behavior as a species adaptation to (or interaction with) an environment
- Cultural anthropology understands and explains health behavior as part of a pattern of living that integrates action with meanings, symbols, and values, as these are connected to a larger social structure. In other words, the behavior cannot be separated from its larger *context*.

- You find that recent immigrants are more likely to have "traditional" Country X beliefs about disease causation; that is, some diseases or illnesses are attributed to spiritual causes, rather than physical/biological ones.
- You also find that the new health clinic has no services and disseminates no messages that correspond to these beliefs—they have, for example, no involvement with traditional curers.

You can do a number of things with this information. You could, for example, work with community leaders in both the recent and long-term immigrant segments of the community so that the more recent immigrants hear the experiences of the older immigrants with respect to using the clinics. Or, you could *co-locate* traditional, spiritual healers at the clinics, so that services would be available for a broader range of health conditions *as perceived by the community*.

Anthropological approaches have been used in a number of situations: Engaging indigenous healers in the prevention and treatment of HIV/AIDS; understanding local practices in order to improve malaria prevention; mapping social networks among injection drug users to better understand risk for HIV/AIDS; and many others.[32,33]

Things to Think About/Critiques

Critique one: One common misperception about developing culturally tailored health promotion approaches is that culture is necessarily homogenous; that is, *one* approach is thought to fit an entire group of people. The fact is, however, that culture is complex, and one group does not typically share all elements of a culture to the same degree. There may be factions and subgroups as well. So if a cultural approach is used too easily, it may "go right past" a significant part of the intended target population.

Critique two: Changes in the way culture and behavior interact may take time. Such changes are often necessary for long-term impact, but in the short-term, changes in the environment, whether they are new laws, regulations, or a physical change (like the building of sidewalks to promote walking), may have a more immediate effect, at least to start up the process.

Chapter Questions

1. What does "encoding" and "decoding" information refer to in communications theory? Why is this important for communicating about health behavior?

2. In terms of an ecological model, what kinds of things does a community mobilization effort address?

3. What is meant by "organizational culture"? How does it relate, for example, to work-related health behavior?

4. Using HIV/AIDS as an example, what issues would a political economic approach address in terms of potential action?

5. What is *cultural* about an ethnomedical system?

REFERENCES

1. Lasswell H. 1948. "The Structure and Function of Communication in Society." In L. Bryson (Ed.), *The Communication of Ideas*. New York: Harper & Row.

2. Shannon C, Weaver W. *The Mathematical Theory of Communication*. Urbana: University of Illinois Press; 1949.

3. McGuire W. Theoretical foundations of campaigns. In: Rice R, Paisley W, eds. *Public Communication Campaigns*. Thousand Oaks, CA: Sage Publications; 1991.

4. Labov W. *Sociolinguistic Patterns*. Philadelphia: University of Pennsylvania Press; 1972.

5. Gumperz JJ, Hymes D, eds. *Directions in Sociolinguistics: The Ethnography of Communication* (rev ed.). New York: Blackwell Publishers; 1986.

6. Hymes D. *Foundations in Sociolinguistics: An Ethnographic Approach*. Philadelphia: University of Pennsylvania Press; 1974.

7. Labov W. *The Social Stratification of English in New York City*. Washington, DC: Center for Applied Linguistics; 1966.

8. Foucault M. *The Order of Things: An Archaeology of the Human Sciences*. New York: Pantheon Books; 1971.

9. Gerbner G, et al. *Invisible Crisis: What Conglomerate Control of Media Means for America and the World*. Boulder, CO: Westview Press; 1996.

10. Gerbner G, et al. *Communications Technology and Social Policy: Understanding the New "Cultural Revolution."* New York: Interscience Publication; 1973.

11. Maibach E, Parrott RL. *Designing Health Messages: Approaches from Communication Theory and Public Health Practice*. Thousand Oaks, Calif.: Sage Publications; 1995.

12. McAlister A, Morrison TC, Hu S, et al. Media and community campaign effects on adult tobacco use in Texas. *J Health Comm*. 2004;9(2):95–109.

13. Alinsky SD. *Rules for Radicals*. New York: Random House; 1972.

14. Freire P. *Pedagogy of the Oppressed*. New York: Seabury Press; 1970.

15. Lewin K. *Resolving Social Conflicts: Selected Papers on Group Dynamics*. In: Lewin GW, ed. New York: Harper & Row; 1948.

16. Lewin K. *Field Theory in Social Science: Selected Theoretical Papers*. In Cartwright D, ed. New York: Harper & Row; 1951.

17. Cummings , Worley . *Organization Development and Change*, 6th ed. Boston, MA: South-Western; 1997.

18. Nielsen EG. *Becoming an OD Practitioner*. Englewood Cliffs, N.J.: Prentice-Hall; 1984.

19. Beyer JM, Trice HM. *Implementing Change: Alcoholism Policies in Work Organizations*. New York: Free Press; 1978.

20. Steckler A, Goodman RM, Kogler MC. Mobilizing organizations for health enhancement: theories of organizational change. In: Glanz K, Rimer BK, Lewis FM, eds. *Health Behavior and Health Education: Theory, Research and Practice*, 3rd ed. San Francisco, CA: Jossey-Bass; 2002.

21. Fullerton JT, Killian R, Gass PM. Outcomes of a community- and home-based intervention for safe motherhood and newborn care. *Health Care Women Int*. 2005;26(7):561–576.

22. McPhee SJ, Nguyen T, Euler GL, et al. Successful promotion of hepatitis B vaccinations among Vietnamese-American children ages 3 to 18: results of a controlled trial. *Pediatrics*. 2003;111(6 Pt 1):1278–1288.

23. Wolf E. *Europe and the People Without History*. Berkeley: University of California Press; 1982.

24. Mintz SW. *Sweetness and Power: The Place of Sugar in Modern History*. New York: Viking; 1985.

25. Singer M. AIDS and the health crisis of the U.S. urban poor: the perspective of critical medical anthropology. *Soc Sci Med*. 1994;39(7):931–948.

26. World Bank. *The Role of Microcredit in the Eradication of Poverty: A Report of the Secretary General*. New York: World Bank; 1997.

27. Brown PJ. Cultural adaptations to endemic malaria in Sardinia. *Med Anthropol*. 1981;5:3.

28. Ritenbaugh C, Goodby CS. Beyond the thrifty gene: metabolic implications of prehistoric migration into the new world. In: Brown PJ, ed. *Understanding and Applying Medical Anthropology*. Mountain View, CA: Mayfield; 1998.

29. Tylor EB. 1924 [orig. 1871] Primitive Culture. 2 vols. 7th ed. New York: Brentano's.

30. Foster GM. Disease etiologies in non-Western medical systems. *Am Anthropol*. 1976;78:4.

31. Hahn RA. *Sickness and Healing: An Anthropological Perspective*. New Haven, CT: Yale University Press; 1995.

32. Hahn, RA. (Ed.). 1999. *Anthropology in Public Health: Bridging Differences in Culture and Society*. New York: Oxford University Press.

33. Trotter, RT. 1995. "Drug Use, AIDS, and Ethnography: Advanced Ethnographic Research Methods Exploring the HIV Epidemic." In EY Lambert, RS Ashery, and RH Needle (Eds.) *Qualitative Methods in Drug Abuse and HIV Research*. NIDA Research Monograph 157. Rockville, MD: National Institute on Drug Abuse.

CHAPTER 7

Doing Something About It: The Ecological Perspective and the Move From Theory to Practice

LEARNING OBJECTIVES

By the end of this chapter, the reader will be able to:

- Understand the role of the planning process as a way to link theory to a particular health situation, community, and population
- Discuss the three basic components of any program planning process
- Describe the PRECEDE-PROCEED and Risk/Protective Factors models as examples of planning approaches

"An ounce of action is worth a ton of theory."

—FRIEDERICH ENGELS (1820–1895)

"Progress is impossible without change; and those who cannot change their minds cannot change anything."

—GEORGE BERNARD SHAW (1856–1950)

"One change leaves the way open for others."

—NICCOLO MACHIAVELLI (1469–1527)

WHERE DO YOU START? PICKING YOUR BATTLES

Now we get to the point where we have to move from theory to action. Contemplating and discussing reasons for human behavior has its own fascinations, but, ultimately we have a job to do! This is where the fun begins.

Not so fast. This is actually one of the most difficult things to accomplish—the transition from theory to practice.

In the field of public health, that transition, and how to do it well, must be one of the most-discussed topics in journals, meetings, and policy-making agencies. Why is it so difficult? You now know about the complexity of identifying causes and factors related to health behavior. You have learned about individual theories of behavior, social and group theories, organizational theories, political-economic theories, cultural theories, and others. Most importantly, you have learned that each of these theoretical approaches is a piece of an interrelated puzzle. The transition from this kind of knowledge to practice means grappling with the complexity and figuring out a specific intervention, program, policy, communication strategy, message, or coordinated approach that will potentially have an impact on the behavior(s) relevant to a health problem.

In the previous chapters, we went through the "layers of the onion," so to speak, and discussed the wide range of factors that have an impact on what people do. That is the holistic or *ecological* perspective, which is generally viewed in the field of public health as the most useful framework for understanding problems as they exist in the real world. At the same time, unless you have unlimited resources and unlimited time, you are not going to be able to address every factor you identify with a program component. So, you have to pick and choose.

Using previous examples, what factors would you try to tackle in the situation of the young women involved in the sex trade in Thailand? The larger political economy and social factors related to the sex trade in Thailand (e.g., urbanization, class, and poverty), or individual knowledge and skills? What about the blues musicians and cancer?

Would you focus on social support and networks first, or individual awareness?

If you have to pick and choose in order to put in place a public health/health promotion intervention, it is best to do so with some rationale or planning framework in mind. There are a number of frameworks out there to help with this process. Most combine assessments of the problem (your assessment of factors related to the health-risk behaviors) with some means for selecting from those factors and using theory to develop or adapt program components/themes, together with an assessment of the resources (funds, people, materials, time, etc.) you have available. We're going to discuss several of these in this chapter.

PLANNING APPROACHES—A SAMPLER
PRECEDE-PROCEED

One of the most well-known approaches for planning, implementing, and evaluating health promotion programs is called PRECEDE-PROCEED.[1,2] The title of the approach says a lot about what it entails: a process of assessment and planning before putting a program in place (PRECEDE), followed by implementation and evaluation of the program (PROCEED). In fact, this is more or less characteristic of all such planning approaches, which basically involve three steps:

1. *Assessment* (or diagnosis) of the health problem and its causal/supporting factors
2. Development of an *intervention* (health promotion program) based on the assessment, targeting selected factors identified in the assessment (and utilizing appropriate theory to guide intervention components)
3. *Evaluation* of the intervention, to determine if it has been implemented as planned and if it has actually affected the causal or related factors (identified in the assessment) that it was intended to affect

Regardless of the specific planning model, this general three-part process just makes common sense. And, all three parts should work together in a kind of continuous feedback loop: What you assess as the nature of the problem, causes, the ecological context, and so on will direct what theories are applicable, what kind of intervention should be undertaken, and what variables should be evaluated to determine effectiveness of the intervention. At the same time, the way your program works or doesn't work in the real world will in turn affect your assessment, which leads to a modification of your program again, and so on.

Although there are many planning frameworks, the PRECEDE-PROCEED approach is in part useful because it is so comprehensive. It is an approach that is designed to work within an ecological framework for understanding a health problem, and to help guide the selection of factors to target. It is also oriented towards addressing health problems at the community or local level, where it is easier to identify the factors and issues related to a health problem *as it occurs in that community*—assuming that the best way to organize and target resources is at that level. Emphasizing the community ecological orientation of PRECEDE-PROCEED, Green and Kreuter reiterate that health behavior "is seen increasingly not as isolated acts under the autonomous control of the individual, but rather as socially conditioned, culturally embedded, economically constrained patterns of living."[1(p17)] It is worth noting that Green and Kreuter's definition of lifestyle as it relates to the PRECEDE-PROCEED approach parallels in important ways the view presented throughout this book that "health behavior" is not really a distinct domain from "behavior" in general. Under this definition, lifestyle is:

> A complex of related practices and behavioral patterns in a person or group, maintained with some consistency over time. It includes conscious health-directed behavior as well as unconscious health-related behavior and practices pursued for non-health purposes but with health consequences or risks.[1(p18)]

The PRECEDE-PROCEED framework is organized in *stages*, beginning with the broadest level of assessment of the problem to the more targeted and specific, then including assessment of administrative and community resources relevant to the proposed program, implementing the program, and culminating in evaluation of the program to determine whether the program has made the desired impact. The stages are as follows.

Phase One: Social Assessment and Situational Analysis

This is the broadest level of assessment, and it's not one that you will always have the luxury to do in public health projects. The general purpose is to understand something about the health problem you want to address as it fits into the larger community context. It can also be used as a way of identifying which health problems a community believes are most important. The basic questions to be answered in this phase are:

- How does the health problem relate to what else is happening in the community?
- At what problems/issues should a community direct its resources and attention—which should receive priority?

In reality, most of the time you won't have a chance to complete this first assessment stage in its full form, though parts of it can be worked into other stages. Or if you do, it will be completed before you seek funding for a specific project. Typically, the health problem you are going to be addressing is one that is already defined by federal, state, local, or private (foundation) funding sources. This means that you will be implementing a program that responds to agency/organizational priorities, or looking for an organization that funds programs concerned with the health problem you have identified as important.

To understand the social assessment, think, for example, of a hypothetical community in the northeastern United States. Let's assume this community comprises an entire county; we'll call it North Hill County. The county has, in the past 20 years, experienced a serious economic decline typical of many "rust belt" communities where the industries that once fueled the local economies have disappeared, resulting in high rates of unemployment and few economic resources. Among other health problems, the county has relatively high rates of alcohol abuse and several related—or *comorbid*—conditions, including liver disease, drunk-driving accidents, and others. You could look at those health problems by themselves, or you could try to understand them in the context of what has been happening in recent years. The latter approach would involve a social assessment, in which you could ask the following kinds of questions:

- What are the *quality-of-life* issues that may be related to health problems in North Hill County?
- More specifically, what are the kinds of quality-of-life issues that may be related to alcohol abuse?

- Is the alcohol abuse related to unemployment? In other words, are people treated for alcohol problems unemployed? Lack of services (due to a lack of resources) may be another factor. Maybe young people in the county simply don't have much to do and don't see much available for them in the future.

What you might find out is that the alcohol abuse problem is really inseparable from the larger situation. If true, what do you think that means in terms of developing a program or set of programs to address alcohol abuse?

Phase one is summarized in Table 7-1.

Phase Two: Epidemiological Assessment

This assessment phase is more specific than the social assessment, and is often where you will actually begin a planning process. In the epidemiological assessment, your goal is to identify the nature and extent of a health problem, who is affected (what population groups), and what the trends are. This will help you *narrow your target*, both in terms of the health conditions to be addressed and the specific populations to target—information you need to know before making decisions about applicable theory. This kind of information is often available at the local level from public health departments, or from national surveillance data such as that collected by the Centers for Disease Control and Prevention (CDC). So, for example, if your local data showed that women experienced a high rate of smoking-related cancers, and that young children in the community were reporting a higher-than-average prevalence of respiratory problems (related to tobacco smoke), you may have three populations to target in a potential health promotion program:

TABLE 7-1 Summary of the Social Assessment (Phase One)

What It Is	Sources of Information	What This Tells You
Assessment of quality of life and social factors surrounding one or more health problems; ranking or positioning the health problems in context.	Social indicators like employment rates, availability of health care services, education, crime, housing, parks/recreation facilities, and so on.	From an ecological perspective, the social assessment provides you with an overview of the interplay between health and other factors, as well as potential social or quality-of-life outcomes for your program. It also may give you an indication of the importance placed on a particular health issue in the community.

- Women generally, and in particular women who smoke
- Mothers who smoke, because they are exposing their children via secondhand smoke
- Children in smoking households

Here are a few terms to know in understanding the kinds of information you need to conduct an epidemiological assessment:

- *Morbidity data:* Data on the incidence and prevalence of disease.
- *Mortality data:* Data on deaths due to disease and other factors.
- *Comorbidity:* Some health conditions are related or comorbid. For example, obesity and diabetes are co-morbid, because obesity is a risk for diabetes.
- *Incidence:* New cases; or the *current* rate at which a disease or health problem is being reported. This may be higher or lower than the prevalence rate, if the disease/health problem is on the rise or dropping.
- *Prevalence:* Existing case rates of a disease or health problem in a population; the spread or distribution of the problem in a population (or an area).

Table 7-2 summarizes Phase Two.

Phase Three: Behavioral and Environmental Assessment

At this point you have a good idea of what and who you will be targeting with your program. That does not, however, tell you *how* to address it. For that, you need a better idea of some of the factors that may be causing or at least contributing to the spread of the health problem. This third assessment phase, the *behavioral/environmental assessment*, begins to get at that by identifying such *risk factors*. Some of these are behavioral, as we have discussed extensively in previous chapters, and others are environmental. One way to characterize the two:

- Think of behavioral risk factors as *internal* or related to persons—they are what people do.
- Think of environmental risk factors as *external* to persons—conditions or situations that exist, such as a factory upstream that is causing pollution in the drinking water.

Using the brief examples mentioned earlier: *alcohol use/abuse* is the behavioral risk factor related to liver problems (such as cirrhosis) and drunk driving accidents in North Hill County; *smoking* is the behavioral risk factor that is related to the health problem of cancer in women and respiratory problems in children. There may be environmental risk factors present as well. For example, the roads in North Hill County may contribute to accidents if they are narrow, have poor visibility, or are not well lighted.

How do we find out what the behavioral and environmental risk factors are? This is not quite as easy as obtaining epidemiological information, which is usually kept by public health departments. Behavioral and environmental risk factor data are not so regularly collected or maintained. There are, however, some good sources. The CDC collects a wide range of data on risk behaviors in both adults and youth across the country from its Behavioral Risk Factor Survey. These data are available from the CDC, and may include information about the community you are working with. The National Center for Health Statistics (NCHS) has national data from many surveys concerning such behavioral risks as diet, smoking, and exercise. The National Household Survey on Drug Abuse collects data on substance abuse among young people, and these data are available in regular published reports through the Substance Abuse and Mental Health Services Administration (SAMHSA). The World Health Organization (WHO) and a number of United Nations agencies collect data on global health problems such as HIV/AIDS that in some cases include behavioral information (for HIV/AIDS,

---

TABLE 7-2 Summary of the Epidemiological Assessment (Phase Two)

What It Is	Sources of Information	What This Tells You
Assessment of prevalence/incidence of a health condition, comorbid conditions, and affected populations.	Local surveillance data from public health sources, or other relevant sources such as schools, emergency rooms, and police (depending upon the issue).	The nature and extent of a health problem or problems, patterns and trends, and the affected populations.

this would be mode of transmission). At the local level, counties or states may conduct surveys or collect information about behavioral risk factors; occupational health and safety organizations, environmental organizations and agencies, and even public housing agencies (among other organizations) may have data on environmental risks.

This phase is summarized in Table 7-3.

Phase Four: Educational and Ecological Assessment

Once behavioral and/or environmental risks (contributing to the health conditions identified in the epidemiological assessment) have been identified, the next step is to go back one more "causal level" and try to get at factors that contribute to those risks. These factors are very much related to the theoretical issues discussed so far in this book—attitudes, decision-making processes, social and cultural influences, and, to a certain degree, broader social and economic factors.

Using one of our examples, we can ask: What kinds of attitudes, beliefs, and social rewards promote heavy alcohol use in North Hill County? As you know by now, this can be complex. Thinking about youth alcohol abuse, let's assume that, because there is not much to anticipate in terms of local jobs, young people either leave the area or try to carve out some social role where they are. One of the ways to carve out a social role is to drink a lot and "do crazy things," which are then talked about (glorified) and contribute to a person's reputation. This is a social act, because there is a group of people involved who are participants in the whole process. They are the ones who legitimize the reputation of the person doing those crazy things. *Shared* attitudes and beliefs are therefore involved. Conducting a Phase Four assessment in this situation would involve an attempt to understand what these beliefs/attitudes are, and the role of alcohol abuse (the behavior) in gaining a socially legitimized reputation. What you find out will provide you with important direction in choosing theory and in developing health promotion activities that target those attitudes and the social system that supports them.

Of course, it could just be about boredom! But even then, such information would be useful in understanding attitudes related to drinking.

Green and Kreuter, in their key volume on health promotion planning,[1] categorize the information sought in the Phase Four educational/ecological assessment in the following way:

- *Predisposing factors:* A population's knowledge, attitudes, beliefs, values perceptions, genetic predispositions, etc.
- *Enabling factors:* Skills, resources, and barriers that help or hinder the desired behavior.
- *Reinforcing factors:* What rewards are received or available when people adopt the desired behavior? (For example, do people get reduced insurance rates for safe driving?) Or, what rewards are available when people engage in unhealthy alcohol-related behavior?

Using the North Hill County example, the *predisposing factors* would include the attitudes about alcohol use mentioned earlier, along with any other knowledge, perceptions, and values that contributed. The *enabling factors* might include easy availability of alcohol at stores and bars with minimal concern about driving, or lack of programs and public information about the risks of drunk driving/excessive alcohol use. *Reinforcing factors* (for reducing alcohol abuse) might include preferential hiring (for limited available jobs) of people with clean driving records.

TABLE 7-3 Summary of the Behavioral/Environmental Assessment (Phase Three)

What It Is	Sources of Information	What This Tells You
Assessment of the behavioral and environmental risk factors linked to the health conditions you want to address as identified and described in the epidemiological data.	Local survey, focus group, or other data from public health sources, or from schools, community groups, or work-related sources (e.g., unions); environmental risk data from environmental agencies, public health agencies, occupational health agencies, or organizations.	Behaviors and environmental conditions that you may need to target in an intervention in order to address the identified health problem(s).

Question: What theories/approaches address the issues raised in this assessment?

- Social norms and attitudes about drinking and risk
- Skills related to alcohol use/nonuse
- Availability of alcohol
- Lack of programs and public information

How do you get the kind of information needed in this assessment? Readily available data of this kind may be even more limited than behavioral or environmental risk data. You may have to locate special studies or research conducted with your target population or with similar populations (e.g., funded by a local hospital, or a Ph.D. thesis). For international populations, this information is often collected by nongovernment organizations (NGOs) that are working in this area. Some of the behavioral/environmental data sources mentioned in Phase Three, though, like the CDC Behavioral Risk Factor Survey, do collect information on attitudes/beliefs. More than for any other PRECEDE-PROCEED assessment phase, however, for this one you may just have to go out and collect some information yourself.

This phase is summarized in Table 7-4.

Phase Five: Administrative and Policy Assessment

By this time, you will have developed a kind of connected picture, or the beginnings of a "logic model" framework that ties individual, social, environmental, and behavioral factors to the health conditions you want to change. This becomes a guide for what kinds of intervention components you ought to include. The Phase Five assessment, however, is more practical. After you have come up with a brilliant program design that hits on key factors you have identified, you are still faced with the challenge of implementing it in the real world, in an actual community. To do that, you are going to need to take stock of what resources you have in the community—organizations, committees, task forces, local politics, and in general the barriers you face and assets that are available. You'll also need to know what kind of staff, equipment, facilities, and funding you need. Taken together, this is what the Phase Five administrative/policy assessment is about.

Once again, let's think about North Hill County. In the Phase Four assessment, we identified easy availability of alcohol and lack of concern among bars about driving after drinking as enabling factors. Consider the following scenario: Given the general socioeconomic conditions identified in the Phase One assessment, bars are desperate to have as much business as possible to keep afloat in hard economic times. When the county council tries to pass a law that will hold bars liable for injuries resulting from drinking and driving, the local bar and restaurant association successfully opposes it, claiming that it will force bars to adopt policies that will cost them business. That is an example of a political barrier you might face. So you are going to have to identify resources in the community that you can draw on to counter that influence or at least provide support for your cause. After some thinking, you are able to convince local car dealers to back an initiative that will reduce interest rates on car payments for drivers who have a DUI-free record, and to drivers who can document that they were designated drivers at least four times during a year. The car dealers become a community resource (because they believe it will help their business).

Another aspect of this assessment has to do with project funding and resources. If you don't have a great deal of program funding, what kinds of resources are available

---

TABLE 7-4 Summary of the Educational/Ecological Assessment (Phase Four)

What It Is	Sources of Information	What This Tells You
Assessment of attitudes, knowledge, social norms, patterns of social and community organization, and similar factors that contribute to the risk behaviors and environmental risks identified in Phase Four. These can be categorized as predisposing, enabling, and reinforcing factors.	Local survey, focus group, or other specialized data from public health sources, local research institutions (universities, private research organizations), NGOs, schools, and work-related groups. In addition, you may need to collect such data yourself.	In order to influence behavior, as we have seen throughout this book, you will often need to begin by addressing the attitudes, norms, social support systems, and other close-in factors that are involved. This assessment helps you identify some of these.

in the community to help, for example, staff your project adequately? Maybe there is a community college or volunteer organization you can draw on. Maybe there are businesses that will donate materials or services, such as printing of flyers and brochures.

Question: What theories/approaches address the issues raised in this assessment?

- The process of implementing policies and regulations
- Working with organizations and community structures
- Funding
- Public and community involvement in the issue

Phase Five is summarized in Table 7-5.

Phase Six: Implementation

This phase does not need a long explanation. Basically, it just means putting your program in place, after using your assessment process to design it. That is what is meant by "proceed."

A reminder: In today's health promotion program environment, there is often a requirement to use *evidence-based* or *model* programs that are responsive to the community situation. In other words, once you have made an assessment, there may be programs that have been developed before and that show consistent evidence of effectiveness in targeting a similar population and situation. If so, it is sometimes advisable to use such programs instead of developing one of your own. Many agencies now have good resources for identifying such programs. (See Chapter 13 for a more detailed discussion.)

Phases Seven, Eight, and Nine: Evaluation

The last three phases of the PRECEDE-PROCEED planning approach involve *evaluation*, which refers to the data you collect about whether your health promotion program is "working" in the sense of making a change in the health problem it is intended to affect. This is a very important part of any program you put in place. Why? The simplest answer is so that you know whether you are accomplishing anything. In addition, dollars are often scarce, and programs have to be accountable for their effectiveness so that the available dollars can be directed to programs that show evidence of success. If your program works, but you have no data to show it, then 1) the program may not continue to receive funding; 2) other communities who might benefit from a program you develop won't have the data to argue for its adoption; or 3) if you develop an innovative approach to a particular health problem, that innovation may not get the attention it deserves from the health promotion field.

In addition to that kind of "external accountability," evaluation is extremely important as a way of letting you know—internally—whether your program is working or not, and in what ways it is or is not working. With this information, you can make adjustments and improve the outcome.

There are basically three types of evaluation, and these three correspond to Phases 7, 8, and 9 of the PRECEDE-PROCEED model. Sometimes these evaluation types are referred to by different names, but the idea is the same. The following is a brief review of these; Chapter 13 covers evaluation in more depth.

Process Evaluation (Phase Seven). This is an assessment of program implementation: Did you do what you said you were going to do (implement the components)? If you said you were going to develop brochures and flyers as one program component, for example, did you develop them? Did you distribute them? To how many people? Did you distribute them to the people your program is trying to reach? The *data* you collect in process evaluation primarily involves *tracking records*—records of what you did. These kinds of

---

TABLE 7-5 Summary of the Administrative/Policy Assessment (Phase Five)

What It Is	Sources of Information	What This Tells You
Assessment of administrative, organizational, and political resources available to support the development and implementation of a health promotion program.	Key community leaders and sources, focus groups, surveys of nonprofit sectors, colleges, and universities.	The practical details about putting a program into action.

records are useful for tracking purposes; they are also helpful in assessing "how much" of the program led to the result.

Impact Evaluation (Phase Eight). This is an assessment of the *short-term* effects of your program—the kinds of effects that might happen in a year or two, maybe even three. Of course any health promotion intervention has as its ultimate goal elimination of a disease or health condition (a change in the epidemiological data identified in the Phase Two assessment), and improvement in the quality of life of the community. But change of this magnitude doesn't usually happen very quickly; not in a couple of short years anyway. So the impacts usually refer to shorter-term changes that, it is hoped, will eventually contribute to a change in the health condition itself. These are usually changes in knowledge, changes in policies and practices, changes in community awareness and systems, and maybe changes in the way people use health services, the kinds of changes that are related to what you identified in Phase Three and Phase Four.

To assess the short-term impacts, you will need to collect information about the factors you think will change before you begin the intervention, then follow up at later intervals with the same collection of information.

Outcome Evaluation (Phase Nine). This is an assessment of the *long-term* effects of your program—the kinds of effects that might happen in several years or more. In contrast to the kinds of effects you might expect from a short-term evaluation, outcomes refer to changes in the health condition itself, quality of life indicators, health behavior if significant, utilization patterns, or substantial policy or system changes. These are factors usually identified in the Phase One or Two assessment (sometimes Phase Three). Many health promotion programs are not funded for a long enough period of time to track long-term change; to do this may require a separate study that follows a community or group of people for many years.

To assess the long-term impacts, you will typically need to collect information about the factors you think will change before you begin the intervention, then follow up at intervals over a long time period with the same collection of information.

The Risk and Protective Factors Planning Model

The *risk and protective factors* model is another example. It is widely used by a number of federal agencies* as a framework for planning and funding health promotion and other interventions focusing on youth or adolescent health risk behavior, including HIV/AIDS risk; early sexual activity;

adolescent pregnancy; tobacco, alcohol, and drug use; and violence, among others. It is different than PRECEDE-PROCEED in some ways, but the basic idea is similar. There are still three basic processes—assessment, implementation, and evaluation. A key difference is that it is a *theory-based* planning model that focuses on certain health risk behaviors as the targets of change. The model was developed based on a synthesis of research about factors that appeared to be correlated with the kinds of health risk behaviors listed above.

This risk factor planning model lays out a set of *risk factors* that are said to be precursors to or predictors of risky behavior by young people. These include, for example:

- Problems in child development and mother–child or parent–child interaction[3-5]
- Family structure, family conflict, and abuse[6,7]
- Poverty (for early onset of violence)[8]
- Previous violence victimization or regular witnessing of violence[9-11]
- The absence of a positive adult role model[12]
- Differences in individual personality traits, affective states, and behavioral skills[4,13-15]

Most of the risk behavior research has consistently pointed to multiple causes, cumulative exposure, or interactions among individual, family, and community risk factors affecting youth over the course of their development.[3,16-20] So, there is a kind of "web" of risk factors involved.

Hawkins, Catalano, and colleagues[18,21,22] synthesized the risk/protective factor research into a widely used, comprehensive approach that functions as a planning tool like PRECEDE-PROCEED, though different. In brief, the model lays out an algorithm of factors (or forces) that, over the youth development process, are said to increase or decrease the likelihood that a given youth will engage in problem behaviors (violence, delinquency, substance abuse, school dropout, HIV/AIDS risk behavior, or others): *risk factors* increase the likelihood of problem behavior; *protective factors* reduce the likelihood of problem behavior. So you can almost think of the process—the way it is abstracted in the model—as a "box" with inputs and outputs. Put in a lot of risk factors, but not many protective factors, and you are highly likely to get health risk behavior as an output. Put a few risk behaviors in, with a lot of protective factors, and you are less likely to see an output of health risk behavior.

Under the Hawkins and Catalano model, risk factors are organized into the following domains:

- *Individual:* e.g., biological and psychological dispositions, attitudes, values, knowledge, skills, problem behaviors

---

* For example, the Department of Health and Human Services (e.g., SAMHSA, CDC), and even the Office of Juvenile Justice and Delinquency Prevention (Department of Justice).

- *Peer:* e.g., norms, activities, attachment to specific peer groups
- *Family:* e.g., family function, management, bonding, abuse/violence
- *School:* e.g., bonding to school, school climate, policy, performance
- *Community:* e.g., bonding, norms, resources, poverty level, crime, awareness/mobilization
- Sometimes, the domain of *society/environment:* e.g., norms, policy/sanctions

Protective factors under this model are not as well specified, and have been organized into a smaller set of similar domains:

- *Individual:* e.g., gender, intelligence, temperament
- *Social bonding:* Attachment/commitment to positive, prosocial individuals and groups
- *Healthy beliefs* and *clear standards for behavior:* In families, schools, communities

Table 7-6 summarizes these risk and protective factor domains.

But not every youth exposed to risk factors is involved in risk behavior[18,23] Many are not, and are said to have in their lives a range of protective factors that *counter* or *buffer* the risk factors. A number of programs and research efforts have focused on these, under the general term *resilience.*[24-28]

In general, the complex and fluid interaction between an individual and risk/protective factors in one or more domains has been described as a "web of influence," and draws from the *ecological* perspective of Brofenbrenner[29] now widely accepted in public health approaches.[1]

How is this approach used to plan, implement, and evaluate health promotion programs targeting adolescents and young adults? Thinking about it in the same way we discussed PRECEDE-PROCEED, there are several phases of use.

Phase One: Assessment

Suppose a community wanted to address particular health problems of adolescents; for example, violence and alcohol/drug use. Using this approach, an agency, committee, or other organization would have to collect information and identify what key risk factors/protective factors were relevant to the violence and drug abuse occurring in the community. So, let's say the agency came up with the following:

- In the individual domain, a high *prevalence* of attitudes that consider violence as one of the ways in which a person gained a valued "reputation" among peers
- In the community domain, easy access to weapons and a high crime rate

TABLE 7-6 Risk and Protective Factor Domains
Risk Factors
Individual
Peer
Family
School
Community
Society/environment
Protective Factors
Individual
Social bonding
Healthy beliefs and clear behavior standards

- In the school domain, disorganized enforcement of no-violence policies

But the agency also came up with at least one protective factor: A relatively large number of volunteer and civic organizations that were interested in helping youth in their community.

That information may come from surveys like the CDC Youth Risk Behavior Survey, data on violence from the police, and information from the schools.

Question: What theories/approaches address the issues raised in this assessment?

- Social norms and attitudes about violence
- Easy access to weapons in the community
- Lack of adherence to no-violence policies in schools

Phase Two: Implementation

Based on the risk factor assessment, the agency could: 1) design a program that targets the risk factors, or 2) identify a model or "evidence-based" program that has already been developed and is intended to target just those risk factors that were identified, and adopt that program. It happens that, for the risk and protective factors model, there is a well-developed system for identifying such model programs and for getting that information out to the public. The program may have several components that address the risk factors you identified:

- A media campaign at schools and in the community focusing on attitudes about violence and "reputation"

- Advocacy activities for strict enforcement of local weapons possession laws
- A school component, drawing on community volunteers to increase the adult (supervisory) presence at school

Question: What theories/approaches are useful for the intervention components listed above?

So, the agency decides to adopt and implement the program.

Phase Three: Evaluation

Evaluation involves the same three types discussed for PRECEDE-PROCEED: process, impact, and outcome. In this planning model, however, there are a significant number of surveys and other evaluation tools already developed that are designed to determine if your program actually had an effect on one or more of the identified risk factors, and if it helped support any of the protective factors you identified. So, your *process* evaluation would emphasize the recording and tracking of program activities; your *impact* (short-term) evaluation would assess whether or not you were able to make any change in attitudes about violence and enforcement of gun laws and school violence policies; and your *outcome* (long-term) evaluation—if you were able to do one—would try to determine if you actually made any change in levels of violence among adolescents.

The two models discussed in this chapter are not the only planning models for health promotion programs. They were chosen in order to give you a sense for what planning such programs can involve, and how this opens the door to selecting and applying theory. The key is that assessment-implementation-evaluation process, which, hopefully, will help ensure that your program is tailored to the real-life situation of a community.

Chapter Questions

1. What does "picking your battles" mean in the context of a health promotion program?

2. What are the three basic parts of most planning models?

3. In general, what role does assessment play in the kind of health promotion program you decide to develop and implement?

4. Why is it important to evaluate health promotion programs?

5. How are the two planning models discussed in this chapter different? Similar?

REFERENCES

1. Green LW, Kreuter MW, eds. *Health Promotion Planning: An Educational and Environmental Approach,* 3rd ed. Mountain View, CA: Mayfield; 1999.

2. Green LW, Kreuter MW, Deeds SG, Partridge KB. *Health Education Planning: A Diagnostic Approach.* Mountain View, CA: Mayfield; 1980.

3. Yoshikawa H. Prevention as cumulative protection: effects of early family support and education on chronic delinquency and its risks. *Psychol Bull.* 1994;115:28–54.

4. Brook JS, Brook DW, Gordon AS, Whiteman M, Cohen. The psychosocial etiology of adolescent drug abuse use: a family interactional approach. *Genetic Soc Gen Psychol Monogr.* 1990;116:111–267.

5. Webster-Stratton C. Parent training with low-income families: promoting parental engagement through a collaborative approach. In: Lutzker JR, ed. *Handbook of Child Abuse Research and Treatment.* New York: Plenum; 1997:183–210.

6. Johnston LD, O'Malley PM, Bachman JG. *National Survey Results on Drug Use from Monitoring the Future 1975–1995.* Vol. I: Secondary School Students. Vol. II: College Students and Young Adults. Rockville, MD: National Institute on Drug Abuse; 1996.

7. Loeber R, Hay DF. Key issues in the development of aggression and violence from childhood to early adulthood. *Ann Rev Psychol.* 1997;48:371–410.

8. Lipsey MW, Derzon JH. Predictors of serious delinquency in adolescence and early adulthood: a synthesis of longitudinal research. In: Loeber R, Farrington DP, eds. *Serious and Violent Juvenile Offenders: Risk Factors and Successful Interventions.* Thousand Oaks, CA: Sage Publications; 1998.

9. Dembo R, Williams L, LaVoie L, et al. Physical abuse, sexual victimization, and illicit drug use: replication of a structural analysis among a new sample of high risk youth. *Violence Victims.* 1989;4(2).

10. Bell CC, Jenkins EJ. Community violence and children on Chicago's southside. *Psychiatry.* 1993;56:46–54.

11. Osofsky JD, Fenichel E, eds. *Caring for Infants and Toddlers in Violent Environments: Hurt, Healing and Hope.* Arlington, VA: Zero to Three/National Center for Clinical Infant Programs; 1994.

12. Beier SR, Rosenfeld WD, Spitalny KC, Zansky SM, Bontemp AN. The potential role of an adult mentor in influencing high risk behavior in adolescents. *Ann Pediatr Adolesc Med.* 2000;154(4):327–331.

13. Kumpfer KL, Turner CW. The social ecology model of adolescent substance abuse: implications for prevention. *Int J Addict.* 1990–1991;25:435–463.

14. Simons et al. 1994. "Two routes to delinquency differences between early and late starters in the impact of parenting and deviant peers." *Criminology* 32:247–275.

15. Petraitis J, Flay BR, Miller TQ. Reviewing theories of adolescent substance use: organizing pieces in the puzzle. *Psychol Bull.* 1995;117(1):67–86.

16. Dahlberg LL. Youth violence in the United States: major trends, risk factors, and prevention approaches. *Am J Prev Med.* 1998;14(4):259–272.

17. Grizenko N, Fisher C. Review of studies of risk and protective factors for psychopathology in children. *Can J Psychiatry.* 1992;37:711–721.

18. Hawkins JD, Catalano RF, Miller JY. Risk and protective factors for alcohol and other drug problems in adolescence and early adulthood: implications for substance abuse prevention. *Psychol Bull.* 1992;112:64–105.

19. Dryfoos JG. *Adolescents at Risk: Prevalence and Prevention.* New York: Oxford University Press; 1990.

20. Tolan P, Guerra N. *What Works in Reducing Adolescent Violence: An Empirical Review of the Field. Report to The Center for the Study and Prevention of Violence.* Boulder, CO: Center for the Study and Prevention of Violence; 1994.

21. Hawkins et al. Predictors of youth violence. *Juv Justice Bull.* Washington, DC: Office of Juvenile Justice and Delinquency Prevention; 2000.

22. Catalano RF, Hawkins JD. *Risk-Focused Prevention: Using the Social Development Strategy.* Seattle, WA: Developmental Research and Programs; 1995.

23. Garmezy, N. 1991. Resiliency and Vulnerability to Adverse Developmental Outcomes Associated with Poverty. *American Behavioral Scientist* 34(4): 416-430.

24. Pransky J. *Prevention: The Critical Need.* Springfield, MO: Burrell Foundation and Paradigm Press; 1991.

25. Benson P, Galbraith J, Espeland P. *What Kids Need to Succeed.* Minneapolis, MN: Search Institute and Free Spirit; 1994.

26. Search Institute. 1998. Developmental assets: an investment in youth. January 4, 1999. Available at: http://www.search-institute.org/assets/index.htm. Accessed November 2006.

27. Benard B. *Mentoring: New Study Shows the Power of Relationship to Make a Difference.* Research Report. Berkeley, CA: Resiliency Associates; 1996.

28. Development Services Group, Inc. October 2003. The Model Programs Guide and Database. Bethesda, MD: Development Services Group, Inc. (sponsored by the Office of Juvenile Justice and Delinquency Prevention, U.S. Department Of Justice)

29. Bronfenbrenner U. *The Ecology of Human Development.* Cambridge, MA: Harvard University Press; 1979.

SECTION III

Putting Theory Into Practice

CHAPTER **8**

Communities and Populations As Focus For Health Promotion Programs

LEARNING OBJECTIVES

By the end of this chapter, the reader will be able to:

- Understand the difference between community (health promotion) interventions and interventions in a community
- Understand the interaction between community characteristics and interventions
- Define population-based health promotion
- Understand tailoring and sustainability with respect to health promotion interventions

"Whatever affects one directly affects all indirectly. I can never be what I ought to be until you are what you ought to be, and you can never be what you ought to be until I am what I ought to be. This is the interrelated structure of reality."

—MARTIN LUTHER KING, FROM *STRENGTH TO LOVE,* **1963**

COMMUNITY INTERVENTION, OR INTERVENTION IN A COMMUNITY?

After all we have said about the ways in which individuals are embedded in communities, cultures, and societies, it should be clear why interventions commonly occur in the context of communities. Communities are the mixing pot, the place where multiple factors interact. The situation you are trying to address is in a community, in which a *particular* set of individuals, social groups, cultures and norms, economic patterns, politics, and resources all interact to help create that unique situation.

Your assessment process (see previous chapter) is going to guide you in terms of what health issues, factors, and people to target. There are lots of decisions to be made and battles to be picked. One decision has to do with *scale*. Based on the assessment, does it make more sense to target the community in general with a broad-based or multilevel intervention? Or should you be trying to reach a smaller, targeted setting? Broader interventions can be called *community* interventions; the more targeted kind can be called *interventions in a community*. These terms are related to the way in which the Institute of Medicine classifies different types of interventions[1]:

- *Universal* prevention interventions are those that target a general population.
- *Selected* prevention interventions are those that target individuals or groups that are at high risk for a particular health problem.
- *Indicated* preventive interventions are those targeting families, groups, or individuals with multiple risk factors for a health problem; in other words, programs that may combine multiple types of activities and treatments to address multiple factors that occur together, such as poverty, high diabetes risk, and poor diet.

Community interventions tend to result in smaller changes, but over a larger number of people—a larger absolute number. Let's say a community mass media intervention resulted in a 3% decrease in smoking. This may not seem like a big decrease, yet over the whole community it might mean that hundreds or thousands of individuals actually quit. Not bad.

On the other hand, it might be more useful to focus the intervention on a segment of the community that is highly affected by or at risk for a health problem (this is an intervention in a community). For example, an HIV/AIDS intervention might focus on people who use intravenous drugs, because if they share their equipment, they run a high risk of being infected, and in turn infecting others. They can serve as a *multiplier* or *bridge* for transmission of the virus. So you might work with a few social groups of injection drug users (IDUs). The percentage in that group who, for example, stop sharing equipment after your intervention, might be 32%, a big change! But it represents a big change over a relatively small subset of the community, so not as large in terms of absolute numbers as a community intervention.

Or, you might not be focusing on individuals at all, but on systems or policies in the community. Policies and regulations may have a substantial impact—take, for example, laws/regulations concerning smoking in restaurants and indoor spaces. It may also be true that the community does not have systems set up to effectively handle prevention or intervention for health issues. The Centers for Disease Control and Prevention (CDC) is well known for incorporating a community focus into preventive interventions. For example, the CDC's National Center for Chronic Disease Prevention and Health Promotion REACH (Racial and Ethnic Approaches to Community Health) program funds community coalitions and other capacity-building efforts, and has developed one of the few evaluation protocols that targets nonmedical factors related to minority health disparities. The program framework and the evaluation protocol assume five stages that can be thought of as strategies towards the goal of eliminating these health disparities:

- *Capacity building:* Community coalition actions to reduce disparities
- *Targeted actions:* Intervention activities believed to bring about a desired effect
- *Community/systems change:* Changes to the community environment and to the knowledge, attitudes, beliefs, and behaviors of influential individuals and groups
- *Widespread risk/protective behavior change:* Changes in rates of risk-reduction behaviors among a significant percentage of community members
- *Health disparity reduction:* Narrowing gaps in health status

Example of a Community Intervention: Minnesota Heart Health Study/Intervention[2]

The goals of this long-term community intervention trial were to examine the effects of a 5–6 year multifaceted individual, group, and community level intervention in six upper Midwest (U.S.) communities on health behaviors, population levels of serum cholesterol, blood pressure, cigarette smoking, and physical activity, and ultimately on reducing morbidity and mortality from coronary heart disease (CHD) in three interventions as compared to three reference communities. The major hypotheses of this heart health program were that a systematic and multiple strategy community-wide health education program was feasible and would lead to a change in the way people think about heart disease and its prevention; in environmental structures which support risk behaviors and their change; and to changes in physiologic risk factors and ultimately in reduced rates of CHD.

The intervention advocated hypertension prevention and control, heart healthy eating behaviors, nonsmoking, and regular physical activity. These interventions were carried out at the micro (individual) and macro (community) levels and embraced a wide range of intervention strategies and therapies. The program alerted people to health issues, informed them of effective behavioral alternatives for health promotion, provided incentives for new behaviors, and provided reinforcements to maintain new behaviors. Community leaders and organizations were engaged as active participants in the intervention programs to support risk reduction activities and provide input to community planning for program continuation. The program included a high-intensity educational campaign through the use of mass media. Primary care physicians and other health professionals were recruited as role models and opinion leaders. Systematic risk factor screening and education programs were carried out to reduce the risk of CHD. Direct education programs for school age children were developed to promote health enhancing behaviors in youth and their parents and discourage negative lifestyle behaviors. The intervention activities were carried out for approximately 5-6 years.

Evaluation of the success of the program was based on the results of annual cohort surveys as well as independent cross-sectional samples of the general adult population of the respective communities. Resting blood pressures, serum total cholesterol, cigarette smoking, height and weight, and extent of leisure time activity were measured in a standardized manner. Surveillance systems for the collection of morbidity and mortality data in residents between the ages of 30 and 74 years were also established.

Commit (A Second Example)

In the 1980s the National Cancer Institute (NCI) funded a number of smoking cessation studies to combat the continuing high levels of smoking. One of the most significant was the Community Intervention Trial for Smoking Cessation (COMMIT).

Elements

- One community in each of 11 matched pairs (10 in the U.S., 1 in Canada) was randomly assigned to the intervention, which was a four-year program (and research component).
- Cohorts of about 10,000 heavy smokers and 10,000 light/moderate smokers were followed by telephone.
- The idea was to involve diverse organizations and individuals together in a comprehensive community intervention that would maximize smokers' exposure to quit messages.
- The focus of the interventions was *solely* on quitting smoking, not on any other risk factors, as was the case for previous interventions.
- The primary target group was heavy smokers (25 or more cigarettes a day). The assumption was that if this group was reached, light/moderate smokers would be impacted as well.
- *Outcome goal:* Higher quit rates in intervention communities, where quitting was defined as cessation for 6 months.

The Intervention

- *Community mobilization:* Each intervention community formed a community board with oversight and coordinating responsibility.
- *Channels:* 1) Public education through media and community events, 2) health care providers, 3) worksites and other organizations, and 4) cessation resources. Each channel was "managed" by a community task force. Key issues were awareness of quit programs, recognition that smoking is a public health problem, and a change in the social desirability of smoking.
- *Other:* Training for pharmacists, mass media campaigns.

Although COMMIT was national in scope, it was done in communities, with a balance struck between national uniformity and local tailoring. Each intervention had a field director, intervention staff, office manager, and the like.

Evaluation

The process included a program records system, monitoring process objectives for every program element and the outcome of self-report quit rates. In order to evaluate the quit rates and their meaning, the COMMIT study developed something called the *receipt index*, which was a measure of how much of the intervention individuals received and/or

participated in. That way, quit rates were not just assessed between intervention and control communities, but in relation to how much exposure someone received.

Results

- More variation across communities than by pairs, showing that the intervention had differential effects depending on *where* it was implemented, and the particular mix of components, commitment, target population, and so on.
- There was a decline in the amount smoked in intervention communities (number of cigarettes)—about 1.3% more quit (over 5 years) in the intervention communities, with similar rates across men and women.
- The hoped-for decline among the key target population (heavy smokers) did not occur to a significant degree. There was little variation in quit rates between intervention and control communities.
- The *major impact* turned out to be with light/moderate smokers, with 3% more quitting in the intervention communities (total of 3,000 across all intervention communities). The impact here was similar for men and women. And, impact was more among those less educated than college educated, probably reflecting the fact that the college educated were already educated, had already reduced their smoking, and the COMMIT intervention did not add much to what they were already doing.

Questions

Why was it not effective with heavy smokers? (Not a big enough dosage? Is a different type of intervention necessary?) In any case, other studies have also shown that it is very hard for heavy smokers to quit.

Example of Intervention in a Community: The Long Beach (California) AIDS Community Demonstration Project

Problem

The HIV/AIDS epidemic grew rapidly in Long Beach, California. By the mid-1990s, the city had 2,800 cases of AIDS. The CDC started funding AIDS Community Demonstration Projects in the mid-1980s to address the spread of the disease in specific populations. The Long Beach AIDS Community Demonstration Project[3] was one of a number of projects that were based in storefront or community locations and attempted to make extensive use of peer education models.

Theory

Program designers attempted to base the project in theory—the Health Belief Model, Theory of Reasoned Action, Trans-Theoretical Model, Social Cognitive Theory, and Diffusion of Innovations were considered. None was viewed as adequate to account for the complexities of HIV risk, which were also driven (in the target population) by social networks, illegal activities, stigma, marginalization, and other factors. So, a "composite theory" was developed, where behavior was said to be correlated with:

- Individual perception of risk
- Anticipated results of a recommended behavior change (positive and negative)
- Perception that others in the community also were changing (social network support)
- Perception of self-efficacy to make change
- Intention and commitment to change
- Acquisition of social and physical skills to make the change

Purposes

The goals of the program were to increase condom use by key population members—injection drug users, their female sex partners, and female street sex workers—and to increase the use of bleach to disinfect injection drug equipment (needles, syringes). It was implemented in a neighborhood with a high incidence of drug abuse and prostitution. The population was primarily low income and Latino, Cambodian, Vietnamese, and African American.

Program Components

Components included the following:

- *Development of "role model stories"*: These were concise, personal vignettes describing the manner in which a local population member had overcome barriers to HIV prevention and adopted more consistent use of condoms or bleach. (Touched on network norms, self-efficacy, modeling, and risk perception.)
- *Dissemination of role model stories:* This was accomplished through 1) small media (flyers, cards, booklets) distributed by community volunteers; 2) posters in intervention neighborhoods; 3) mass media public service announcements or news stories; and 4) audio or video recordings distributed to the target population.
- *Creation of an identity:* The overall project identity was "Healthwise" (from "streetwise"). For publications, the program used "Road Dogs" for at-risk

male IDUs, and "Risky Business" for female IDUs, sex partners, and sex workers. (Road dogs is a street term among inmates and drug users for hangout buddies.)

In the process of implementing this program, project staff learned that mass media components were probably not effective because they would cover too wide of an audience. That activity eventually was dropped. The Road Dogs logo was revised several times based on audience reaction. And, it was discovered that females were also reading the Road Dogs publication. They did not like the "Risky Business" title and did not want to be seen with it (stigma). Eventually "Healthwise" was dropped because it was not readily identified by the population, and the whole program was called Road Dogs. However, it still needed a publication for women. Therefore, the program introduced a new four-page flyer called "For Women Only" that contained information targeting women at risk, but also including issues and information of general interest to women. The program also distributed bleach and condom kits to IDUs, but had to make many changes. For example, IDUs had no access to clean water, so a water bottle was included in the kits.

The peer outreach staff recruited a total of 386 volunteers, 125 active at any given time. These were members of the target population. Their role was to distribute information and bleach kits and disseminate messages that also were distributed by paid outreach staff. Twenty local businesses also volunteered to be distribution points for project materials. These businesses were very effective.

Results

Surveys collecting information about the factors to be changed were collected several times over the course of the project in the intervention and a comparable "control" community (see Chapter 13). These measured exposure to the project (process), (change in) stage of change, behavior (carrying condom, using condom, using bleach kit, risky sex, sharing needles), and attitudes and norms (perceived behavioral control over bleaching, perceived risk of needle sharing without bleach, attitudes to risk, social norms regarding risk, etc.).

An average of 70% were exposed to materials/activities (process). There was a significant increase in condom carrying and condom use among those exposed to the intervention. There was also a change in "stage of change" in terms of condom use (moved from precontemplation). More impact was made with nonmain partners than with main partners. Finally, bleach usage increased significantly among those exposed to the intervention.

COMMUNITY INTERVENTION AND THE COMPLEXITY OF COMMUNITIES

One truism for community interventions, whether large or targeted, is that the intervention itself is almost always just part of the picture. Because a community is involved, the interests, needs, politics, resources (or lack thereof), and social structures of the community will inevitably play a role in some way. Let's take a look at some of these community factors.

Politics of Selecting the Target Population and Health Issue(s)

In any community, at any time, there could be a number of health issues that are important in some way. Let's say you are working with a mining community in West Virginia, where the community is rural, incomes are relatively low, and access to health care services is not particularly good. Let's name this community *Minerville*. Health issues might include:

- Mine safety/occupational health, with mine accidents a particular concern
- Lack of health insurance coverage
- Cardiovascular health
- Cancer (smoking-related)
- Alcohol abuse and driving accidents among youth
- Tobacco-related cancer

How do you choose which one, or two, to focus on? Each of the health issues may have a political dimension to it, in the sense that an advocacy group or particular interests within the community are trying to increase the attention and resources directed to that issue.

Not only that, but the health issue you focus on may be dictated by the source of funds. For example, the Maternal and Child Health Bureau of the Health Resources and Services Agency (HRSA) gives out funds related to its specific maternal and child health mission. The Center for Substance Abuse Prevention (CSAP) within the Substance Abuse and Mental Health Services Administration (SAMHSA) gives out funds for community substance abuse prevention efforts. So, the funds you have may be limited in a way that clashes with strong community interests.

Here are some potential scenarios:

Scenario One: Somehow, you receive an open-ended grant of funds from the "Do Good Foundation" to support health promotion in a selected community. In this case, the funding does not specify a health issue. You are in both a good and potentially difficult position. The good part is that you have some room to tailor efforts to community interests and needs. The bad part is, well, that you have some room to tailor your efforts. Why? Because you may walk right into the politics of competing health issues in the community, with individuals and organizations lobbying you to direct your funds to the health issue they think is most important. Of course you could, as in PRECEDE-PROCEED, simply make a decision based on the epidemiological data about morbidity and mortality. But it isn't always that simple. Some health issues are critical because of what *might* happen, not what has already happened.

Scenario Two: You have received some funding from a federal agency to assess risk for HIV/AIDS as it relates to substance abuse among youth. The funding is part of a larger federal effort to assess these risks in both rural and urban communities, and to make sure that services are appropriately tailored to the risks. You have something of a dilemma. There is a small HIV/AIDS prevention program within the Minerville City Department of Health, but it is very small. Primarily, it serves to obtain and distribute small numbers of HIV/AIDS pamphlets and information to local health providers, and, to a limited extent, schools. On the other hand, there is a larger department within the Health Department that handles alcohol and other drug abuse, and a vocal group of substance abuse treatment providers who have formed an association, the Minerville Drug and Alcohol Abuse Treatment Providers Association (MDAATP). When you approach the schools, they don't want anything to do with an HIV/AIDS assessment, saying they have more important issues to focus on and that HIV/AIDS is too controversial. MDAATP, on the other hand, sees that you have funds and is interested in directing those funds as much as possible to assessing drug and alcohol abuse, and they want to include adults if possible, as well as youth. Your task will be to negotiate these political waters and to try and 1) find some way to increase the willingness of schools or other youth-serving organizations to participate in the assessment (you need access to youth), and 2) rein in the desire of MDAATP to dominate the effort while still involving them in the project.

Coalitions and Community Structures of Power

Even beyond the selection of target populations and health issues, when you implement a project in the community you are typically doing so through—or at least in collaboration with—community structures of some sort. These may include, for example:

- Government agencies or a specific leader (e.g., mayor, governor, head of the public health department, etc.)
- Task forces formed by government agencies but including community leaders and organizations
- A *community advisory board* composed of health providers, members of a particular population that is the focus of your program, faith community representatives, businesses, and advocacy groups
- Grassroots community organizations
- Professional groups, including organizations or associations of health providers
- Community coalitions

Any of these kinds of groups and partnerships may have their own motives related to the politics of the community, of preserving or enhancing their position in the community, of gaining control over a particular (health) issue in order to be able to set the agenda, or other reasons. In addition, any of these groups may have internal conflicts and divisions that stem from individual rivalries or different goals/interests. For example, consider the following scenario:

Scenario Three: You are trying to implement a smoking prevention effort in a well-defined community within Minerville consisting primarily of large buildings with apartments. As part of the project, you are supposed to work through a community coalition, which you have gone to great lengths to assemble—a coalition of small local businesses, two local churches, one woman who is known in the community for her advocacy on tenant issues, and two small health clinics. In preparing your application for grant funds, the coalition seems to have been a stroke of genius. All members expressed their desire to work together and to reduce smoking in this community, which all agree to be a problem for both adults and children. However, after the funds come in, you begin to notice some splits within the coalition. The two churches have been at odds with each other about how to work with the community, and the tenant rights advocate is going around the community acting as if this were "her project," clearly using it as a means of increasing her power base. She has had some success in this respect, but also increased the ire of those who do not like her, potentially creating a wedge with the community. You have to manage this fractious coalition and try to keep the focus, the resources, and the activities directed towards the prevention goal.

In short, you may have but one issue in mind—addressing a specific public health issue. Carrying that out in a com-

munity context, however, requires that you recognize the multiple social and political forces that often intersect with what might seem to be a straightforward issue.

COMMUNITIES AS EXPERTS

Despite all the complexities noted in the previous section, there is no better expertise on the community than expertise from the community itself and the diverse groups within it. These are the people who know community habits and customs, knowledge and attitudes, social groups, where things happen (locations), and much more.

That is why an increasing number of health promotion and related research efforts require the integration or participation of the community in the project itself. Suppose, for example, you were trying to disseminate prevention messages related to obesity in a particular community. How would you know the best places and ways to disseminate the information? How would you know what kinds of themes to emphasize? How would you maximize the likelihood that key members of the community would reinforce/support the messages? Community participation would be necessary.

In working on a number of HIV/AIDS prevention programs targeting high risk groups such as injection drug users, for example, it has been clear that one of the best strategies is to involve people who were members of these high risk populations as *community health outreach workers (CHOWs)*; that is, people who go out into the community to connect injection drug users to the project, disseminate information, and provide advice on how best to reach this target population. The CHOWs know drug use patterns in the community, the appropriate ways to talk about HIV/AIDS, customs and practices that relate to HIV/AIDS risk, and so on. Even more important, because they are closely connected to the target population, they are perceived as "knowing how it is," and bringing legitimacy to the project.

POPULATION-BASED HEALTH PROMOTION

Extending our discussion of communities as a locus for health promotion is the broader issue of *populations* as a focus of such efforts. We have talked about communities and their dynamics. In talking about communities we are talking in reference to a geographic component—communities exist in a specific place, where there are particular blends of populations, resources, climates, economies, social structures, and so on. However, as we know, health problems exist in aggregates of people, whether at the global, national, regional, or local level. These aggregates of people may be aggregates just because they live in a certain place. They may also be aggregates because they already are a social group of some kind, whether that is a socioeconomic group, a national or ethnic group, a gender or age group, a geographic group, or an occupational group. So, what we have discussed about working with communities is one subset of the larger topic of working with populations.

We are in the business of *public health*. That, by nature, is the business of addressing the health of population aggregates. Health issues often affect specific populations or aggregates of people because of the very reason they are an aggregate. For example:

- A particular group of people has a genetic predisposition to a health problem, such as sickle-cell anemia among African Americans or Tay-Sachs disease among Eastern European (Ashkenazi) Jewish immigrants.
- A particular group of people is at high risk for smoking-related diseases because they live in an area or areas where prevention services are limited and regulations on the sale of tobacco are minimal or nonexistent.
- A particular age group (e.g., adolescents) is at risk for alcohol-related driving accidents because it is characteristic of that age group to hold/share beliefs about personal invulnerability, and to focus on the immediate situation as opposed to broader or longer-term considerations.

Over-emphasizing shared characteristics of a specific group can be dangerous (stigmatizing, stereotyping). Still, in order to develop a health promotion approach towards a population/group that is at risk for a particular health problem *because of factors common to the group*, you will have to gain familiarity with the population and work with its environment, dynamics, social structures, patterns of behavior, and other issues, similar to what we discussed earlier concerning communities.

TAILORING

A key to developing and implementing health promotion efforts in communities and with populations is *tailoring*. This is really what we have been discussing all along in this book. Among other things, it means that an intervention or program you put in place needs to:

- Be developed based on an assessment and understanding of the health problem *as it takes shape in a particular population, subgroup, or community.*
- Be inclusive, as much as possible, of the target community in designing the program.
- Refer, as much as possible, to situations, people, and

issues relevant to the target community/population.
- Use language and materials appropriate for the audience.
- Schedule activities (hours, locations) so that members of the target population can participate.

But just because a program targets a particular population, it doesn't always mean that the program has to be developed from scratch, or that it needs to be completely unique to one situation! If this were true, a lot of energy would be expended on design and development every time a program was put in place. Fortunately, there are often at least some commonalities across situations and communities with respect to a particular health problem, and programs that have been developed before that you can draw from. So, tailoring becomes a process of *adapting* an existing program to a new situation, community, or population, as much as it is developing a new program. The problem here, though, is that if you are going to adapt a program, you want to adapt one that is effective. That is why so much importance is placed now on "best practice" or "evidence-based" programs. This is discussed further in Chapter 13, on evaluation. You can find existing, relevant health promotion programs through:

- Federal agency clearinghouses
- Nonprofit associations focused on a particular health problem
- Federal "model programs" databases—the National Registry of Effective Programs (SAMHSA) is one example
- Professional associations

The process of developing a program, or adapting an existing one, usually involves the following steps:

1. Assessment of the problem (as in a PRECEDE-PROCEED or similar assessment).
2. Formative research (e.g., using interviews, focus groups) with members of the target population. This can be used to see what kinds of adaptations to an existing program are needed, or to gain specific information about what kinds of components, messages, materials, or other elements are appropriate.
3. Ongoing evaluation/assessment to track how well the program is going during implementation, so that changes can be made if necessary.

SUSTAINABILITY

Finally, another important issue that arises with respect to any kind of community intervention is the question of *sustainability*. Most of the time, the funding that is available for community programs is for a relatively short period of time, such as three or four years. Thinking about some of the community issues mentioned earlier in this chapter, it may take at least a year, if not more, before a program even gets established.

So what happens when the funding dries up? This is an ongoing problem. It's very awkward to "up and leave" a community just when a needed program gets going. It certainly does not help relations with the community.

To address this, you have to plan for it when you are developing or implementing the program. If the program funding ends in three years, add in steps along the way that help build community capacity to run the program when funding is finished, and to link with other sources of funding. For example, such steps could include:

- Make sure to train and hire members of the community to operate the program.
- Bring in community stakeholders (businesses, civic organizations, etc.) that will have a stake in keeping the program going (if, of course, it is effective).
- Search for other sources of funds, including local, state, and national (or international).
- Write grant applications or letters seeking those funds, and be sure to train community members in finding funding and writing applications.
- Help link the program to others like it and to practitioners in the field.

Whatever the steps you take, the idea is to connect the program with the community and build the community's capacity to carry it out.

Chapter Questions

1. Why is it that communities are the primary settings for public health/health promotion interventions?

2. What is the difference between a community intervention and an intervention in a community?

3. What kinds of community politics might you encounter? What theoretical approaches could you use to address some of these political situations?

4. Explain what it means to "tailor" an intervention to a community or population.

5. How can you keep an intervention going? What does sustainability refer to?

REFERENCES

1. Gordon R. An operational classification of disease prevention. In: Steinberg JA, Silverman MM, eds. *Preventing Mental Disorders.* Rockville, Md.: Department of Health and Human Services; 1987.

2. Corby NH, Wolitski RJ, eds. *Community HIV Prevention: The Long Beach AIDS Community Demonstration Project.* Long Beach, CA: The University Press; 1997.

3. Perry CL, Klepp KI, Sillers C. Community-wide strategies for cardiovascular health: the Minnesota Heart Health Program Youth Program. *Health Educ Res.* 1989;4(1):87–101.

CHAPTER 9

Application of Theory: Schools and Worksites*

* I am grateful for feedback and input in this chapter from Deborah M. Galvin, Ph.D. (workplace setting issues) and Dr. Julia Lear, Director of the Center for Health and Health Care in Schools at George Washington University (school setting).

LEARNING OBJECTIVES

By the end of this chapter, the reader will be able to:

- Understand key issues with respect to implementing health promotion programs in a school setting
- Understand the kinds of social/behavioral theories that could be applicable to school-based health promotion programs, and describe examples of theory-based programs in school settings
- Understand key issues with respect to implementing health promotion programs in the workplace
- Understand the kinds of social/behavioral theories that could be applicable to workplace health promotion programs, and describe examples of theory-based programs in the workplace setting

---

"If you think education is expensive, try ignorance!"

—FORMER HARVARD UNIVERSITY PRESIDENT DEREK BOK, 1978

SETTINGS FOR INTERVENTION

Whatever your intervention, it will be implemented in a community or population *setting*; that is, the program components or messages will be delivered in one or more specific places (e.g., in schools, in hospitals, at worksites, in mobile units) or through one or more channels (e.g., print media, community groups, the Internet). Different settings and channels have their own unique characteristics, and can usefully draw on theoretical approaches that make sense for the setting and population. In other words, a school-based intervention is likely to have a curriculum delivered in a classroom setting. So, community mobiliza-

tion is probably not the theoretical approach you would use in this case.

In this chapter we will discuss the kinds of theoretical approaches that make sense for structuring interventions in schools and worksites, because these two settings share at least a few characteristics.

SCHOOLS

When you think of *health education*, schools are a classic setting. And no wonder. There are a lot of good reasons for conducting health promotion interventions through schools. Here are just a few:

- Health and education are intertwined. Students can't learn, and sometimes can't come to school, if they are not healthy. Their attention and ability to learn is affected by health, nutrition, and mental health, among other factors. So, health and educational goals go together.
- Students spend a great deal of time at school during the day—in that sense, they are a "captive audience."
- Families often interact in some way with schools, so schools become an important channel for reaching them as well.
- There is a history of health promotion in schools, from relatively early in the 20th century, so the experience and the infrastructure (e.g., school nurse, health classes) are already there.

Because the format of school activities is classroom-based, school health programs have typically been structured to fit in that setting. In other words, they are usually *curricula* of some kind, and usually educational or skill-building in nature.

However, there have been many efforts, especially in recent years, to try more comprehensive school health approaches.[1] Comprehensive school health education has been defined as: "classroom instruction that addresses the physical, mental, emotional, and social dimensions of health; develops health knowledge, attitudes and skills; and is tailored to each age level."[2] Even broader than this definition is the kind of coordinated approach represented by the Coordinated School Health Program (CSHP), funded and supported by the Centers for Disease Control and Prevention (CDC), as well as the American School Health Association (ASHA). The CSHP includes eight components:

- Health education, as a K–12 curriculum, covering a wide range of health topics, from nutrition to injury prevention; personal, family, and community health; sexuality; substance abuse; and more
- Physical education, also as a K–12 curriculum
- Health services
- Nutrition services
- Counseling and psychological services
- Healthy school environment (e.g., facilities, social conditions at the school)
- Health promotion for staff
- Family/community involvement

If you have understood what we have described in this book as the *ecological model*, these kinds of approaches will make a lot of sense, though they certainly require resources to put them in place. These eight components cover a lot territory, including education, health services, physical and mental health for students and staff, the environment of the school, and the involvement of family and community. Along the same lines, Greenberg and colleagues at the Collaborative for Academic, Social, and Emotional Learning (CASEL) have advocated an approach to school health that is part of a coordinated effort to develop students not only academically, but also in terms of their social competencies and values; healthy behavior; contribution to peers, family, and community; and work habits.[3]

Whatever the model, interventions in a school setting are complex for a number of reasons:

- The intensity and effects of a developmental stage with respect to the youth involved in an intervention, where social pressures, the process of forming an identity and affiliating with social groups, and biological changes all impact what you may be trying to achieve
- The politics of implementing social and health programs in schools
- The greatly increased demand on schools to act in a much broader social capacity

- Competing priorities and scarce resources

Schools are in a difficult position. They are being asked to take on a much greater role than before, in part because of the weakening of community bonds and social structures, increased economic and other pressures on families, and other factors that have displaced much of the task of "bringing up" children from families and communities to schools.[3] Schools are also increasingly responsible for the education of a range of children with disabilities and other high needs,[4] and there are increasing connections between school and other community social/health activities. At the same time, school health has typically been a low-priority issue,[4] and the school environment is not always welcoming to outside intervention or programs. Building a working relationship with schools is therefore a typical part of the process.

Health Behavior Theory and the School Setting

Let's take a look at the school setting and think about what kinds of social/behavioral theory might be applicable. First, it will be useful to go through a brief assessment process, PRECEDE-PROCEED-style, in order to identify issues and factors to address through a theoretical perspective.

Social Assessment

To set the stage, it is helpful to consider the overall community context or environmental design[5] for school-based intervention. Given the broad and often complex relationship among school, family, and community, the potential kinds of useful information are diverse. To gauge the overall situation and "climate" relative to one or more health problems with a focus on schools, you could look at:

- Community/neighborhood environment—Is it safe? What is the physical setting? Are there recreation areas? Libraries?
- Level of poverty, nutrition, and well-being of families
- Existence of barriers to education, including economic, language, class size, and resources for the learning disabled
- Stability of teachers and staff at local schools; teacher pay and morale
- Community participation or involvement in school
- Student attitudes or "bonding" to school

So, if you have a school or schools in a setting where the economy is down, funding is very tight, teacher pay is low, there is a high incidence of conflict or violence at and near the school, and teachers rarely stay very long, the setting is, well, problematic. Not impossible, but a challenge.

Epidemiological Assessment

In this setting, what are the health problems of primary importance for the schools? What kinds of data will help you understand the types of health problems that exist? One approach is to use local public health data to assess the health issues of importance for school-age children in the target area—or, if this information is not available for the local population, for the largest relevant unit (and then estimating for the local population). The school or school district is likely to keep some epidemiological data as well on its student population, but these data are not easy to obtain (nor should they be). This material may include attendance records, accidents, injuries, school disciplinary actions, nurse visits, disease outbreaks, health effects from environmental hazards in the school and community (e.g., water quality, mold, lead poisoning, etc.), and other data. Schools are very sensitive about releasing any data about their schools that might appear in public with a negative spin! This could affect student enrollment and family involvement, as well as local property values, school board politics, and resource allocation.

Behavioral/Environmental Assessment

What are the behavioral and environmental risks that may contribute to school health issues? Environmental risks may include, for example, hazards related to the physical condition of the school—heating or air conditioning systems that don't work, chemicals used to repair facilities, holes in the outdoor basketball courts, and so on. To find this out a number of diverse federal, state, and local databases and resources may be accessed, including those from the Centers for Disease Control, Agency for Toxic Substances and Disease Registry, National Institute of Environmental Health Sciences, Consumer Product Safety Commission, Environmental Protection Agency, National Association of Local Boards of Health, and individual state and local departments of health.

Behavioral risk, of course, refers to the things that school personnel, students, and their families do or don't do that pose health risks; for example, if bathroom facilities don't supply soap, if a large percentage of families don't immunize children, if a significant percentage of students carry weapons, or if hate speech is tolerated at school. A lot of health and risk behavior data come from surveys of students, including surveys done at schools. These surveys include the CDC Youth Risk Behavior Survey (YRBS) and the Monitoring the Future survey on alcohol and drug use.[6] The Search Institute also conducts surveys of community and youth risk factors, assets/supports, and attitudes.[7] The CDC data may be available for your state, or even for your metropolitan area.

And, because the overall administration of K–12 education is primarily a state function, state departments of education may be a source for health and behavioral data, though this varies by state. Getting school-specific health risk data is not easy, however.

Educational/Ecological Assessment

Now we get to the assessment that touches on a lot of theoretical issues related to behavior—the issues of what students, staff, families, and the community know; prevalent attitudes related to health risk; kinds of health-related skills that are or are not common; social, cultural, and community norms that reinforce behavior; and so on. Understanding these kinds of factors is also important for a school-based setting because *education* is the organizational purpose of the school environment in the first place, and as such, educational interventions fit in most naturally.

Where can you find out about attitudes, knowledge, social norms, resiliency, and enabling factors for a given school or group of schools? These are hard to come by other than from specific studies, though some of this information is collected in the YRBS and other surveys mentioned in the previous section. The U.S. Department of Education conducts the National Assessment of Educational Progress (NAEP), National Household Education Survey, Early Childhood Longitudinal Study, and a series of elementary, secondary, high school, and baccalaureate surveys. There may be state data/surveys on attitudes and knowledge, or data from nonprofits like the Alan Guttmacher Institute, Annie E. Casey Foundation, Children's Defense Fund, and others.

Administrative/Policy Assessment

Finally, you also have to consider, for example, the policy and systemic environment you face in trying to put an intervention in place. Schools and school boards tend to be very political bodies if for no other reason than that education is such an important community issue, one that touches on peoples' values and the way they think children should be brought up. Although you may not have much trouble if you are addressing dental health, you may run into a political minefield if the health issue being addressed is HIV/AIDS prevention, adolescent pregnancy prevention, or substance abuse. Before a school-based intervention is implemented, approval from the school board is typically necessary, along with many other difficult and time-consuming efforts to gain support and approval within the school. As noted earlier, health interventions are often not the highest priority, and are competing with multiple demands and requirements faced by a school.

Understanding the policy environment is important, and including as an intervention component organizational and community advocacy may be necessary. And sometimes it's not the school board. Think for a minute: What kind of opposition might you encounter if you wanted—as an obesity prevention measure—to advocate for a regulation, say, banning the sale of high-fat or unhealthy snacks at schools, and even in a limited area surrounding the school? Furthermore, if you wanted to evaluate these strategies or programs, you would need consent from schools, students, and their parents in order to collect data. In cases where there is stigma surrounding the health issue, such as with HIV/AIDS, obtaining any type of consent might be difficult.

Question: Thinking about the more comprehensive school approach described earlier, where parents, education of staff, and consideration of other environmental factors are included, what theories might be applied to a school-based program?

Relevant Theory

Taking the issues and factors discussed in the previous sections into consideration, what kinds of theories will help you understand school health-related issues and shape interventions?

First, think about theory that might help guide a classroom-based intervention. What skill building, awareness, or attitude issues can be addressed in the school environment? Here are a few:

- Knowledge about the consequences of risky behavior
- Personalizing risk
- Skills to counter risk
- Resources where youth can go for information or support
- Confidence-building, role-playing, and other exercises
- Building social networks to support healthy behavior
- Addressing the physical environment of the school

School interventions may not focus just on students in the classroom. Think about our assessment. What do you do if you find that a major problem lies in crumbling and degenerating school facilities? This has to be addressed by repairing or replacing such facilities, which is an issue of funding and resource allocation, which is then a political issue related to the priorities of, say, the local school board or the state legislature. What kinds of theories and approaches make sense for this purpose? Or, what if the key to a particular health issue is reaching families? What theories apply to a planned effort to do that?

In short, many theoretical approaches are applicable, depending upon the situation. Consider the following list:

- Theories focusing on individual knowledge and attitudes, like the Health Belief Model and the Theory of Planned Behavior. Where would these be useful in a school context?
- Theories addressing the interaction between an individual and the environment, including observational learning (role models), developing skills, and self-efficacy, like the Social Cognitive Theory. Where would these be useful?
- Theories and approaches focusing on the mobilization of communities and organizations. Where would these be useful?
- Theories and approaches that address the role and structure of the "built" (physical) environment in health behavior. Where would these be useful?

Program Examples

The following are a few examples of school-based behavioral interventions, with the theory described.

Life Skills Program:[8,9] This is a very well-known school-based health promotion program focusing on substance abuse prevention (including cigarettes, alcohol, and other drugs). It was developed in response to what program developers argue were ineffective programs that either: 1) just presented factual information about substance abuse consequences; or 2) used experiential and classroom discussion to enrich personal development. By contrast, the Life Skills program is said to better address psychosocial *causes/risk factors* associated with early onset of substance abuse, like:

- Drug-related expectancies (knowledge, attitudes, norms)
- Drug-related resistance skills
- General competence—self-management, social skills

Theory:

- Based on a person-environment interactionist approach (Social Cognitive Theory[10]) and the risk-protective factors model[11]
- Addresses the developmental progression of involvement in drug use and risk behaviors, focusing on psychosocial factors such as an increasing emphasis on peers among adolescents and the drive for autonomy.

Components:

- Three-year classroom-based intervention that takes fifteen 45-minute class periods
- Intended for middle/junior high students
- Three components: self-management skills, social skills, and information and skills related to drug use (anti-drug attitudes, resistance skills, anti-drug norms, etc.)
- Booster sessions as well

Evidence of success:

- Almost two decades of implementation—drug use has been cut in half in some instances where the program was implemented.

South Windsor (Connecticut) Schools Obesity Prevention Program[11]: This school-based program used a range of approaches including marketing and environmental-oriented actions to increase intake of lower fat and nutritious foods among students.

Theory:

- Based on a social marketing approach, implementation of regulations/policies, and a general environmental change strategy, where high-fat/unhealthy foods were made less available, better food choices were marketed, and the cost of choosing better foods was lowered
- Seeks to create a multilevel intervention in schools to change eating practices towards more healthy choices

Selected components:

- Change in "food environment" by introducing vending machines that sold healthy food and drink options, providing better lunch food options, and reducing the availability of high-fat foods
- Change in cost of healthy vs. unhealthy food choices—available snack options were evaluated for nutritive value, and those with lower value (e.g., doughnuts) were sold at a higher price
- Use of colorful menus (sent to students' families), coupons, and other marketing strategies to highlight the revised menu choices at school
- Training for school food service and enlisting food service staff in a catering service to increase "buy-in"

Evidence of success:

- Preliminary indicators show strong sales/consumption of healthier food items.

To Think About

Have you ever had a health class in school? What was it about? Do you remember it? Do you think it changed the way you acted in any way? Is there some other approach that might have been more effective?

WORKPLACE SETTINGS

There are also a lot of good reasons to conduct health/wellness and health promotion interventions at the workplace. More people are at the workplace than at most other accessible institutions, and these people are at the workplace for the majority of their waking day. Workplaces and schools have some similarities, in terms of access to the target population and the synergy between health objectives and organizational goals:

- Health, work performance, work safety, and productivity are intertwined. When workers are not healthy, they miss work time and are more prone to accidents.
- Many studies have shown that promoting health in the workplace is cost-effective because it reduces health care expenses and increases productivity. Proctor & Gamble, for example, found that having a workplace health promotion program reduced their health care costs by 29%.[13] Johnson & Johnson, another large company, found that an employee wellness program resulted in an estimated savings of almost $2 million in reduced medical costs, reduced sick leave, and increased productivity.[14]
- Employees spend a great deal of time at work during the day (or evening). In that sense, they, like students, are a "captive audience."
- There is a well-documented, successful history of health promotion and wellness programs in workplaces.

The idea of the workplace as a site for health promotion and intervention has gained considerable currency since the mid-1900s. Workplace health is now a major applied focus for health promotion. The growth in importance of the workplace in public health is likely due to a number of factors, including:

- The growing workforce of women, prompting a need to address maternal health and child care issues, among other health concerns.

- An aging work population.
- The Occupational Safety and Health Act (OSHA) of 1970, which created a federal agency to regulate issues of workplace safety and health, and to set standards.
- The rising cost of worker's compensation and medical care and increased motivation for employers to engage in health promotion to cut down on health problems.
- Managed care, specifically workplace-based managed care plans.
- The rise of employee assistance programs (EAPs) as a vehicle for prevention and intervention with substance abuse and mental health problems. Many EAPs now address family issues, workplace problems, and financial counseling among other areas related to life skills and quality of life. Focusing on these issues has impacted the health/wellness of employees and their families. For example, substance abuse has been a major cause of job-related accidents, absenteeism, and decreased productivity.
- An expanded view of occupational health concerns that has grown to include cardiovascular disease, high blood pressure, ulcers, smoking, repeated motion syndromes, obesity, and other health problems.

The focus of workplace health efforts has evolved from screening (health appraisals and health risk assessments) to an increased concentration on environmental factors that might affect health at the workplace, to broader health promotion and wellness efforts. The same general evolution occurred with EAPs, which moved from an emphasis on substance abuse prevention, early intervention, and treatment including having a Drug-Free Workplace Policy with pre-employment, for cause, and random drug testing, to a much broader health promotion, prevention, and early intervention program. This approach has increased the attractiveness and effectiveness of EAPs for employees—the more comprehensive prevention focus took away some of the stigma that EAPs were just programs for "alcoholics" or "drug abusers." Numerous studies of health/wellness programs indicate a good return on investment (ROI), conservatively estimated from $1 to as high as $30 or more for employers who have adopted these programs.

There remain many barriers to workplace health promotion, including employee reluctance to mix personal health issues with a work context and differences between "wellness" programs and specific workplace cultures that might include social norms and messages related to success such as working very hard, not complaining, and not revealing personal information at work. In some workplace settings such as hospitals or law offices, these programs appear to be redundant to the needs of most employees. In other locations, employees don't have the time or the incentive to take advantage of these programs. Frequently, there is a strong relationship between management and union support of these programs and participation.

Health Behavior Theory and the Workplace Setting

Again, let's do a quick PRECEDE-PROCEED assessment to look at the workplace setting and where behavioral theory might be applicable for health promotion.

Social Assessment

Understanding the overall context surrounding workplace health is somewhat different than it would be for a community or school. Workplaces can be in one or several communities or even global in nature, they have their own workplace culture and norms, and the family of each employee is frequently part of a workplace "family" depending on the orientation of the particular workplace. The famous sociologist Emil Durkheim specifically focused on the workplace in his classic book *The Division of Labor in Society* and remarked on the variations between workplaces and communities.[14] Examples of workplaces that have traditionally had close interactions with the community are Hershey's in Pennsylvania, Kodak in New York, and Weyerhaeuser in Washington State.

General well-being indicators of a community may not be relevant, because the focus of the workplace setting usually is more on measures of productivity, reduction of workplace health hazards and risks, employee continuity, and similar issues. However, you could look at some external factors from the community; for example, if a local economy is down, and there is only one employer, then there will be a lot of pressure on workers to keep their job and not complain, even if conditions are unsafe. Or, external issues such as the cost of health insurance may present a problem for employers, which of course affects employee access to health care. Globalism and competition may also create pressures to lower wages and reduce benefits, affecting worker morale and security.

Epidemiological Assessment

We are focusing on the work setting, so the health concerns and epidemiological data are related to *work-related health conditions* (e.g., carpal tunnel syndrome, high blood pressure, etc.). There are a number of general reports and studies about work-related health problems. Some good places to start in looking for these data are the Occupational

Safety and Health Administration (OSHA) within the U.S. Department of Labor, and the National Institute for Occupational Safety and Health (NIOSH), part of the U.S. Department of Health and Human Services. For problems related to substance abuse at work and drug testing issues, the Workplace Division of the Center for Substance Abuse Prevention (CSAP), also within the Department of Health and Human Services, is a good source. The National Survey on Drug Use and Health, conducted by the Substance Abuse and Mental Health Services Administration (SAMHSA), has addressed a number of substance abuse use and workplace issues in the past. The Bureau of Labor Statistics within the Department of Labor tracks occupational injuries and illnesses via a survey called the Survey of Occupational Injuries and Illnesses.

Behavioral/Environmental Assessment

What are the behavioral and environmental risks related to workplaces? Examples include a truck driver, pilot, or train engineer who drinks alcohol before or while working; wearing/not wearing protective gear; high-stress work norms where employees work very long hours with little break; unsafe storage areas for dangerous/toxic chemicals; exposure to toxic materials; or unsafe equipment or work facilities. Also in this category are workplace environmental factors that contribute to health problems such as obesity or cardiovascular disease. For example, if there are only two food sources at or near a workplace—vending machines with potato chips and donuts, and a burger joint down the road—and no time or place to walk, the environment is going to contribute to diet-related problems and ultimately to the more severe outcome of an increase in Type 2 diabetes. As described in Chapter 2, such environmental conditions are already the focus of recent efforts at obesity prevention in the workplace.

Where can you find data about this? OSHA, NIOSH, and CSAP are sources to start with, but you may also be able to find information from unions, the Chamber of Commerce, business health coalitions, and workplaces themselves.

Educational/Ecological Assessment

What predisposing, enabling, and reinforcing factors are related to work? This is an important domain of information that you need to understand for planning and implementation of workplace health promotion efforts, and for identifying applicable theory. Think about a workplace. It is a kind of small, contained social setting in which people spend a lot of time with each other. It makes sense that a key issue to consider for the application of theory is the role of *social networks,*

Occupational Illnesses and Injuries[16]

Leading injuries and illnesses include:
- Hearing loss
- Lung disease
- Cancer and lead poisoning
- Carbon monoxide poisoning
- Allergic and irritant dermatitis
- Fertility and pregnancy abnormalities
- Infectious diseases
- Low back disorders
- Musculoskeletal disorders of the upper extremities
- Traumatic injuries
- Adverse mental health outcomes

social support systems, and social norms. Workplaces are also organizations, so there are organizational roles and an "organizational culture" to consider. What kinds of rewards are built into the setting, for example, for unhealthy behavior? For healthy behavior? What about employee knowledge and attitudes? If there is a health risk on the job, do employees know that it exists? Do they perceive it as a threat? What is the motivation and intention to do something about it? Or *not* to do something about it?

Administrative Assessment

In order to develop an intervention and select an appropriate theory, you will also want to understand something about policies, structures, and resources in workplace settings. Are there resources available for a health promotion program? Is there, for example, some sort of "workplace wellness committee"? What kinds of workplace health benefits are there? Health insurance? An employee assistance program? Are there discounts for belonging to a gym or fitness club? Are health screenings available at work? What about unions? Are there unions at the worksite? What kinds of policies and programs do they have? Are there any community organizations or businesses—for example, local fitness clubs or YMCAs—that offer workplace-based activities?

Then, of course, what kinds of regulations and requirements pertain to the type of worksite you are considering? Are there state or federal laws that govern safety or occupational conditions? How are these carried out and monitored?

Relevant Theory

Based on the discussion and assessment, what kinds of theories will help you understand workplace health-related issues and shape interventions? First, think about the context for employee education. When would a workplace be able to offer such programs? At lunch? After work? These are sometimes difficult settings because employees want to eat lunch, or they want to leave and go home. What about health fairs or similar events? These might work, and have in many situations such as in Sandra Lapham's Substance Abuse Prevention, Workplace Managed Care, Project Wise (see examples below). And how will you present the information? Employees are not students, and they are adults. If they attend an educational session or health fair they are more than likely doing so by choice, so your educational approach should be engaging and hands-on, or "sell" the benefits of the behavior (e.g., getting health screenings, quitting smoking). What theory/theories might apply? Social marketing? The Health Belief Model? Diffusion of innovations?

As noted, workplaces are also social and organizational institutions, with organizational cultures. Some characteristics that are relevant for identifying appropriate interventions are:

- In organizations, there may be individuals who are "leaders" or "influencers."
- Groups of employees may also be friends.
- The workplace may have social norms about health-related behavior. These may even be related to what people consider a "good employee."
- People are at a job, and they want to do well and be rewarded.

What theories are relevant to those workplace characteristics? Diffusion of innovations? Social Network Theory? Social Cognitive Theory? Theory of Planned Behavior? Culture Theory?

Finally, in order to impact the workplace culture, or to build support for the availability of a health intervention or health-related policy, it may be necessary to engage in organizational change, and to bring to bear influence from the surrounding community. What theories are applicable?

Program Examples

The following are a few examples of workplace-based health promotion programs/interventions, with the applicable theory described. The descriptions come from the SAMHSA National Registry of Evidence-Based Programs and Practices (NREPP), accessible via http://dwp.samhsa.gov/index.aspx.

The Healthy Workplace Program: This is a set of workplace substance abuse prevention interventions that reduce unsafe drinking, illegal drug use, and prescription drug abuse while improving the health practices of adult workers. Cast in a health promotion framework and rooted in social-cognitive principles of behavior change, the program integrates substance abuse prevention material into popular health promotion programs, seeking to defuse the stigma that accompanies substance abuse and removing barriers to help-seeking behavior. The Healthy Workplace program:

- Reaches the mainstream of workers through the positive vehicle of health promotion
- Raises awareness of the benefits of healthful practices and the hazards of using alcohol, tobacco, and illegal drugs, and misusing legal drugs (Health Belief Model)
- Teaches employees specific techniques/skills for improving health and reducing use of alcohol, tobacco, and illegal drugs (Social-Cognitive Theory)
- Uses carefully constructed videos to raise self-efficacy and provide models for how healthful practices can be embraced and substance abuse reduced (Social Cognitive Theory)

It has been recognized as a *model program* by SAMHSA based on evidence of effectiveness.

Coping with Work and Family Stress: A Workplace Preventive Intervention: This is a 16-session weekly group intervention designed to teach employees how to develop and apply effective coping strategies to deal with stressors at work and at home. The model is derived from Pearlin and Schooler's hierarchy of coping mechanisms[17] as well as Bandura's social learning theory.[10] Previous NIH-funded research provided the basis for development of the Yale Work and Family Stress Program. The curriculum that guided the intervention for these two studies placed a major emphasis on the role of stress, coping, and social support in relation to the occurrence of substance use and psychological symptoms. Ultimately, a 16-session program was created to teach employees effective methods for *reducing risk factors* and *enhancing protective factors*. The two studies provided evidence that those who participated in the program showed significantly greater decreases in substance use and psychological symptoms compared to control group participants.

The program results in:

- Actual reduction in work and family stressors
- Increased use of social support
- Changes in the meaning of stressful events
- Less reliance on avoidance coping strategies
- Increased use of a wider range of stress management approaches
- Prevention or reduction of alcohol and drug use
- Prevention or reduction of psychological symptoms such as depression and anxiety

It is also a SAMHSA model program.

To Think About

Think about a work setting you know about. Are there any health risks you can think of? How does the work setting contribute to the risks, or to their prevention? What could you do about it?

Chapter Questions

1. What are some characteristics of school and workplace settings that are similar? How might this affect relevant theory?

2. What is a comprehensive school health approach?

3. What are some of the political issues you might face in trying to implement a school-based health promotion program? (Think administrative/policy assessment.)

4. What connections are there between schools and their communities that might affect the type of program (and theory) selected? What about connections between workplaces and communities?

5. How have workplace health programs changed over the years, and what does this mean in terms of the kinds of programs and theoretical approaches that would be applicable?

REFERENCES

1. Marx E, Wooley S, Northrup D. *Health Is Academic: A Guide to Coordinated School Health Programs*. New York: Teacher's College Press; 1998.

2. Education Development Corporation, Inc.

3. Greenberg MT, Weissberg RM, O'Brien MU, et al. Enhancing school-based prevention and youth development through coordinated social, emotional and academic learning. *Am Psychol.* 2003;58(6/7):466–474.

4. Lear JG. Children's health and children's schools: a collaborative approach to strengthening children's well-being. In: Lear JG, Isaacs SL, Knickman JR, eds. *School Health Services and Programs (Robert Woods Johnson Series on Health Policy)*. San Francisco, CA: Jossey-Bass; 2006.

5. Jacobs J. *The Death and Life of Great American Cities*. New York: Vintage Books; 1961.

6. Johnston LD, O'Malley PM, Bachman JG, Schulenberg JE. *Monitoring the Future, National Results on Adolescent Drug Use: Overview of Key Findings 2005*. (NIH Publication No. 06-5882). Bethesda, MD: National Institute on Drug Abuse; 2006.

7. Search Institute. Developmental assets: an investment in youth. January 4, 1999. Available at: http://www.search-institute.org/assets/index.htm. October 2006

8. Botvin GJ, Griffin KW, Paul E. Preventing tobacco and alcohol use among elementary school students through life skills training. *J Child Adolescent Substance Abuse*. 2003;12(4):1–17.

9. Botvin GJ, Schinke SP, Epstein JA, Diaz T, Botvin EM. Effectiveness of culturally-focused and generic skills training approaches to alcohol and drug abuse prevention among minority adolescents: two-year follow-up results. *Psychol Addict Behav*. 1995;9:183–194.

10. Bandura A. *Social Foundations of Thought and Action*. Englewood Cliffs, NJ: Prentice Hall; 1986.

11. Hawkins JD, Catalano RF, Miller JY. Risk and protective factors for alcohol and other drug problems in adolescence and early adulthood: implications for substance abuse prevention. *Psychol Bull*. 1992;112:64–105.

12. U.S. Department of Agriculture/Food and Nutrition Service, Centers for Disease Control and Prevention/DHHS, U.S. Department of Education. *Making it Happen! School Nutrition Success Stories*. Alexandria, VA: 2005.

13. Goetzel RZ, Jacobsen BH, Aldana SG, Verdell K, Yee L. Health care costs of worksite health promotion participants and non-participants. *J Occup Environ Med*. 1998;40(4):341–346.

14. DeMoranville CW, Schoenbachler DD, Przytulski J. Wellness at work: boost wellness center participation with target marketing strategies. *Marketing Health Serv*. 1998;18(2):14–24.

15. Durkheim E. *The Division of Labor in Society*. New York: Macmillan; 1993.

16. Friis RH. *Essentials of Environmental Health*. Boston: Jones & Bartlett; 2007.

17. Pearlin LI, Schooler C. The structure of coping. *J Health Soc Behav*. 1978;19:2–21.

CHAPTER 10

Application of Theory: Communications Campaigns[*]

* Written with Lorien Abroms, PhD

LEARNING OBJECTIVES

By the end of this chapter, the reader will be able to:

- Understand key issues with respect to the use of communications and media for health promotion
- Understand the kinds of social/behavioral theories that could be applicable to communications campaigns
- Describe examples of theory-based communications campaigns

"The new electronic interdependence recreates the world in the image of a global village."

—MARSHALL McLUHAN, 1962

"The highly masculine figures and the tattoo symbols set Marlboro cigarettes right in the heart of some core meanings of smoking: masculinity, adulthood, vigor and potency."

—PIERRE MARTINEAU, ON CIGARETTE ADVERTISING, IN VANCE PACKARD'S INFLUENTIAL BOOK, *THE HIDDEN PERSUADERS*, 1957

COMMUNICATING THROUGH THE PUBLIC MEDIA

The effort to communicate or disseminate information through the public media, and in so doing have an impact on people's behavior, is one of the most well-known applications of behavioral theory in public health programs. Why? Think about it. As human beings, we are highly sophisticated creatures of communication and symbol; processors of symbolic information. Communication is our primary tool in the basic process of interacting with other human beings (as it is for all species); but more importantly, human life is inseparable from the complex world that is represented, stored, transmitted, and altered through the incredible range of communication processes that we use. We live a life that is built around shared (and conflicting) meanings, ongoing social interaction, and group-related behavior, much of which is encoded and acted upon based on the various ways in which we communicate (see our extensive discussion of communication in Chapter 6).

How do you know, for example, what kinds of clothing to wear at any given time? How do you know what is fashionable? Such a simple thing. Not really. Much of what you know comes through the communication of images in the media, and through all the talk that occurs about clothing and dress. You know what it means to wear one thing versus another, and in what situations wearing a particular kind of clothing will mean one thing versus another. Or at least you know what it means for the social group that you are attached to.

That is exactly why the mass media—television, film, video, DVDs, the Internet, radio, and print publications—have taken on such an importance in contemporary society. Because what you see, read, and hear in the public media becomes a major storehouse of information influencing how you act, look, sound, and think about things. The language you hear, the patterns of social interaction you see, the way situations are presented and characterized, the way symbols are used, all shape your understanding of the world. People and characters in the media provide models for behavior.

If you remember your theory, the latter phenomenon was described in social learning theory (later SCT) as "observational learning"—where people model their own behavior based on the behavior of others, and what happens to them when they engage in that behavior. Models in the media help people develop understandings, for example, about when it might be appropriate to use violence, or if smoking is an attractive thing to do. The mass media can also be seen as a "playing field" for representing oneself (especially through the Internet) and interacting with others.

As we have discussed throughout this book, *behavior* is action infused with intent and meaning, and interconnected with the social and environmental sphere. We know that the mass media are a major component of this social environment, affecting the health of people in intended and unintended ways. The question that we will explore in this chapter is how the media can be intentionally harnessed to promote the public's health.

Recent Technologies and Their Emerging Role

The Internet

Although the "traditional" types of mass media—TV, newspapers, and radio—are and remain important, the Internet (or the "Web") has emerged since the 1990s as a primary, and global, means of both interpersonal and mass communication. All major broadcast media have parallel Internet operations, and Weblogs, or "blogs," have become a major source of information and opinion. E-mail and instant messaging are the standard communication channels for daily work and personal interaction. There are now an astonishing number of Web sites—over 85 million, according to some sources.[1] And with the continued growth of satellite communications, streaming media (sound and video), and wireless connectivity, access to the Internet, as well as the wide range of available information, is expanding at breakneck speed. Importantly, the Internet and wireless communication media have become the primary communications channel for young people who came of age during this time, prompting a dramatic shift in patterns and styles of communication. The implications for health communication are significant.

Cable Television and Satellite Broadcasting

Cable television and the recent advent of satellite radio have also added new dimensions to the spectrum of communications channels. Cable TV has been around for some time, and from the beginning—with MTV and other youth-oriented channels—created an entire programmatic style and a global site for the dissemination of pop culture. People around the world now have access to shared cultural symbols, language, and behavior.

COMMUNICATIONS CAMPAIGNS

A *communications campaign* can be thought of as a planned process of disseminating messages to influence behavior in a particular group or population (typically called a "target audience" when referring to a communications effort) through a coordinated process that involves the following:

- Identifying your key target audiences (who do you need to reach), and often subgroups within target audiences (known as *audience segmenting*)
- Identifying the best communications channels to reach one or more target audiences and subgroups
- Determining the messages to be communicated—for each target audience and subgroup, and communications channel—and the most effective way to format or present the message (e.g., tone, language, image)
- Identifying a sequence of activities—in other words, the specific "unfolding" of a campaign, with the different activities and media products introduced over time to achieve the intended effect
- The use of formative research with the target audience(s) in order to be sure that the messages and channels are effective

Communications campaigns usually, and most effectively, use a combination of different modes of communication and channels.[2,3] Many use channels of communication besides the mass media such as public events and interpersonal communication, or use these in combination with mass media. So, public health communications means more than just the mass media. And communications efforts face a challenge. Campaigns are most effective when they are heard and remembered against the din of other competing messages in the media—and there are a lot of competing messages! This is one reason why a major difficulty for communication campaigns is that the campaigns often don't adequately expose the target audience to the campaign message, and are less than effective not because of problems with the design of the message, but because they don't reach their audience.[3]

Let's try a hypothetical example. Your assignment is to design and carry out a communications campaign in a metropolitan area that will: 1) increase awareness among both adults and young people about the need for physical exercise and better eating to address obesity; and 2) convince these *target audiences* to adopt better eating and exercise habits. First of all, think about the two target audiences named in your assignment. Is it sufficient to think of them just as two target audiences? Probably not, and here's why:

- Your adult audience may include several subgroups that will have different issues to consider about diet and exercise. Adults who are parents, for example, are more likely to think not only of themselves, but also of their children. They may want to be good examples, and to do what they can to keep their children healthy. Messages and information targeting parents should therefore help them in these tasks. By contrast, single adults may have more time to exercise, to cook for themselves, or to eat out. Their focus is more on themselves and the quality of their personal lives; thus, communication efforts should address different themes than for parents. There are many other potential subgroups: by age, cultural background/language, or region, to name a few.

- Your audience of "young people" is also likely to include many subgroups whose relationship to diet and exercise is different. A big factor here may be age—eating patterns vary between youth who are, say, 9 years old and those who are 16 years old. And, of course, 16 year olds are likely to be concerned about how they look in ways that most 9 year olds don't yet fully grasp. Another factor may be geography. Young people living in a suburb or rural area may have a lot more *space* to exercise, in parks or other open areas. Urban young people have to find creative alternatives to that kind of open space.

It's not hard to see that, even with this simple exercise, you will probably need to *segment* your two basic audiences at least into the following kinds of groups: 1) Single adults, 2) adults who are parents, 3) youth who are approximately 12 and younger, and 4) youth approximately 13 and older.

Assuming we now have four target audience segments, what are some communications channels appropriate for each of them? This is a question for which *formative research* is very helpful in identifying answers. .

From this kind of research, you may find out, for example, that your best channels of communication break out like this, for each target audience group:

- *For adults who are parents:* Health and family-related stories on the evening news; communications received from pediatricians; communications received from schools; information they hear in person from other parents (word-of-mouth)

- *For adults who are single:* Health stories on the evening news; articles and ads in fitness and lifestyle magazines; information from work; Web sites on the Internet; information from other single adults in activity-related settings

Formative Research

To understand one or more target audiences for purposes of a public health communication campaign, you may conduct formative research.

- Formative research can consist of *interviews, focus groups (something like a group interview),* or *surveys* with members of the target audience who have agreed to participate in the research.

- The information you collect will help you identify: channels of communication, the best "tone" for a message, themes to emphasize (or not emphasize), potential spokespersons or influential social models (What theory does this refer to?), and the knowledge levels and attitudes of your audiences concerning the health issue

- *For younger youth:* Information from parents; television programs and ads; information from teachers; ads and information on Web sites geared to younger children; what celebrities say; what they are told by older siblings

- *For older youth:* Information from parents; television programs/ads; Web sites geared to older youth; things they hear from downloads/podcasts; movies; what they hear from friends and from peers involved in similar activities; views and information from celebrities

You can see that there is some overlap between the two adult groups and some overlap between the two youth groups, but very little overlap between youth and adult channels. But for each audience group, there seems to be a combination of mass media channels, views from authority figures or admired figures, and interpersonal sources.

You may also have found out from the formative research that it is only adults who think of physical activity as "exercise," and are aware of the need to do it for health reasons. For now, assume that young people in your research said that they don't think too much about it, and are not generally worried about their health. Some play sports like soccer when they can. Both boys and girls in the over-13-year-old group are very aware of how they look, and if they think about diet or physical activity it is related to appearance. Some of your urban young people also said that they have nowhere to go except school playgrounds. For all the young people in your research, video games take up a lot of what would otherwise be physical activity time.

At this point, you may be able to start thinking about messages, themes, and tone. Your adult parents have said that they value being good parents, so if information is "pitched" to them as helping to achieve that goal, it may catch their attention. Also important, if they hear the same message by word-of-mouth, they might feel an extra imperative to incorporate the information by a kind of peer pressure (this could, for example, involve communication through parent groups like school PTAs). For single adults who (according to your research) are most concerned about keeping healthy and being able to do a lot of activities, the pitch needs to focus on healthy diet and exercise as part of what active people do. These single adults may also be responsive to messages that emphasize a theme of "newness," like a new activity or new food to try.

Finding the right pitch to the two youth audiences is not so simple. Let's say that the younger youth have said, in your research, that they don't want to be talked to like little kids. They pay attention to messages that are cool and fun, give them guidance, but are not patronizing. It's a subtle balance. At the same time, scare messages may have more impact on them than they would on older youth, who say that they "blow off" those kinds of messages as transparent attempts to scare them into doing something "that the adults think is right." The older youth don't want to be told what to do, and respond better to *examples* of young people who, for example, eat healthy and are still looked on with approval by other peers. They also like to hear these messages directly from friends, or from adults they think are admirable, and who aren't just trying to "act like adults" towards them.

Are you getting the idea of how this works?

Finally, you put together all this information, working together with experts in developing Internet content, print materials, community events, press/news stories, and television advertisements, and design a whole package of messages and materials that fits into the needs identified in your research. Then, you think strategy. What should go first? Should you have a general "kickoff event"? Based on your research, that might not be the best idea. Why? Because, among other reasons, your older youth audience might be "alerted" that it is a health campaign, and your younger youth might not even pay attention. The kickoff might then be useful only for adults. For youth, you may want to begin with a whole series of messages that show up on, say, Web sites, or during broadcasts of sports events. When you have worked this out, you have a campaign.

The Four-Stage Planning Approach for Communications Campaigns

Thinking about this more systematically, a widely used book on developing, implementing, and evaluating health communications programs describes a four-stage process.[2] The stages are:

- *Stage One: Planning and Strategy Development:* This includes a determination of how communications can be used effectively for a particular organization or program; identification of intended audiences; the conduct of consumer (formative) research to develop a strategy and objectives; and the drafting of *communications plans* that set out activities, partnerships involved, and baseline surveys to be used as a basis for evaluating program outcome (see Chapter 13).
- *Stage Two: Developing and Pretesting Concepts, Messages, and Materials:* This entails the development of relevant, meaningful messages (using the formative research); planning activities and drafting messages; and *pretesting* messages and materials with members of the target audience(s).
- *Stage Three: Implementing the Program:* This includes beginning communications activities as planned; tracking exposure among the target audience(s) and determining if adjustments to the program are necessary; and periodic review of all program components to ensure that they are meeting the need.
- *Stage Four: Assessing Effectiveness and Making Refinements:* This requires assessing the program and identifying refinements that will increase the effectiveness of future implementation.

As you may have guessed, this process is very much like the planning approaches discussed in Chapter 7, but applied to communications.

MEDIA ADVOCACY

Another important kind of communications activity, which can be an integrated part of a communications campaign, is called *media advocacy*. Media advocacy is the strategic use of mass media to apply pressure to advance healthy public policy.[4] The primary purposes of media advocacy campaigns are to:

- Influence public opinion
- Influence policy makers
- Influence policy

In this sense these campaigns indirectly aim at health behavior change by seeking to change social institutions and their policies, and in doing so getting at the environment that surrounds behavior. Well-known and very effective advocacy efforts have focused, for example, on establishing smoking regulations/policies such as clean indoor air ordinances, and on increasing the funding for HIV/AIDS research and prevention.

Like any other communications effort, media advocacy begins with a goal. The goal may not be behavior change of *individuals*, but instead focuses on behavior change of policy makers within an institution such as a school, city, or state. Efforts may be aimed at, for example:

- Policies or regulations concerning the sale of alcohol to minors
- Policies or regulations regarding smoking and the prevention of secondhand smoke inhalation
- Policies to increase access to health care facilities in an urban neighborhood
- Policies mandating the cleanup of polluted water

Media advocacy may consist of a full scale mass media campaign with advertising to gain public support for a particular type of policy, or to get policy makers to vote in a particular way. Additionally, media advocacy efforts may seek to influence the public and/or policy makers through *access* to the news media. This type of media advocacy is typically called "news outreach." The first step is to gain media access and see to it that your topic is getting adequate news coverage so that the public and policy makers are aware of your health issue. A second and equally important step is to make sure that your topic is being covered in a particular way. In other words, your task is to help shape media coverage so that it presents the issue in a way that advances the promotion of public health.

Generally speaking, there are several strategies to think about in working with the news media:

- *Developing and maintaining a relationship:* This is important because news organizations often have to work fast, and they tend to go to "known sources" or at least sources with whom they already have a relationship. So if you develop a relationship, by making contact, providing background information, and establishing yourself or your organization as a *source*, you have created a foundation.
- *Providing information in a format that is useful:* Broadcast media, by and large, do not allot much time to any given story, so when you provide information that you want to be reported, package it with that in mind. Think of it as a headline with key supporting details. Also, remember that the media are looking

A Communications Plan

Typically, a communications plan will summarize the rationale for, elements of, and timetable for implementing a communications campaign, including, for example:

- Campaign name
- Agency
- Health problem to be addressed
- Overall health objective
- Communications campaign objective(s)
- Primary target audience(s)
- Secondary target audience(s)
- Formative research activities, purpose, and results
- Messages by audience/segment
- Materials to be developed/used
- Message dissemination—channels, materials by channel, and rationale
- Time line/sequence of campaign
- Staff and resource allocation
- Partners, collaborations
- Evaluation plan

for *stories*, not rambling expositions. Wherever that story can have a "human face," showing its impact on people, so much the better.

And of course, the information, the story, that you provide should be crafted to make the point you want made—that, for example, there are no health care facilities in certain sections of the city and the city council is not doing anything about it.

The kinds of materials and activities typically used in media advocacy include[4,5]:

- Press or news releases
- Letters to the editor
- Opinion (Op-Ed) pieces
- Making presentations to an editorial board
- Interviews
- Conducting media events (designed for news coverage)

There are many resources that provide more detailed guidelines for conducting media advocacy, including a manual available from the American Public Health Association (www.apha.org).

HEALTH BEHAVIOR THEORY AND COMMUNICATIONS CAMPAIGNS/MASS MEDIA CAMPAIGNS

As you might have guessed by now, much of the health behavior theory we have talked about is useful in communications campaigns and mass media efforts. Hornik cites three general types of theoretical models used[6(p14)]:

- *Individual models:* Focusing on change in awareness, knowledge, and skills
- *Social diffusion models:* Focusing on processes of change in public norms, which lead to behavior change among groups
- *Institutional diffusion model:* Emphasizing change in "elite opinion," which is then "translated into institutional behavior, including policy changes, which in turn affect individual behavior"

We can map a wide variety of theoretical approaches onto those general models. Using the hypothetical example of an obesity prevention campaign, for *individual models*, remember that the ultimate goal of your campaign is to promote change in individual diets and exercise. So, for example, the Health Belief Model[7,8] may be a useful guide to messages—in the campaign discussed earlier—targeting youth and seeking to increase their perception of susceptibility to health problems such as diabetes as a consequence of obesity, or in minimizing the "cost" of preventive behavior. Or the Transtheoretical Model[9,10] may help direct your messages to the "stage" of one or more of the target audience segments, and help you determine what change process you need to emphasize in order to help move them towards action. Youth may be more in the precontemplation or contemplation stage, with respect to obesity, whereas adults may be ready for action.

In terms of social diffusion, Diffusion of Innovations[11] and Social Marketing Theory[12-14] are highly applicable—both of these approaches provide important guidance with respect to factors to consider in structuring campaigns and the processes by which people receive and implement information. General communications theory and culture theory are very useful in highlighting these issues as well as the role of communications channels, language, and "packaging" (encoding). Some specialized campaigns may also use a social network approach, disseminating messages and risk behavior alternatives through close networks of individuals. Other campaigns concentrate on reaching *community leaders*, which is an example of targeting "elite opinion," identified as institutional diffusion in the scheme above, and which may involve media advocacy. For example, say you experienced considerable resistance among school principals for implementing a new obesity awareness education component in schools. If you were able to change the opinion of key school board members, or of the leadership within a broad organization such as a national association of school principals or the National Education Association ("elites" insofar as schools are concerned), this might result in local policy requiring schools to implement the program (and possibly guidelines for implementation), which in turn would influence the behavior of principals, teachers, and ultimately students.

New communications technologies are ripe for the application of theory.[15] The opportunities for innovative diffusion have multiplied. Images/social models of behavior can be disseminated instantly. The possibilities of working through social networks (for support or information dissemination) via e-mail and the Internet have opened virtually an entire subfield of study and practice. E-mail counseling, for example, has been used to effectively change a variety of health behaviors including weight loss[16] and smoking.[17,18] Support groups on the Internet for people diagnosed with breast cancer have been shown to reduce negative emotions, increase women's participation in health care, and increase their information competence.[19]

Theory and the Development of Messages

What information should you communicate? How should you package or "encode" the information you want to communicate? These are questions that are very much informed by theory as it pertains to the situations and characteristics of particular target populations.[20] If you hope to influence behavior among a particular group or population, your messages must have some meaning for that population. We talked about this in the brief example earlier in the chapter in terms of finding the right "pitch" for an audience.

Using this example again, let's explore some of the issues that have to be addressed and their connections with theory. Remember that the older youth audience is not likely to pay attention to messages that appear to be asking them (or scaring them) to conform to what "adults think is right." Now, let's say your formative research tells you that this age group does not think itself *susceptible* to obesity or its consequences. Sounds like the Health Belief Model may be relevant? All you have to do is come up with a message that increases their perceived susceptibility, right? In this case, you have to take into account a number of factors, for example, that adolescents and young adults typically do not think themselves vulnerable across a range of potential health or other problems. So to try that route may be running into a brick wall related to the developmental stage of those youth.

So what other behavior change theories might be developmentally relevant in helping you develop messages? Adolescents and even young adults in the United States tend to focus on peers for guidance in terms of how to behave. What theory or theories provide you some insight here? What about Social Cognitive Theory and its vicarious learning (learning by models) component? This might be more applicable, and you may be more effective in developing a message that employs a peer social role model to create *value* for exercise and healthy eating behavior, without—at least for the moment—focusing on scare tactics or the negative health effects of bad diet and lack of exercise. This could still be relevant in terms of the Health Belief Model, because what you are doing is playing up the *benefits* (as understood by young adults) of healthy behavior.

Now, what if you are developing messages for young adults from another country or culture. The peer emphasis so common in the United States may not be as important or relevant. In some cultures, great respect is given to older adults. Culture theory informs us that we live and behave in subjective worlds of meaning, where behavior and meaning are linked. So if age-respect is important, and if young people are viewed as *representing family* as opposed to asserting individuality (a common sentiment, for example, in many Asian cultures), then a message associating exercise/good eating with approval from elders and representing one's family well may be much more effective.

Here again, as in so many other instances we discuss in the book, the selection of applicable theory is very much tied to population and circumstance.

PROGRAM EXAMPLES

There are many well-known and visible health communications campaigns that illustrate how theory is applied. The following are just two examples.

National Youth Anti-Drug Media Campaign

This has certainly been one of the most visible media campaigns in the past few years, and is a very good example of a coordinated, strategic media campaign at the national level. The campaign was funded by Congress in 1998, and was launched and managed by the White House Office of National Drug Control Policy (ONDCP). It was and is a public-private partnership. Many nonprofits participate, including the YMCA, Boys and Girls Clubs of America, National Education Association, and others. The Partnership for a Drug-Free America (originally organized in 1987), a coalition of communications professionals, including the pro bono (unpaid) involvement of major advertising agencies such as Ogilvy & Mather and Fleishman Hillard, is responsible for the development of advertising messages.

The campaign includes the following components (see www.mediacampaign.org):

- *Advertising:* Television, radio, print, and Internet
- *Media:* News media outreach and media initiatives
- *Internet:* A set of Web sites for youth/teens (www.Freevibe.com), parents (www.TheAntiDrug.com), and other potential "influencers"
- *Entertainment outreach:* Information and resources provided to entertainment writers, media roundtables, and others
- *Multicultural outreach:* Advertising and outreach targeting African Americans, Hispanics, Asian Americans, and American Indians/Alaskan natives with materials developed in several languages
- *Partnerships:* For dissemination of prevention information and messages; a broad group of nonprofit agencies are involved, including a number of organizations representing multicultural populations
- *The @Work program:* Intended to reach parents at worksites, and to serve as a vehicle for dissemination of messages via worksites

As you can see, messages and campaign activities target both youth and parents to reach those involved or potentially involved in substance use, their peers (and social norms), and adults who can influence them. It has been implemented in several phases.

Has it been effective? Results are mixed. According to one recent evaluation[21]:

- Exposure (recall of messages) was relatively good for both parents and youth, particularly in the more recent "waves" of the campaign.
- The campaign appeared to have a positive effect on parents, with 80% of parents reporting change in attitudes and behavior (such as talking to kids about drugs, monitoring). Change varied with exposure to the campaign.
- However, there has been little evidence of campaign impacts on youth. There was no statistically significant decline in marijuana use or improvement in attitudes/beliefs between 2000 and 2001, and no relationship between increased exposure and change. There was even some apparent evidence that more exposure to ads for young girls made them more likely to report use than girls with less exposure.

The Truth Campaign

The Truth Campaign is the largest national youth-focused anti-tobacco mass media campaign. It was launched in 2000 by the American Legacy Foundation. Rather than talking up the ill-health effects of smoking, Truth was designed to appeal to the need for independence among teens. It strove to reach teens by letting them know—in innovative ways and with cutting-edge style—that the tobacco industry was out to manipulate them through their marketing and manufacturing practices.

There is substantial evidence that the Truth Campaign worked:

- Seventy-five percent of all 12- to 17-year-olds can accurately describe one or more of the Truth ads.

- Nearly 90 percent of youths aged 12 to 17 said the ad they saw was convincing.
- Eighty-five percent said the ad gave them good reasons not to smoke.
- Exposure to ads was associated with being more likely to believe that cigarette companies lie and that taking a stand against smoking is important.
- It is estimated that the campaign is responsible for 22% of the decline in youth smoking between 1999 and 2002.[22]

Question: Why did one campaign succeed with youth and the other not succeed? What do you think might be going on to cause these results?

Chapter Questions

1. Explain how the modern mass media have become so important as influences on human behavior and health behavior.

2. What is a communications campaign?

3. How are target audiences and communications channels related?

4. How does *formative research* help you select and use theory for a communications campaign?

5. In the example of an obesity-related communications campaign in this chapter, explain how Diffusion of Innovations theory would help explain how exercise (as a behavior) was diffused among adults and youth.

REFERENCES

1. Netcraft.com

2. Department of Health and Human Services. *Making Health Communication Programs Work,* rev ed. Washington, D.C.: National Cancer Institute, National Institutes of Health, U.S. Department of Health and Human Services; 2002. (Also known as the "pink book.")

3. Hornik RC, ed. *Public Health Communication: Evidence for Behavior Change.* Mahwah, NJ: Lawrence Erlbaum Associates; 2002.

4. Wallack L, Diaz I, Dorfman L, Woodruff K. *News for a Change: An Advocate's Guide to Working with the Media.* Thousand Oaks, CA: Sage; 1999.

5. American Public Health Association. *Media Advocacy Manual.* Washington, D.C. Available at: www.apha.org.

6. Hornik RC. Introduction. Public health communication: making sense of contradictory evidence. In: Hornik RC, ed. *Public Health Communication: Evidence for Behavior Change.* Mahwah, NJ: Lawrence Erlbaum Associates; 2002.

7. Becker MH, ed. The health belief model and personal health behavior. *Health Ed Monogr.* 1974;2:Entire issue.

8. Janz NK, Becker MH. The health belief model: a decade later. *Health Ed Q.* 1984;11(1):1–47.

9. Prochaska JO, DiClemente CC. Stages and processes of self-change of smoking: toward an integrative model of change. *J Consult Clin Psychol.* 1983;51:390–395.

10. Prochaska JO, Velicer WF. The transtheoretical model of health behavior change. *Am J Health Prom.* 1997;12:38–48.

11. Rogers EM. *Diffusion of Innovations,* 4th ed. New York: Free Press; 1995.

12. Kotler P, Roberto EL. *Social Marketing Strategies for Changing Public Behavior.* New York: Free Press; 1989.

13. Kotler P. *Marketing for Non-Profit Organizations.* Englewood Cliffs, NJ: Prentice-Hall; 1975.

14. Manoff RK. *Social Marketing.* New York: Praeger; 1985.

15. Owen N, Fotheringham MJ, Marcus BH. Communication technology and health behavior change. In: Glanz K, Rimer BK, Lewis FM, eds. *Health Behavior and Health Education: Theory, Research and Practice,* 3rd ed. San Francisco, CA: Jossey-Bass; 2002:.

16.v\ Tate DF, Jackvony EH, Wing RR. Effects of Internet behavioral counseling on weight loss in adults at risk for type 2 diabetes: a randomized trial. *JAMA.* 2003;289(14):1833–1836.

17. Abroms LC, Windsor R, Simons-Morton B. A formative evaluation of an email-based program for smoking cessation in young adults. Under Review.

18. Cobb NK, Graham AL, Bock BC, Papandonatos G, Abrams DB. Initial evaluation of a real-world Internet smoking cessation system. *Nicotine Tob Res.* 2005;7(2):207–216.

19. Gustafson DH, McTavish FM, Stengle W, et al. Use and impact of eHealth system by low-income women with breast cancer. *J Health Commun.* 2005;10(Suppl 1):195–218.

20. Institute of Medicine. *Speaking of Health: Assessing Health Communications Strategies for Diverse Populations.* Washington, D.C.: National Academy of Sciences; 2002.

21. Westat, Inc., Annenberg School of Communication. *Evaluation of the National Youth Anti-Drug Media Campaign: Fifth Semi-Annual Report of Findings (Executive Summary).* Unpublished report for the National Institute on Drug Abuse, National Institutes of Health; 2002.

22. Farrelly MC, Davis KC, Haviland ML, Messeri P, Healton CG. Evidence of a dose-response relationship between "truth" antismoking ads and youth smoking prevalence. *Am J Public Health.* 2005;95(3):425–431.

CHAPTER 11

Application of Theory: Global Health*

* I am grateful for the review and expert advice from Laurie Krieger, PhD and Richard Skolnik, MPA in preparing this chapter.

LEARNING OBJECTIVES

By the end of this chapter, the reader will be able to:

- Understand key issues with respect to health promotion in a global setting
- Understand the kinds of social/behavioral theories that could be applicable to global health promotion programs
- Describe examples of theory-based global health promotion programs

---

"Give me health and a day, and I will make the pomp of emperors ridiculous."

—RALPH WALDO EMERSON, "BEAUTY," *NATURE* **(1836)**

THE SETTING: HEALTH IN THE GLOBAL CONTEXT

Before proceeding with this chapter, it is useful to reiterate that the discussion that follows is not a comprehensive overview of global health, but a brief and selective introduction to one of the arenas in which social and behavioral theory can be applied. A full review of issues in global health can be found in *Essentials of Global Health* (Richard Skolnik), a companion volume in this series. That said, in many ways, it becomes less and less useful to think about "global health" as separate from "domestic health." As the HIV/AIDS pandemic and recent threat of avian flu demonstrate, the two settings have increasingly merged into one, at least in terms of the epidemiology.†

† However, the organizations and practitioners involved in global health remain, for the most part, separate from those addressing domestic health.

And although the term *globalization* is typically used in an economic context, it really refers to much more, including health. Movements of people, of images and information, of resources, and of environments all have done much to reduce the distinction between global and domestic. HIV/AIDS, for example, is prevalent 1) where there are international transportation and trade routes; 2) where rapidly developing economies create an urban-rural divide and people flow into urban areas to find sources of income; 3) where there are migrant worker flows, and men and women are separated from their families for long periods of time; and 4) where people travel to seek pleasure. It is also prevalent in economies that are hard-pressed, and don't have the resources or capacity to mount prevention efforts or provide access to anti-retroviral therapies that are manufactured and controlled in more industrialized and wealthier economies.

Another example is the threat of an avian flu epidemic. Avian flu is a complex global phenomenon that has been around for a long time, but as a virus that could infect humans it first surfaced in Hong Kong, in 1997. The bird flu then spread to Thailand, Vietnam, Indonesia, China, Japan, and South Korea. In some of these countries poultry is both a major export product (as in, for example, Thailand) and a cultural tradition—most rural homes have chickens, and fighting cocks are prized possessions. As a disease borne by birds, its spread is also determined by the flight patterns of migratory birds, which have nothing to do with national borders. More recently, there have been outbreaks in Europe and elsewhere.

Globalization

What is it? There are many definitions, but in general it refers to the way in which the operation of businesses, production, and markets are integrated across national boundaries. For example, a clothing item is produced in a factory in the Philippines, using cotton that comes from Egypt, and then sold under different brand names at shopping malls in Tokyo, London, and Los Angeles. The whole operation is run by a company headquartered in the United States. However, customer service and data processing operations are "outsourced" to India.

Broader implications: In a broader sense, globalization refers not just to the integration of economic production and markets, but to the social and political consequences of this trend. There are many views about whether these consequences are positive or negative (see, for example, "Globalization: Threat or Opportunity?" International Monetary Fund Issue Brief, April 12, 2000. Washington, DC: International Monetary Fund). For public health, globalization has several implications, including the following:

- Increasing complexity in terms of ensuring workplace health and safety across globalized operations
- Increasing complexity in terms of ensuring environmental responsibility where facilities and production are segmented and located in different countries, under different regulations and conditions
- Much more rapid routes of transmission for infectious disease around the globe
- Much more rapid avenues for communication and dissemination

So how shall we think of global health as a setting for the application of behavioral theory in public health programs? Despite the powerful impact of globalization in all its aspects, health problems follow different *trajectories* in different nations or regions due to variations in at least the following *ecological* factors:

- *Environmental risks:* The presence of diseases carried or vectored in a particular location via contaminated water, insects, pollution, or climatic factors that cause food shortages or famine. According to one recent report, for example, 24% of the global burden of disease was attributed to environmental causes.[1]

A recent, severe cholera outbreak in Angola was said to be caused by polluted water from the Bengo river trucked to slum dwellers in the capital, Luanda, together with mountains of garbage and sewage in and around standing water.[2] And in situations like this, it may or may not be the case that people are aware of the need to wash hands, for example, increasing the risk.

- *System capacity and infrastructure:* The presence or absence of adequate health care services, planning, or prevention functions. For planning that means at least the capacity to collect and analyze epidemiological data so that problems can be identified and resources allocated. The level of basic health care capacity is critical: To what extent do the physical facilities exist, and are there trained health professionals to staff them? To what extent are they located where people can access them? To what extent do class, caste, or ethnicity present barriers to service? Also important and in this category are basic infrastructure characteristics such as transportation capabilities and the availability of water and power. It goes without saying, for example, that sanitation is difficult when clean water is not available—a substantial percentage of diarrheal disease is directly related to inadequate sanitation facilities (e.g., water, toilets, sewers).[3,4]

- *Socioeconomic conditions:* The nature of the economy and its relationship to the global economic system, and the impact of this context on social factors, which in turn affect health conditions and system capacity. For example, if a country is dependent on just a few export crops subject to the fluctuations of the global market, resources available for health will be uncertain, and long-term planning and services less likely. If the economy has shifted to an urban and industrializing or service related economy, with substantial gaps in income and education, as well as decreasing resources outside urban areas, there may be population flows to these urban areas leading to crowding, poor living conditions, and the easy transmission of disease. The presence of a highly valued commodity like diamonds, water, or oil may provide the resources to restructure and improve health care; or, it may end up supporting debt repayment or entangled in other political issues and conflicts as the source of conflict over resources.[5,6,7]

- *Political conditions:* The presence of instability or conflict, or, at worst, armed conflict and civil war. It goes without saying that such conditions are devastating for health and for the ability of health systems to function. Political rivalries and factionalism can also divert resources and attention from pressing public health needs.

- *Social patterns and cultural traditions:* These impact health and health behavior in numerous ways, as we have described in earlier chapters. Gender roles, for example, affect the transmission of HIV because they may determine the options a woman has for prevention. Social stratification, whether by class, race/ethnicity, caste designations, or any other grouping, determines the kinds of health care people have access to. Language barriers fall in this category as well. In many countries, there may be an official "national language," but in fact 70 or 80 or more languages exist! The ways in which different peoples and cultures view the relationship between their diet and well-being, as well as the use/abuse of alcohol and drugs (for example, if alcohol use is associated with male gender behavior) can also result in situations that are viewed as public health issues.

In addition, the overall pattern of illness and disease varies in important ways between industrialized/developed countries and those that are less developed. As countries develop in broad socioeconomic terms, life expectancy increases and the pattern of morbidity and mortality shifts from infectious disease to lifestyle-related health conditions (e.g., chronic disease, heart disease, cancer). This is known as the *epidemiologic transition* or *health transition*.[8,9] The wide spread of diseases like HIV/AIDS and, potentially, avian flu have also blurred the distinction between these two general patterns of health. Moreover, lifestyle-related diseases such as heart problems and others have increasingly appeared in the developing world due to longer lifespans, as well as differential economic development among population sectors within countries—that is, where some population groups live in more developed conditions than others.

Thinking about global health truly highlights the idea of an ecology of health. Although such ecologies are always the case, in a global context there are more concentric circles or "layers of the onion" involved. In this chapter, we will touch on some of these and discuss the kinds of theoretical approaches that have applications in global health programs.

THE GLOBAL HEALTH SYSTEM

Before proceeding, it is useful to consider the systemic context. Who are the agencies and organizations involved in global health through which interventions and prevention

Example: The Epidemiological Transition and Health Attitudes in Refugees

Of major importance in global health is the flow of migrants and refugees, for both political and economic reasons. When the refugees/migrants are coming from a rural or less developed country to a more developed one, a number of issues arise. Take, for example, the problem of obesity. In the home country, food scarcity may be an issue, the diet may not include many processed foods, and there is an integration of physical work into food preparation. Because of food scarcity, those few individuals who are wealthy, have plenty of food, and are large in stature may also have high prestige.

When migrants arrive in a country where food is less scarce, more likely to be processed, and higher in sugar, fats, and carbohydrates, and at the same time they enter at low levels of socioeconomic status, a pattern of obesity may ensue (and has been documented).[10,11] For some populations, the prestige attached to "being large or fat" as a signifier of wealth and well-being may be retained[12] and contribute to obesity.

efforts are conducted and/or funded? It is a complex system, with many levels. To give you a general idea, here is a brief breakdown:

- *Government-level organizations:* Only a relatively few countries have public health agencies that carry out extensive (typically bilateral—government to government) activities beyond their borders. Examples of such agencies include the Centers for Disease Control and Prevention (CDC), the National Institutes of Health (NIH), the U.S. Agency for International Development (USAID), the German International Aid Agency (GTZ), and the United Kingdom's Department for International Development (DFID).
- *Regional organizations:* These include international organizations that focus on health issues in a particular region. The Pan American Health Organization (PAHO), which focuses on the Americas, is one example.
- *Public international or multilateral organizations:* These include, of course, the World Health Organization (WHO, based in Geneva, Switzerland), and the

UN agencies: UNAIDS (HIV/AIDS), UNICEF (child health and survival), the United Nations Population Fund (UNFPA), and the UN Development Program (UNDP).

- *Public/private partnerships:* The Global Fund to Fight AIDS, Tuberculosis, and Malaria (usually referred to as the "Global Fund") is one prominent example. Other partnerships include those that produce *products,* such as vaccines and other pharmaceuticals. The International AIDS Vaccine Initiative and the Global Alliance for TB Drug Development are examples.
- *Public or private financial institutions:* These include the World Bank, Asian Development Bank, InterAmerican Bank, and others.
- *Nongovernmental organizations (NGOs) and nonprofits:* These are key players, particularly with respect to implementation as well as funding of programs, and in providing assistance in some of the most difficult situations. Examples include CARE, Medicins Sans Fontiers (Doctors Without Borders), the International Committee of the Red Cross and Red Crescent (ICRC), the Bill and Melinda Gates Foundation, the Ford Foundation, Bread for the World, and many others.
- *Parastatal organizations:* These are somewhat unique, like the Millenium Challenge Account in the United States, a "government corporation."

Depending upon the situation, different combinations of these "global health actors" may come into play. For a disaster or short-term health crisis, the ICRC and CARE, or Doctors Without Borders may be involved, with funding and logistical support from national agencies such as USAID or regional organizations, such as the European Community or Association of Southeast Asian Nations (ASEAN). For a long-term effort to prevent the spread of an infectious disease, WHO may coordinate activities, and collaborate with public/private (e.g., Ford Foundation) and national health agencies (e.g., the National Institutes of Health in the United States, the Ministries of Health in affected countries). NGOs such as CARE will likely participate as well, for example, by distributing medications in a relief capacity and in some cases implementing prevention programs.

THEORY AND ITS APPLICATION

What kinds of social/behavioral theory might be applicable to health promotion and health interventions in a global context? This is a complex question, because many of the behavioral theories discussed in this book originated in a Western, industrialized country context. Again, for purposes of a general understanding, let's go through a brief PRECEDE-PROCEED–style assessment to identify issues and factors to address, then discuss theory as it applies to those factors.

Social Assessment

What do you think are key elements of the social context for global health? Take all the situational diversity you would find across communities and populations in the United States and multiply it a hundred-fold, and you might come close. The division between rich and poor nations is a major structural factor, as is the division of wealth and resources *within* nations. The character of the global economy— patterns of production, labor, capital, finance, regulation, and markets—also help determine the distribution of resources among nations and variation in the social and environmental impact of industrial and agricultural production. Both the high level of mobility of modern life and international flows of labor resulting from a globalized economy contribute to the movement of health problems from one place to another. A wide variety of cultural traditions, health beliefs, and practices also form an important part of the overall context—Western medicine (biomedicine) in a global perspective is one of many competing paradigms for understanding and treating disease and illness, along with, for example, other types of biomedicine; Chinese medicine; Vedic traditions (India); various spiritist traditions from Africa, Latin America, and the Caribbean, and shamanic practices from Eurasia and the Americas. Sites of conflict have impacts on health: Long periods of civil war in Sudan and Somalia have been devastating in this respect.

Many of these socioeconomic indicators are available through global or regional demographic and health surveys (from the United Nations Population Fund or UNFPA, at www.unfpa.org), and *Population Bulletins* or other fact sheets from the Population Reference Bureau (go to www.prb.org).

Epidemiological Assessment

Where to start? First of all, trying to get data on global health issues is both easy and problematic. Although the World Health Organization compiles its World Health Report and manages the Global Burden of Disease database (originally developed by Harvard University), the degree to which mortality and morbidity data are kept varies greatly by country and there are often problems with defining health conditions in a uniform manner.

Country health ministries are a potential source of data, particularly where those countries have set up and maintained surveillance operations. Sometimes universities establish research centers that may be a source of data. Major global health issues include:

- HIV/AIDS, particularly in sub-Saharan Africa, South Asia, Southeast Asia, parts of Eastern Europe, Russia, and the Ukraine
- Tuberculosis
- Malaria
- Child health and survival, neonatal disease
- Reproductive health
- Immunization
- Lower respiratory infection
- Cholera and waterborne disease
- Diarrheal disease

Behavioral/Environmental Assessment

Environmental and behavioral risks vary widely by disease, region, and country. There is no complete source of information to help you in this area—specific countries and organizations compile information on such risks, as do country-specific studies, research and intervention efforts, and other sources. Risk factors listed in the WHO's *Global Burden of Disease* reports are important indicators of broad global patterns of risk. "Grey literature" (unpublished reports) from specific projects and interventions, available through project or organizational Web sites, is another important source.‡ A sampler of environmental and behavioral risks includes the following:

- Industrial development with little or no environmental control
- Limited access to health care in rural areas
- Flood or drought conditions
- Rapid deforestation and environmental destruction
- Forced marriage and childbearing at very young ages
- Female genital cutting
- Injection drug use and substance abuse in general
- Unsafe sex
- Smoking/tobacco use
- Poor diet
- Immunization practices

Just thinking of immunization alone, according to the CDC, about 1.4 million children die each year from vaccine-

---

‡ Listings of projects can often be found, by country, on the USAID Web site.

Social Inequalities and Emerging Infectious Diseases[13]

Dr. Paul Farmer is founding director of Partners in Health and is widely known and respected for his work in addressing HIV/AIDS and other infectious diseases among the poor in Haiti and other countries. In a 1998 article, Dr. Farmer summarized some of the connections between poverty and health in a global context:

- Think about the *trajectory* of disease. We can look at infectious diseases not in terms of the infectious agent, but based on the conditions that contribute to their emergence—because human actions have contributed so greatly to mutations, resistance, and spread.
- One of the key political ecologies contributing to the emergence of infectious disease is the structure of poverty.
- For example, *malaria*—This was a disease of "first world" countries, prevalent in the U.S. at one time. It was controlled as a by-product of agricultural development, with better housing, land drainage, mosquito repellants, nets, etc. But these things were not available for poor people, so the malaria lingered longer in those populations.
- *Tuberculosis*—Though viewed in recent years as an emerging disease, tuberculosis was once thought to be controlled. But even while effective therapies have been in place for many years, TB has never been eradicated in many poorer nations. And when therapies exist, they still have to be delivered, stored, and used according to protocol—not easy where resources are poor. TB has gained prominence (as a part of the Gates-funded Global Fund to Fight AIDS, TB, and Malaria) due in large part to its role as an opportunistic infection in those with HIV/AIDS and the increasing incidence in developed countries due to increasing immigration from developing countries.

preventable diseases because 30% of the world's children do not receive all of the available vaccinations.[14] Moreover, as noted in one recent bulletin from the Population Reference Bureau,[15] most of these risk factors interact to form a web of interrelated risk.

Educational/Ecological Assessment

Here you face the incredible diversity of knowledge, attitudes, normative, cultural, and social factors influencing behavior and risk around the world—and all the possible implications these have for applying social and behavioral theory. And again, there is no key source for this kind of information, other than specific research, studies, reports, intervention results, or other less formal sources. National health ministries are one starting point, international health behavior research is another, and reports published or distributed by NGOs and nonprofits that focus on a particular health area are another. The box on the following page takes a look at a few examples of the kinds of issues you may encounter in this category, but remember that it is dangerously easy, in a short summary like this, to stereotype examples of diverse global attitudes and norms as something different, something that "other" peoples have, as if that diversity was not characteristic of all peoples.

What is important here is that you cannot make quick assumptions about attitudes and knowledge that influence behavior. Effective global health intervention, if addressing knowledge/belief/normative issues, means *partnering* with individuals and organizations familiar with local capacity, knowledge, beliefs, norms, and culture, and/or taking the time to *conduct research* that will help you understand some of these factors, and/or working with communities in a *participatory collaboration*. In this process you learn something about the structure of incentives and motivation for behavior (predisposing, enabling, reinforcing factors), so that you can effectively incorporate these into an intervention. Globally, as in the United States, health promotion and interventions are *inherently human in nature*; a willingness to learn, to understand, and to respect will take you a long way.

Administrative/Policy Assessment

Needless to say, books can and have been written on policy and administrative environments for global health. As already discussed, there are many layers to consider in an intervention, and the complexity of the political situation is typically a factor. So, for example, let's say you are trying to address the issue of sexually transmitted infections (STIs) in Country X. There are funds available from a domestic U.S. agency, but those funds are restricted to parent education or school-based education. You also have funding from a global nonprofit that does not have those restrictions, but does require that you partner with an in-country organization (which makes sense in any case). In Country X, there are two nongovernmental organizations that address, among other health issues, STIs. One of them is closely tied to family members of the

Minister of Health. The other is not. The second, independent organization, however, has better access to schools around the country, which would help you leverage funds from both sources. Finally, there is a small but vocal contingent of Country X medical professionals who oppose any kind of direct education to youth about sexuality, on moral grounds. Yet there is a growing STI problem, which may increase the risk in Country X for HIV/AIDS if nothing is done.

How would you negotiate this thorny situation? And what if you did not know about all these political crosscurrents?

HEALTH BEHAVIOR THEORY AND THE GLOBAL SETTING

There are clearly many broad areas to consider in thinking about theory as it applies to global health interventions. We will look at some of these briefly.

Theories Related to Understanding and Addressing the Diversity of Cultural Knowledge and Practices

Much of the theory we have reviewed concerning knowledge, health beliefs, intentions, social norms, and culture is potentially applicable, at least in its basic form. But you will in many cases have to "fill in the blanks" with different kinds of information. For example, if you are trying to use the Health Belief Model to guide an intervention, what you address as *barriers* need to be relevant to the population you are working with. That is always the case, but in a global context this may require an extra effort to make sure your intervention is meaningful and relevant. Second, remember that much of the individual theory we reviewed makes certain kinds of assumptions about individuals as decision makers and individuals in general—assumptions that may not be applicable in societies or cultures where the individual is not understood as the "primary social unit" or primary decision-making unit as it is (generally speaking) in Western societies (see the brief discussion of "individual" in Chapter 4).

In addition, as discussed in Chapter 6, cultures and peoples across the world have varying *ethnomedical systems*—systems of knowledge and practice that tie together culturally shared ideas about what causes illness and disease, how to treat/cure illnesses, and who the appropriate healers are. Ethnomedical systems are closely tied to the elements of many behavioral theories—they influence people's understandings and expectations about utilization of health care, norms related to patient and healer behavior, the values and meanings attached to particular (health) outcomes, and many other issues.

Yet all the cultural variety can be seen as a strength from which to build interventions. Indigenous communications

Example: Gender Attitudes/Roles, Sexuality, and HIV/AIDS Risk in India[16]

Eighty-four percent of AIDS cases (at the time of the article) in India are attributed to sexual transmission. Although specific population subgroups were initially at high risk, it has increasingly spread to the general population. Although India is highly diverse, with Hindu, Muslim, Christian, and Sikh populations, a number of cultural traditions cut across these lines:

- Patriarchal family structure—Family name, inheritance, etc. go through the male line, from father to son. After marriage, a woman lives with her husband in her father's house.
- Female purity before marriage is a prized quality, whereas men are encouraged to have premarital sex. Marriages are still often arranged for women near the time they reach puberty, even though the legal age of marriage for women is 18. Thus men may be infected prior to marriage.
- If women enter marriage with knowledge about HIV risk and preventive methods, they may be suspected of having premarital sex.
- Because of the patriarchal structure, and because family wealth and resources are inherited by males, women find it difficult to leave a marriage even if there is abuse or if the husband has extramarital sex.
- The female duty to procreate conflicts with condom use, and female social position is often related to childbearing.
- In addition, condom use also is associated with sex workers—it is stigmatized. Sterilization is more common as a contraceptive than condom use. Women are sometimes sterilized when their families are "completed."
- Health beliefs include concepts of health and balance related to flow of body fluids and regulation of heat. Condoms are sometimes viewed as interrupting this flow and thereby threatening male health.
- Women sometimes believe that their husbands are better off going to sex workers when on the road than having lovers, so that their flow is maintained without threat to the relationship.
- There are strong cultural beliefs that the marriage relationship itself is a protection from HIV/AIDS—that a woman cannot get HIV from her husband.
- A certain acceptance of fate as part of Karma may increase acceptance of risk situations.
- In addition, in cases of men having sex with men, it often involves men who are married.

practices, breastfeeding, and many other traditions have already been incorporated effectively in public health interventions.[17]

Theories Related to Communication and Information Dissemination with Diverse Populations

As described in Chapter 6, communications theories address, among other things, the process of encoding, sending, receiving, and decoding messages, where "encoding" and "decoding" refer to the ways in which a message or information is packaged so that a particular population or group will understand the meaning as intended, and the information will make intuitive sense as well. In the global context, this requires careful thinking and a decent knowledge of the many possible target populations. How would you, for example, target information to migrant Latina mothers in the United States? What would you need to know about themes, about words and symbols to use or not use, about communications channels through which to disseminate the information?

Communication programs in global health are one of the areas of application where theory is most explicitly used. Such programs draw on communication theory in general, as well as social marketing, diffusion of innovations theory, and community mobilization, for example. In fact, there is a specific term, *behavior change communication (BCC)*, that is used almost exclusively in a global health context.

Theories Related to Organizational Change and Advocacy

Working with these kinds of approaches may be necessary when there is an organizational or policy problem that needs to be addressed in order for there to be improvement in a specific health problem, or the general health of a population or group. If, for example, health resources are not directed to a population that needs them because the public health agency or network of agencies has no system for identifying who is affected by a health problem, and feed-

Behavior Change Communications (BCC)

BCC is an approach developed primarily in the global health context, originally in the area of nutrition, and later widely used concerning HIV/AIDS. Its roots are in several of the behavior change theories discussed in this book (and some that are not):

- Diffusion of Innovations
- Stages of Change/Transtheoretical Model
- Self-Efficacy (from SCT)
- Social marketing (and its accompanying consumer research)
- The Behavior Change Continuum (from the World Bank—not discussed in this book)

Like many programs in global health, a combination of theories is used.

Very similar to the general process that is part of any communications campaign, BCC involves a series of steps:

1. State program goals
2. Involve stakeholders
3. Identify target populations
4. Conduct formative BCC assessments (formative research, designed to better understand risk behaviors, their context, attitudes, and understandings)
5. Segment target populations
6. Define overall behavior change objectives
7. Design a BCC strategy, consisting of current behavior, concepts/themes, key messages, channels of communication, addressing barriers and supports for change, implementation partners, and monitoring and evaluation
8. Implement and evaluate the strategy

In general, the goals of a BCC program are to change behavior and therefore address a health problem (epidemiology), through the following processes:

- Increase knowledge
- Stimulate community dialogue
- Promote essential attitude change (e.g., regarding perception of risk, etc.)
- Reduce stigma and discrimination
- Create demand for information and services
- Advocate
- Promote services for prevention, care, and support
- Improve skills and sense of self-efficacy

ing that information to decision makers. An organizational change effort is needed where a new system for linking epidemiological data and program planning is developed and put in place, and the internal organizational resistance to change is addressed. These theories may also be important when the effort for change needs to come from within a community—people have to be aware of a problem and motivated to take *collective action*, holding public awareness events, gathering signatures for a petition, organizing a mail campaign directed towards a legislator, and so on.

Theories Related to Community Mobilization

Advocacy and mobilization approaches are very much a part of public health work in a global context, particularly the kinds of *participatory* approaches that come from Paolo Freire,[18] in which there is a collaboration with the community in defining the problem and identifying solutions.

Theories Related to the Political-Economic Context

As we have described in this book, there is often a macro-level political-economic context that shapes the trajectory of a particular health condition. A country's pattern of economic development may create vulnerabilities in specific populations. The rural-urban transition may, for example, be the result of political decisions about what kinds of businesses or industries to focus on. Let's say that the effect of such decisions is to create a geographic class of people (rural) who have less and less access to work, cash income, resources, education, and medical care. If this is the case, an intervention targeting the political-economic context is likely to focus on *identifying* key elements of the political-economic context that have an impact on one or more health issues, then using a range of approaches, including community mobilization, advocacy, and direct programmatic action. The object might be to redirect economic activity to rural areas, organize rural health collaboratives to maximize scarce resources, or pass a law that makes it difficult for businesses to relocate from rural to urban areas without providing some kind of compensatory service. The microcredit approach discussed in Chapter 6 (Grameen Bank) falls in this category.

Multi-theory Approaches

Global health programs are often developed as pragmatic approaches to real-world situations, and the emphasis on theory is not always as pronounced as it is for domestic health programs. Programs that are theory-based may use combinations of theoretical approaches, or constructs from different approaches. An example of this is the *AIDS Risk Reduction Model* (ARRM).[19] This approach focuses on sexual transmission of HIV, and incorporates elements of the Health Belief Model, efficacy theory (from Social-Cognitive Theory), as well as the role of emotion and interpersonal processes. There is also an influence from Stages of Change theory (Transtheoretical Model), because the change process envisioned in the ARRM approach includes three stages:

- *Stage 1:* Recognition and labeling one's behavior as high risk
- *Stage 2:* Making a commitment to reduce high-risk sexual contacts and to increase low-risk activities
- *Stage 3:* Taking action—seeking information, obtaining remedies, and enacting solutions

Question: Thinking about other theories discussed in this book, do these stages sound familiar? What parallels can you draw with other theories?

PROGRAM EXAMPLES

The following are a few examples of global health behavior-related programs.

Avian Influenza Communication Program

The U.S. Agency for International Development (USAID) developed and implemented a communications program intended to inform target audiences about avian influenza and preventive strategies. The program includes:

- Interpersonal communications employing agriculture and veterinary extension agents, patient counseling by clinic health staff, and peer educators (farmers, vendors, etc.)
- Organizational and community channels, such as workplaces, schools, village or community meetings, and "affinity group" meetings (e.g., farmers associations, community organizations, etc.)
- Mass media—television, radio, print
- Public relations and advocacy—including leader conferences, press briefings, and training of public spokespersons
- Private sector partnerships

Social Marketing for STI Prevention

Population Services International (PSI) conducted a social marketing campaign to reduce sexually transmitted infections (STIs) and unwanted pregnancies in Cameroon, West Africa (Example from Murphy 2005, referenced above). The program reached about 600,000 sexually active urban youth ages 15-24. Components included:

- Young Cameroonian peer educators, journalists, comic-strip artists, radio personalities, and script-writers helped develop messages and activities
- Focusing on the *100% Jeune* (100% Young) condom brand, messages promoted images of youth who challenged social norms and protected their health—more than 40,000 of these condoms were sold in 2002
- The effort included a serial radio drama and a call-in talk show
- Face-to-face sessions for school-age youth (in and out of school) reached about 10,000 youth per month

Program evaluation showed that knowledge increased, attitudes about buying condoms were more positive, and condom use was up (with regular partners).

Albania Family Planning Project

In Albania, The Manoff Group (a research and program consulting organization), participated on a USAID-supported family planning project led by John Snow, Inc. It designed a BCC strategy based on cognitive anthropology, social interaction theory, behavior change theories derived from commercial market research, and gender role/status theory. The goal of the project was to help Albanians to adopt and use effective modern family planning methods.

The steps in designing and implementing the BCC portion of the project were:

1. A literature review
2. Formative (qualitative) research
3. Trials of improved practices (TIPs)§
4. Development of a comprehensive behavior change strategy
5. A national baseline survey
6. Development of two television spots portraying (symbolically and socially) the cognitive domains elicited through the formative research and advocat-

7. ing locally feasible behaviors based on TIPs results
8. Broadcasting the spots
9. A national media recall survey
10. Development and implementation of a community outreach program based on research findings
11. Broadcasting a call-in show to answer common family planning questions (formative research and a CDC-designed national reproductive health survey showed a lack of knowledge of most modern family planning methods)
12. A press workshop to help radio, TV, and print journalists learn about family planning and how to report on family planning and health issues
13. A follow-up national survey

The formative research included eliciting cognitive domains through a projective technique as part of an ethnographic interview. The methodology and BCC design assumed that fertility and family planning are parts of culture that are inextricably linked to gender roles and status as well as to the couple's relationship. A media recall survey showed that over 65% of women in the intended audience and over half of men had seen the spots and the great majority of these discussed the spots with others. Models of culture change suggest that discussing information with others is key to production of knowledge. In this project all BCC steps from design through evaluation were based on culture theories.

---

§ TIPs is a technique developed by The Manoff Group and first used in 1979. Using the results of formative qualitative research, the TIPs researcher develops a menu of behaviors that will help to improve audience members' health or help people reach their fertility goals more safely and effectively. The behaviors may be slightly different than the "ideal" public health recommendations because they must be practical for local people to do. Then the TIPs researcher draws a small sample (15 people or more per audience segment), observes and interviews them in their homes or clinics (for health care provider behavior change), and recommends a behavior for the person (or couple) to try during the coming week. The researcher *negotiates* with the person or couple to find a behavior that they are willing to try. The researcher obtains a commitment to try the behavior from the research participant(s) and then returns after a week to see how the person/couple did. The goal is to learn what behaviors are locally feasible, so researchers often learn more from what people were unable to do than from what they could do.[20] The TIPs researcher analyzes the data according to "barriers" to doing the behavior and "supports" or "motivators" that help people to practice the behavior. TIPs is based on both culture theory (i.e., the importance of understanding the local situation) and behavior change theories.

Chapter Questions

1. Why is "global health" harder and harder to distinguish from "domestic health"?

2. What are some of the key components in the overall ecology of global health? Are these different than the ecological context for domestic health? If so, how?

3. What are some examples of the ways in which social inequality impacts health, and how would you address these examples using theoretical approaches discussed in this book?

4. What do you have to do to adapt behavior change approaches developed in a U.S. context for application in a global context?

5. What are some examples of global health approaches that combine multiple theories and/or constructs?

REFERENCES

1. Pruss-Ustun A, Corvalan C. *Preventing Disease Through Healthy Environments: Towards an Estimate of the Global Burden of Disease.* Geneva: World Health Organization; 2006.

2. LaFraniere S. In oil-rich Angola, cholera preys upon poorest. *New York Times,* June 18, 2006.

3. Esrey S. 1996. "Water, Waste and Well-Being: A Multi-Country Study." *American Journal of Epidemiology* 143(6): 608-623.

4. Tumwine JK et al. September 2002. "Diarrhoea and Effects of Different Water Sources, Sanitation and Hygiene Behaviour in East Africa." *Tropical Medicine and International Health* 7(9): 750-756.

5. Garrett L. 2007. "The Challenge of Global Health." *Foreign Affairs,* January/February 2007.

6. Vidyasagar D. 2005. "Global Minutes: Oil Purse or Oil Curse?" *Journal of Perinatology* 25: 743-744.

7. Bannon A and Roodman D. 2004. "Partners for Development?" *Perspectives in Health—The Magazine of the Pan American Health Organization* 9(2).

8. Omran AR. The epidemiological transition: a theory of the epidemiology of population change. *Milbank Memorial Fund Q.* 1971;49:509–538.

9. Christakis NA, Ware NC, Kleinman AM. Illness behavior and the health transition in the developing world. In Chen LC, Kleinman AM, Potter J, Caldwell J, Ware NC, eds. *Health and Social Change in International Perspective.* Boston, MA: Harvard University Press; 1994.

10. Sundquist J, Winkelby M. Country of birth, acculturation status, and abdominal obesity in a national sample of Mexican-American women and men. *Int J Epidemiol.* 2000;29:470–477.

11. Khan LK, Sobal J, Martorell R. Acculturation, socioeconomic status, and obesity in Mexican Americans, Cuban Americans, and Puerto Ricans. *Int J Obesity.*1997;21:91–96.

12. Renzaho AM. Fat, rich and beautiful: changing socio-cultural paradigms associated with obesity risk, nutritional status and refugee children from Sub-Saharan Africa. *Health Place.* 2004;10(1):105–113.

13. Farmer P. Social inequalities and emerging infectious diseases. In Brown P, ed. *Understanding and Applying Medical Anthropology.* Mountain View, CA: Mayfield; 1998.

14. Centers for Disease Control and Prevention. Programs in brief: global health. Available at: www.cdc.gov. Accessed December 2006.

15. Murphy EM. May 2005. "Promoting Healthy Behavior." *Health Bulletin Number 2.* Washington, DC: Population Reference Bureau

16. Battacharya G. Sociocultural and behavioral contexts of condom use in heterosexual married couples in India: challenges to the HIV prevention program. *Health Educ Behav.* 2004;31(1):101–117.

17. Airhihenbuwa CO. 1995. *Health and Culture: Beyond the Western Paradigm.* Thousand Oaks: Sage Publications..

18. Friere, P. 1970 *Pedagogy of the Oppressed.* New York: Seabury Press.

19. Catania JA, Kegeles SM, & Coates TJ, 1990. "Towards an understanding of risk behavior: An AIDS risk reduction model (ARRM)." *Health Education Quarterly* 17(1): 53-72.

20. Dickin K, Griffiths M, & Piwoz E 1997. *Designing by Dialogue: A Program Planner's Guide to Consultative Research for Improving Young Child Feeding.* Washington, D.C.: Academy for Educational Development and The Manoff Group.

CHAPTER 12

Application of Theory: High-Risk and Special Populations*

* This chapter is adapted from material to be published in a forthcoming article by the author for *Medical Anthropology Quarterly*, entitled "Risk Behavior Theory and Its Discontents: A Generative Approach to Understanding Behavior That Is Risky for HIV/AIDS, Violence, and Other Health Problems."

LEARNING OBJECTIVES

By the end of this chapter, the reader will be able to:

- Understand key issues with respect to health promotion among populations at particularly high-risk for key health issues (e.g., HIV/AIDS, substance abuse, violence, tuberculosis, etc.)
- Understand the kinds of social/behavioral theories, and unique considerations, that could be applicable to health promotion in high risk populations
- Describe examples of theory-based health promotion programs addressing these populations

---

"Illness is a convent which has its rule, its austerity, its silences, and its inspirations."

—ALBERT CAMUS, NOVEMBER 1942, *NOTEBOOKS 1942–1951*

INTRODUCTION

Although public health interventions as a whole target everyone who has or is at risk for health problems towards the goals of maximizing health and quality of life, it is sometimes necessary to focus on particular *populations* (as opposed to individuals) who are said to be at *high risk*, or who for various reasons are difficult to access. As we know from the ecological approach, people can be at high risk for many reasons: exposure to hazardous conditions at work or in their living environments, limited access to health care or prevention information, involvement in behavior or practices that are particularly risky (e.g., having unprotected sex with multiple partners),

involvement in illegal or marginalized activities (e.g., involvement with the commercial sex trade, or in gangs), and other reasons. For example, youth who are involved in substance use, tobacco use, early sexual activity, and other behavior are said to be at high risk for HIV/AIDS, sexually transmitted infections (STIs), delinquency, and violence; injection drug users (IDUs) and their partners are said to be at high risk for HIV/AIDS, and so on. Their risk behavior is viewed as a kind of *abnormal behavior, when viewed only in the context of health*. As we will see, though, understanding what is going on, finding an applicable theory, and developing effective interventions for *populations* at risk may first require looking beyond the behaviors and their implications for health.

In general, for populations whose risk is particularly high for one or more health problems, it is often true that the high risk is related to specific circumstances or conditions that contribute to, or shape, the risk. For example:

- Migrant workers who do not speak English and have limited or no access to health care
- Youth who come from high-crime communities and histories of family dysfunction
- Rural populations where there are few sources of employment, a lack of income, low educational levels, and limited access to health care
- Youth who drop out of school
- Adults or youth returning from prison
- People living in high-poverty communities where there are few sources of income, and the prevalence of "street" income sources (drug sales, sex for money, theft, etc.) is common

TABLE 12-1 Estimated Number of AIDS Cases in the United States in 2004

Exposure Category	Male	Female	Total
Male-to-male sexual contact	17,691	-	17,691
Injection drug use	5,968	3,184	9,152
Male-to-male sexual contact and injection drug use	1,920	-	1,920
Heterosexual contact	5,149	7,979	13,128
Other**	298	279	577

TABLE 12-2 Estimated Number of AIDS Cases in the United States, Through 2004*

Exposure Category	Male	Female	Total
Male-to-male sexual contact	441,380	-	441,380
Injection drug use	176,162	72,651	248,813
Male-to-male sexual contact and injection drug use	64,833	-	64,833
Heterosexual contact	59,939	99,175	159,114
Other**	14,085	6,636	20,721

*Includes persons with a diagnosis of AIDS from the beginning of the epidemic through 2004.

** Includes hemophilia, blood transfusion, perinatal, and risk not reported or not identified.

From CDC Website: http://www.cdc.gov/hiv/topics/surveillance/basic.htm#exposure. Accessed August 5, 2006.

Because of these kinds of circumstances, the following are almost always important issues in working with high-risk populations:

- Building and sustaining trust
- Gaining access
- Finding the right way to communicate
- Confidentiality
- Honesty—making sure that the population you are working with knows what you are doing and why

In this book, we have talked about the multiple levels of motivation and influence on behavior, and about the fact that much of the behavior that has implications for health is not motivated by health concerns—or at least not solely by health concerns. This is typically true for high-risk behavior as well. Public health and health promotion interventions focus on behavior as it relates to health, and categorize groups of people primarily based on those health risk behaviors, without always considering either the context that surrounds them or other key aspects of who they are

and what they do—which are inevitably intertwined with health behavior, as we know. Their primary identity becomes a "high-risk population." If that is all we focus on, though, we limit our understanding about health risk among these populations and consequently the appropriate use of theory and development of effective interventions.

Marginalized and socioeconomically segregated populations (among others) often engage in health risk behavior with goals in mind that relate to life situations of limit (social, economic, gender-based), threat, alienation, and mistrust, with correspondingly different understandings of what is and is not a *risk*. Many of the runaway youth interviewed by the author in a study on HIV and substance use among runaways, for example, believed they would not live beyond, say, age 25—giving them a particular perspective on what was and was not a risk, a perspective very different from the public health agencies trying to develop an intervention for them. In other words, why should people who do not believe they have a long life ahead of them worry about HIV infection, which may take ten years to actually manifest itself as

AIDS, when there are more immediate concerns? In several health research studies working with high-risk populations, the author has listened to people describe extreme violence, drug use, exploitation, transience, and many other circumstances that would otherwise be extraordinary, but are talked about as if they were as common and day-to-day as eating a sandwich. So, in order to be more effective, it may be necessary to step back from the health risk behavior itself and gain a better understanding of the "world" that behavior is coming from. Approaching the risk behavior in isolation from this context just does not capture the situation.

Here is the question: How well does current theory really explain high-risk behavior? After all, the injection drug user that is being categorized as an "IDU" may also be a car mechanic, and a good one, or a cousin, or an uncle, or a very good cook. He may be helping to raise a child. He may live with two other families in a small apartment that has no air conditioning. Which is the most meaningful way to understand this person? As an injection drug user, or as an uncle, or cook, or mechanic, or person coping with a difficult living situation?

As we have talked about in this book, public health theory, and the ecological model in general,[1,2] do acknowledge a range of broader ecological, social, and cultural factors that together influence behavior. Yet most actual interventions have difficulty addressing the broader *interaction* of factors, or what ties them together, because figuring out how to measure the success of an intervention then becomes difficult, and the time necessary to achieve success is more than the typical three to five years allotted for most funded interventions. The need for measurable results in a short period of time favors the use of theories and models that fill the need. This chapter discusses some of the assumptions and strategies used to categorize and address high-risk behaviors and populations, and presents several alternative—and complementary—approaches for understanding and addressing behavior that is risky with respect to health, with a focus on violence and HIV/AIDS risk. One of the approaches presented specifically tries to understand the integration of factors, not just correlations between specific factors and behavior.

Throughout this book, we have talked about the fuzzy separation between "health behavior" and just "behavior." If what people do (even if it has health implications) is often not *about* health, this has implications with respect to theories and models that focus on *health risk* and *high-risk individuals or populations*, and that are used to design, implement, and evaluate intervention programs. So, an important task in working with high-risk populations is to expand our thinking beyond the domain of health behavior per se, and

A Story: The Man in the Wheelchair

While working with one HIV/AIDS risk behavior change project (targeting injection drug users, crack cocaine users, and their sexual partners), I spent time walking the streets with community health outreach workers (CHOWs) who distributed prevention information and "bleach kits" for injection drug users to clean injection equipment and prevent HIV transmission. The CHOWs were almost all recovered and recovering addicts from the communities in which we worked.

One day, as we walked the streets, both CHOWs I was with walked up to greet an older man in a wheelchair. The man was not in good shape—he appeared to be homeless, was dirty, and had two legs amputated, covered in torn rags, as a result of frostbite, they told me. He was also very drunk. The two CHOWs spoke with him for a while, and treated him with kindness and a great deal of respect. They clearly knew him well.

I asked them, "Who is he? You seem to know him pretty well." The answer was illuminating: The man and both CHOWs were once "locked up" in prison at the same time. During their incarceration, the older man became a kind of mentor to the two younger men, trying to keep them free of trouble and encouraging them to read books from the prison library. He basically got them through their time in prison, and they were forever grateful and respectful of him for that. The fact that he was not in the best of shape at this time had no effect on their deeply held feelings.

On hearing their story, it struck me that I would have had no idea about this man's character or his past had I not been told. It would have been all too easy to make assumptions about who he was, and the nature of his health risk behaviors. Those assumptions would have been ill-informed, narrow, and in no way sufficient to address his situation in an appropriate way.

to look for and highlight socioeconomic constraints, motivations, and meanings (not necessarily related to health) that have an impact on "risk behavior."

APPLYING BEHAVIORAL THEORY TO HIGH-RISK POPULATIONS AND CONTEXTS

Let's go back for a moment to some of the theoretical approaches we have reviewed in this book, as they relate to high-risk behaviors. Theoretical approaches to violence, HIV risk behavior, substance abuse, and other health risk behaviors typically conceptualize behavior as an *output* of some set of factors (inputs) or thinking processes (e.g., stages of readiness to change, decisions made based on a cost-benefit analysis). For simplicity, let's refer to these as "output" theories or approaches.

The Health Belief Model (HBM)[3-5] and Theory of Planned Behavior (TPB),[6-8] as we have seen, construct health behavior as the result of individual decision-making processes or attitudes that address health-related issues. To recap: Under the HBM, individuals make decisions about whether or not to engage in health risk behavior (or healthy behavior) based on an assessment of *perceived susceptibility* to a health problem, *perceived severity* of the problem, *costs and benefits of action* to address the problem, a *"cue to action"* (e.g., an event or circumstance that spurs a decision to act), and *self-efficacy* (confidence in the ability to take the action). Under TPB, decisions about risk behavior/healthy behavior are said to be the result of *attitudes* towards a behavior itself, *subjective norms* an individual associates with the behavior (will it be viewed as good/bad?), and *perceptions* concerning the *degree of control* one has over the behavior. In both of these approaches, a relatively narrow, linear process takes place in which the contemplated behavior and its health consequences *are the primary object of attention.*

What if a health-related behavior is *not* the object of the individual's attention, but just one of a number of actions related to motives, goals, and basic needs entirely unrelated to health? Would this kind of linear decision-making process for health behavior be relevant in order to develop an effective intervention? For example, a common type of motivation under which HIV risk behavior occurs has to do with the performance of gender roles. Many studies have documented the great age difference in arranged and other traditional marriages in India, Africa, and elsewhere—a dynamic that contributes to HIV risk because of the power difference between partners, and, for example, the likelihood that the older male has had and will continue to have multiple partners. So, from the viewpoint of the individuals involved, the behavior (risky for HIV/AIDS) is primarily about *gender roles*, not health.

Another very well-known framework for predicting behavioral outcomes—and for designing intervention programs targeting youth—is the "risk and protective factors" model so widely used in violence and substance abuse prevention programs. (This model was discussed in its role as a planning framework in Chapter 7.) To recap: Under the model, *risk factors* are situations and characteristics pertaining to individuals that are said to be precursors to or predictors of high-risk behavior. Most of the risk behavior research

underlying this approach concludes that there are *multiple and cumulative exposures* to risk factors affecting youth over the course of their development.[9-14]

The risk and protective factor approach developed by Hawkins, Catalano, and colleagues[12,15,16] sets up an overall predictive relationship where the nature of exposure (to risk vs. protective factors) increases or decreases the likelihood that a given youth will engage in high-risk behaviors (violence, delinquency, substance abuse, school dropout, HIV/AIDS risk behavior, or others). Exposure to *risk factors* increases the likelihood of problem behavior; exposure to *protective factors* reduces the likelihood of problem behavior. Under the Hawkins and Catalano model, a total of 19 identified risk factors are organized into the following domains:

- *Individual:* e.g., biological and psychological dispositions, attitudes, values, knowledge, skills, problem behaviors
- *Peer:* e.g., norms, activities, attachment
- *Family:* e.g., function, management, bonding, abuse/violence
- *School:* e.g., bonding, climate, policy, performance
- *Community:* e.g., bonding, norms, resources, poverty level, crime, awareness/mobilization
- Sometimes *society/environmental:* e.g., norms, policy/sanctions

Protective factors under this model are not as well specified, and have been organized into a smaller set of similar domains:

- *Individual:* e.g., gender, intelligence, temperament
- *Social bonding:* e.g., attachment/commitment to positive, prosocial individuals and groups
- *Healthy beliefs:*
- *Clear standards for behavior:* in families, schools, communities

In short, this is an epidemiological "exposure" model that determines the likelihood of engaging in risk behavior based on the balance of risk and protective factors to which a youth is exposed. It lends itself well to the development, implementation, and evaluation of programs that target specific risk and protective factors, where the goal is to reduce the risk factors and build up the protective factors. The effect of the intervention on these factors can be easily tracked and measured. The interrelationship of these factors, though, is not as well addressed in terms of what it says about the context of the risk behavior. Where are socioeconomic forces, motivation, meaning, and individual intent, for example?

Researchers working in this area understand that the presence of multiple risk factors among high-risk individuals means more than just the "sum" of these factors. Clustering of risk factors has been treated as indicating an oppositional or "nonconventional" worldview.[17-21] Hawkins and Catalano[22] themselves note that of the 19 risk factors they have identified for adolescent high-risk behavior, 16 are common for both delinquency and substance abuse; 11 are common for violence and substance abuse; and 9 are common for all three. But once again, getting at that worldview, or the relationship between the worldview and the ecology surrounding it, has not been a focus of most intervention research. It is much more difficult to translate into a program, and does not lend itself to typical research, program planning, or evaluation designs.

Figures 12-1 and 12-2 depict the general process implied in output theories.

Have these kinds of approaches been effective in reducing high-risk behavior? One problem is this: If these interventions are designed to target specific risk factors, evaluations of effectiveness tend to focus on measuring change in those risk factors as evidence of impact. There is a substantial literature on evidence-based programs that shows impacts of this type, and a well-developed set of indicators and instruments that measure, for example, a given intervention's impact on, for example, specific risk factors within the model such as bonding to school or self-efficacy.

But if we focus on youth violence as one high-risk behavior of serious concern, there isn't much evidence that the proliferation of such programs has generally made much of a difference. The Surgeon General's Report on Violence concluded that little was known about the effectiveness of hundreds of violence prevention programs used in schools and communities throughout the United States, and that many such programs had been found ineffective.[23] Even the most recent National Institutes of Health Consensus Conference on Preventing Violence and Related Health-Risking Social Behaviors in Adolescents drew a similar conclusion, though noting that some programs had reduced violence *precursors* (i.e., risk factors), and some had actually reduced violence and arrest, at least in the short term.[24]

With respect to HIV/AIDS, the record is better, but the situation is also different: HIV/AIDS prevention programs typically aim to change selected behaviors—sharing injection equipment, condom use, multiple sex partners—*in order to cut off routes of HIV transmission* (the health problem, and desired outcome). It is, in some cases, easier to focus on specific behavioral risks, or social cultural norms, for change, because a change in those factors will reduce HIV trans-

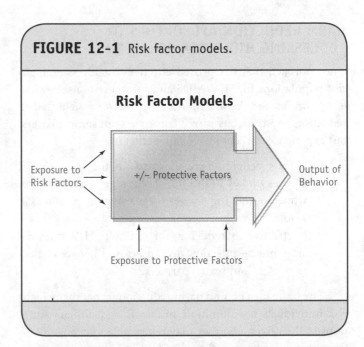

FIGURE 12-1 Risk factor models.

Risk Factor Models

Exposure to Risk Factors

+/– Protective Factors

Output of Behavior

Exposure to Protective Factors

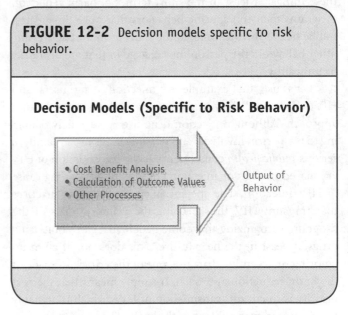

FIGURE 12-2 Decision models specific to risk behavior.

Decision Models (Specific to Risk Behavior)

- Cost Benefit Analysis
- Calculation of Outcome Values
- Other Processes

Output of Behavior

mission. Preventing violence is a little different. The term *violence* refers to a broad category of behavior that is itself a "health" problem, so it is the behavior that is the ultimate target.

The sections that follow summarize two approaches for working with high-risk populations. One is called a *harm reduction* approach, and the other is an approach that focuses on the context and the integration of factors, including the ways that "risk-behaving individuals" construct and organize their actions. I will call the latter a *generative* approach. Each has significant implications for theory and its use.

HARM REDUCTION APPROACHES TO ADDRESSING HIGH-RISK BEHAVIOR

One approach that has proved effective in addressing high-risk populations for HIV/AIDS and substance abuse is what is known as the *harm reduction approach*.[25-27] The harm reduction approach has stirred controversy in some quarters, but experience and data have shown that it

- "Meets people where they are" in the sense that it focuses on key health impacts of a person's behavior while not judging or overcategorizing the person as a whole.
- Is effective in reducing, for example, HIV transmission among injection drug users and between injection users and sexual partners.[28]

The basic idea behind harm reduction is that many high-risk individuals have multiple problems and difficult situations in their lives, and they may not be able to change all of these things, at least in the short term. So, harm reduction programs focus on specific behaviors that pose the greatest public health threat, while, in the short term, not addressing other behaviors the person may engage in that are also risky or unhealthy.

Let's use the example of injection drug users and HIV/AIDS, a well-known application of the harm reduction approach. Although injection drug use is extremely damaging to the person involved, and possibly to his or her family, a serious *public health* consequence is the transmission of HIV via shared needles or injection equipment—a leading cause of HIV infection. The specific injecting drug use practices that transmit HIV thus become the primary focus of the program, recognizing that some people just can't quit using drugs, at least in the near future. This does not at all mean ignoring or accepting drug use, one of the criticisms made of the harm reduction approach. It simply means that the first priority is to cut off transmission of HIV, which is arguably the more pressing public health threat. Then, in many cases, addressing drug use becomes much easier after a nonjudgmental relationship has been established with IDUs through an HIV/AIDS harm reduction program. With this in mind, the following are some components that might be part of such a program:

- *Needle exchange programs (NEPs):* These allow IDUs to exchange their used syringes/equipment for clean equipment. It is important to note that programs seeking federal funding cannot support or advocate for this activity.
- *Dissemination of risk reduction kits:* These typically consist of prevention information, condoms, and bleach for disinfecting needles (along with instructions for their use). If properly used, immersing injection equipment in bleach can kill the HIV virus. The condoms are to help prevent transmission of HIV from an infected IDU to a sex partner.
- *Drug substitution treatment:* The medically supervised treatment of addicted drug users by administering drugs such as methadone or buprenorphine (as a substitute for what they are using) that mitigate the addictive craving without most of the negative consequences.

Typically, such programs employ recovered addicts as CHOWs or "outreach workers" to disseminate kits, provide education, and staff needle exchange programs. Again, in line with the harm reduction strategy, these outreach staff understand the difficulties of addiction and are able to relate to IDUs in a knowledgeable and nonjudgmental way. The role of the CHOWs and outreach workers can be viewed as drawing from at least several theories we have discussed:

- Social Network Theory
- Social Cognitive Theory (where the CHOWs, as ex-addicts, are models)
- Transtheoretical Model (where IDUs are addressed based on their readiness to modify specific HIV/AIDS risk behaviors, or even their drug use)

Harm reduction as an approach has demonstrated applicability for other high-risk health behavior issues as well; for example, changes in alcohol policies towards a recognition that drinking situations occur, and an emphasis on preventing the drinking-related behaviors that present the most risk, such as drinking and driving.[29] With people involved in the sex trade, a harm reduction approach would involve an initial emphasis on building knowledge and skills related to safer sex practices (condom use) and personal safety (recognizing dangerous or abusive situations), where the public health issue of importance is HIV/AIDS or injury/mortality from abuse. Focusing on these public health issues would come before attempting to stop a person's involvement in the sex trade, recognizing that stopping involvement may be very difficult and even dangerous.

One additional outcome of harm reduction approaches is very important for high-risk populations. As mentioned earlier, these populations are often marginalized in one way or another, and are difficult to reach with traditional programs. Because harm reduction programs entail interaction with marginalized groups in a way that does not immediately judge or challenge everything about their existence, an important opening for interaction may be established, a

FIGURE 12-3

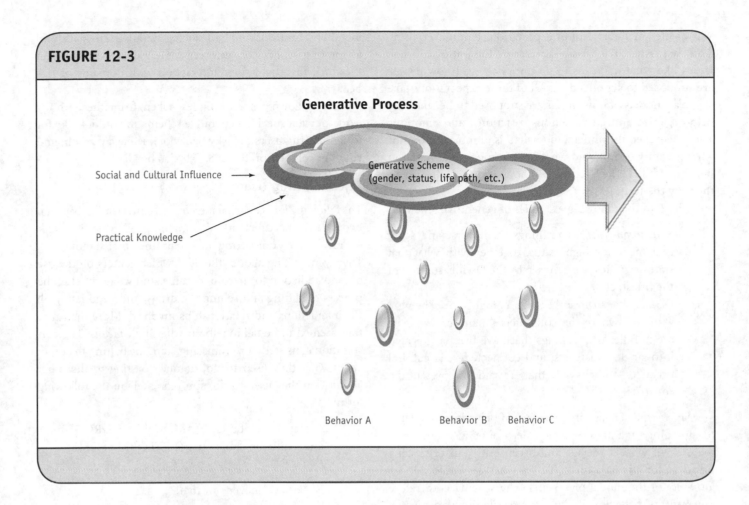

Generative Process

Social and Cultural Influence →

Generative Scheme
(gender, status, life path, etc.)

Practical Knowledge

Behavior A   Behavior B   Behavior C

certain trust and rapport. This becomes an essential building block for interaction about other risk behavior that is also present. In other words, when the bond is established, high-risk individuals may be more open to change in other areas of their life. You could say, then, in terms of the Transtheoretical Model, that the *bond* or *trust* precedes movement towards change.

GENERATIVE APPROACHES TO UNDERSTANDING RISK BEHAVIOR

Another type of approach is what I am calling a *generative* approach. Here, the focus is *not* on behavior conceptualized in terms of inputs and outputs (e.g., risk/protective factors and risk behaviors), but on the organizing (and motivating) processes and structures through which individuals *generate* behavior over time, *including* behavior that has implications for health or that is intentionally health-related. In the theoretical literature from anthropology, social psychology, and sociology, these may be referred to as cultural models, narratives, scripts, discourses, frames, or schema.[30-38] However, they are, by and large, still untapped as theoretical tools in

public health with respect to issues of risk behavior,[†] though there are certainly exceptions, particularly with respect to HIV/AIDS prevention, some global health efforts, substance abuse prevention research, and other areas. And existing health behavior theory could incorporate some of these broader motivating constructs when thinking about intentions, norms, and values.

Figure 12-3 illustrates the difference between generative and output approaches.

Generative approaches assume that a very important human process is to "make meaning" out of what we do. We are geared towards behaving in ways that we think of as coherent and purposeful within a general way of life, and responsive to an environment. So, our actions are meaningful in relation to that way of life. You could say that a

---

† With some exceptions, for example, in the research on HIV/AIDS risk behavior and subsequent development of interventions. In addition, Oyserman and Markus[39] (see also Oyserman and Packer[40]) utilized an integrative construct called "self-concept" and its link to "possible selves" as a way of understanding an internal dynamic behind clusterings of youth risk behavior, a construct that could organize diverse explanations for delinquency.

"way of life" includes a lot of expectations about everything, from big issues like possible career or life paths, to small issues like what it means to go on a date and how people are supposed to act on a date. All of these expectations take shape as models of how things are supposed to be, and they help organize and guide actions, reactions, and emotions. They help people understand what is important or not, what is funny or not, and what others might expect of you. Because of that, they generate action, and we will refer to them by the term *generative schema*.

Think of the following examples of generative schema:

- *Status constructs:* The things, behaviors, and so on that make for high status, together with what that status signifies (e.g., chosen by the Divine, survival of the fittest, etc.)
- *Gender constructs:* "Being a man" or "being a woman," where the constructs "man" or "woman" are bundles of meanings that have been aggregated into single constructs, and connected—via cultural practice—to behaviors that are said to represent the construct

So, we may engage in a number of behaviors all related to pursuing, maintaining, and defending a gender role (because of what it means, and because it is an organizing principle for "living a life"). This is what we would call *performance* of the model or schema. The schema is therefore *generative* of behavior, but *not necessarily* predictive in the positivistic sense, because individuals tend to "assemble" their behavior in ways that carry out an organizing theme.[41] The key is not "exposure to a schema" in an epidemiological sense, like "exposure to a risk factor" (though that is certainly part of the process). Models are internalized, interpreted, and used by individuals—the intersection of a schema with day-to-day life is a process in which an individual pulls from the "life material" available to him or her to *act out or perform the model*.[42]

Therefore, if *pursuing status* is a construct that guides behavior—because of what "having status" means—individuals may be motivated by it to do "something" related to having status, or to behave in a way that coincides with their perceived status or an aspired status. But the status schema *generates* behavior, and is not directly predictive, because today (or in a particular social setting) that behavior may take shape in one form, and tomorrow as another, all related to the process of negotiating how one fulfills the narrative related to the meaningful construct of status.

Therefore, to better understand health-related behavior, more research and its practical application could focus on identifying and working with such generative schemata, and attempting to develop intervention models that focus on these schemata and their interaction with domains of risk behavior.

The following are examples, taken from the author's work, of what specific generative schema might look like for injection drug users (a risky behavior), runaway youth, and youth in colonias on the U.S.–Mexico border.

Injection Drug Users

The following is a scenario taken from a conversation between two older drug addicts in Washington, D.C., who were talking on a corner, one sitting on a chair, the other standing.[43-45] They were talking about "the life," which centers on the use of (and addiction to) heroin, cocaine, and whatever else; the process of getting and selling the drugs; and negotiating all the interactions and relationships involved. More than that, they seemed to be talking about what it all *means*. The conversation consisted of reminiscing, and one baiting the other about what they used to do, or one boasting to the other about what they used to do, approximately in the following form:

> **A:** Hey, I used ta' take (AMOUNT OF DRUG) and still be able to (PERFORM SOME ACTION).
>
> **B:** Naaaw. I never saw that!
>
> **A:** Doncha remember when we (DID SOME ACTION X WHEN WE HAD TAKEN SOME AMOUNT OF DRUG Y)??

In this scenario, a possible *generative schema* is the *drive towards mastery*, framed this time through talk about a time when their drug use was the vehicle through which to show how they could "get over," how they could "fend off a challenge" from the drug (as if it were a rival, a challenger, a competitor) without losing a step as a man, as a master of the universe. Like warfare, the courtroom, the boardroom, the bedroom, or the family room, "the life" (of injecting drug use) could be just another arena in which to play out one's story, one's triumphs and defeats, one's place in the cosmos. It could be argued that it was the arena that for these men was the most accessible in their lives. "The life" also made possible the *negotiation of personal status using stories* within the social world of the injection drug user (it gave people "stories to tell").

I also heard that if someone overdosed on a street corner, other junkies would rush to the corner to see if they could get a hold of whatever the overdoser was using. It is a challenge—to try and play against the odds. Moreover, in talking about the one who overdosed, they might even say that he was just *incompetent*—he couldn't take it. He wasn't a master of the game.

Let's assume that this generative schema is in fact common among IDUs. How could that be used to impact risk behavior? The underlying needs in the scenario are to achieve mastery, to demonstrate status, to have stories to tell. These in themselves are not unusual or necessarily risky. The key would be to develop an intervention that included *other choices of behavior* that would satisfy the generative motivation. Of course that is easier said than done, and substantial research would be needed in order to identify useful choices. But if the schema remains attached solely to injection drug use as its *field of play*, then what, for example, would motivate an IDU to go into drug treatment? In addition to the physical pain and sickness involved in detoxing and treatment, stopping drug use might leave the IDU with nothing around which to leverage his or her identity.

Runaway Youth

In a shelter for youth in trouble, I had a conversation with a 15-year-old African-American boy as part of a study on HIV risk and substance abuse. Like many of the other youth I spoke with who came from the Southeast and other economically depressed sections of Washington, D.C., he was out in the street much of the time, shifting between several potential residences (with relatives and others). And, like others, he was heavily involved in the ubiquitous street economy, which included the drug market, but many other activities as well. It was this economy that mattered. After reciting his various "jobs"—stealing cars, acting as a drug-dealer's lookout, and so on—he smiled and said, "See, I know how to make money without carrying people's bags."

His statements could refer to one of the many generative schema that gave meaning to the "work" he described. It was a matter of pride to him that he knew how to obtain resources without being in a constant position of subordination to others to do so. He was, in his corner of the world, on top for a change.

What could you do with that generative schema? It would be necessary, for example, to address this youth's motivation to do other kinds of work or activities that would result in a sense of independence and status.

I also conducted interviews with runaways on the street in the Washington, D.C., and Baltimore metro areas. These youth were primarily European American. Because they were out on the street, but not cycling between extended family or *fictive kin*‡ type relations (as with many of the African-American runaways), they relied heavily on peer networks for survival, which also had a likely impact on who they thought of as "risky" sex partners or not. The text segment below is from an interview with an 18-year-old "punk" on the street who praised her friends in almost poetic terms. The tenor of that narrative gives some clue as to a generative schema that might have guided her behavior.

> Mainly my homeless experience was with skinheads and punk rockers, and there's a camaraderie between them. If they cannot eat half their dinner and sneak it out to you, they will. If they've got ten bucks and you're hungry, they'll take you out to like Tasty Diner, it's only $2.50 for some ham and eggs. But it's food and you've got it. And if there's beer, they'll share it, and if the cops come, and you get busted for something they did, or whatever, they'll take up for you, I've seen that happen, and it's more than just a friendly camaraderie, it's like family. And I think that the government doesn't understand skinheads. They think that they're all Nazis. But if it wasn't for skinheads, I'd probably be dead or a prostitute, or both. A dead prostitute. They took me in, they were my friends, they helped me find jobs. They cut my hair weird, but they were good people. They didn't leave me for dead in the streets. They weren't like "well, my parents won't like it." They were like, "f___ my parents, we'll sneak in the basement window." "You can't sleep out on the street. It's snowing. It's raining." You know, or "it's cold out tonight, here you can have my favorite sweater. It will keep you warm. You want some clean socks, here's some clean socks. You want to do your laundry here, it's free" . . . .

In this case, a possible generative schema might have been: "The world is against us," and so "my friends are all there is" (much like the ethic of soldiers in battle). Therefore, no risk is too great to preserve that social unit. With that generative schema to work with, it might have been useful to channel HIV prevention efforts through one or more of the local, informal punk houses that had evolved into centers

---

‡ "Fictive kin" refers to a relationship between people that is not technically family, but that is treated (and sometimes talked about) as if it is.

of activity (at the time of this research), organizing outdoor music and fundraisers for free clinics and other causes. These houses could potentially mobilize networks of friends who shared a "misfit" or rebel identity, and messages could include themes about "protecting friends."

Mexican Border Youth, Violence, and the Narcotrafficker Identity

As part of a broader study done in the U.S.–Mexico border region on the cultural persona of the narcotrafficker and its relationship to risk behaviors such as violence,[43,44,46] I interviewed youth in a Ciudad Juarez, Mexico, youth prison. During interviews I tried to draw out any contrasts between what these youth admired in narcotraffickers and what they generally felt were admirable qualities and admirable people. At their relatively young ages, they displayed a remarkable cynicism about many common social roles that carry status or esteem, and expressed a desire to be narcotraffickers, the kind who were famous and had popular songs known as *corridos* written about them.

Corridos, the songs the youth wanted written about them, are a traditional hero-song form in Mexico that have recently become an entire pop-song genre. Many of these recent corridos, however, are about narcotraffickers, their exploits, and their attitude of "braving any risk" and "spitting in the face of death." (These corridos are called *narcocorridos.*) In a high-poverty setting (colonias in the border region), where there are few perceived options among the poor for social status or recognition, having a corrido written about you is one signifier of importance. So, the fact that one may die, or engage in violence, or take other risks to have that corrido written about you may have seemed less important to these youth than the recognition gained. After all, whether in this life or in the next, having a corrido means "you are something."

Thus the generative schema that would be tied to violence in this case had to do with "being something" to offset the kind of facelessness that is often said to be characteristic of concentrations of poverty.[47] Having spent time in Ciudad Juarez, it is not hard to see how this connection is made; it is harder to come up with alternative paths to such recognition in the political and economic context of serious poverty.

Although I was focusing on the relationship between the narcotrafficker persona and violence (as a risk behavior), there appeared to be broader implications. Narcocorridos, among other things, present an image of "willingness to face death" or "willingness to take risks" that is part of the hero persona (in old corridos as well). This can be generalized to a wide range of what would be called "risk behaviors." For example, in an old corrido about California bandit Joaquin Murieta:

> Pistols and daggers
> Are playthings for me
> Bullets and stabbings
> Big laughs for me
> With their means cut off
> They're afraid around here.[48,49]

The recent narcocorrido entitled *Mis Tres Animales* is another example of the "willingness to face death" or "willingness to take risks" schema:

> Death is always near me
> But I don't know how to give in
> I know the government hunts me
> Even under the sea
> But there's a way around everything
> And my hiding place hasn't been found.[§]

In addition, many narcocorridos also include a reference to movement from poverty to riches or power, directly related to the generative schema. From *Joaquin Murieta*:

> I came from Hermosillo
> In search of gold and riches . . .
> From the greedy rich
> I took away their money
> With the humble and poor
> I took off my hat
> Oh, what unjust laws
> To call me a highwayman.[48,49]

Again, from *Mis Tres Animales*:

> I learned to live life
> until I had money
> I don't deny that I was poor
> And that I was a mule skinner
> Now I am a great gentleman
> The gringos covet my pets.[¶]

Applications of a Generative Approach

How can a generative approach be put into practice? Like any other approach, successive demonstration efforts would provide useful feedback with respect to implementation. In general, possible directions include:

§ by Mario Quintero Lara. Copyright Mas Flamingo Music
¶ by Mario Quintero Lara. Copyright Mas Flamingo Music

- Work towards adding less risky behaviors to an "inventory of behaviors" that satisfies the generative schema.
- If an identified schema is related to personal identity and its connection to behavior, work towards the addition of additional identity possibilities or "possible selves" (a term developed by social psychologists Oyserman and Markus).[39]

Suppose, for example, that a young woman involved in the sex trade in Thailand is the oldest daughter of an impoverished family from the rural north. She ended up in the sex trade after coming down to Bangkok to find some way to make money to help her family. One possible generative schema influencing her "risk behavior": As the oldest child (in a Southeast Asian culture), she bears the most responsibility for family support. Her motivational schema is to meet her obligations in this role and support the family that gave her life, even if she must sacrifice herself. Thus in developing an HIV/AIDS prevention program for young women in her situation, would it not be more effective to incorporate the generative schema into program components, to "harness" its motivational force towards other nonrisky behavior? To do this, the program components would have to allow her to "follow her schema" through *substitute behavior or activities* that meet the same need. These may include microcredit or other income producing components through which she can support her family and thus satisfy the schema-related role. In such a case, other traditional HIV/AIDS prevention modalities may not even be necessary, because a simple substitution of behavior is involved (relative to a schema) that will take her out of the risk situation.

Chapter Questions

1. Why should we be concerned with *context* when trying to understand and address high-risk behavior?

2. What is meant by "risk factors for high-risk behavior"? What is meant by the "integration" of such factors?

3. What is a harm reduction approach?

4. What is a generative approach?

5. How do the approaches discussed in this chapter use the kinds of health behavior theories reviewed in this book?

REFERENCES

1. Bronfenbrenner U. *The Ecology of Human Development.* Cambridge, MA: Harvard University Press; 1979.

2. Green & Kreuter, 1999.

3. Becker MH, ed. The health belief model and personal health behavior. *Health Educ Monogr.* 1974;2:Entire issue.

4. Janz & Becker, 1984.

5. Hochbaum GM. *Public Participation in Medical Screening Programs: A Sociopsychological Study.* Public Health Service publication no. 572. Washington, D.C.: Government Printing Office; 1958.

6. Fishbein M, Ajzen I. *Belief, Attitude, Intention, and Behavior: An Introduction to Theory and Research.* Reading, MA: Addison-Wesley; 1975.

7. Ajzen I. The theory of planned behavior. *Organ Behav Human Decision Processes.* 1991;50:179–211.

8. Ajzen I, Fishbein M. *Understanding Attitudes and Predicting Social Behavior.* Englewood Cliffs, NJ: Prentice Hall; 1980.

9. Dahlberg LL. Youth violence in the United States: major trends, risk factors, and prevention approaches. *Am J Prev Med.* 1998;14(4):259–272.

10. Yoshikawa H. Prevention as cumulative protection: effects of early family support and education on chronic delinquency and its risks. *Psychol Bull.* 1994;115:28–54.

11. Grizenko N, Fisher C. Review of studies of risk and protective factors for psychopathology in children. *Can J Psych.* 1992;37:711–721.

12. Hawkins JD, Catalano RF, Miller JY. Risk and protective factors for alcohol and other drug problems in adolescence and early adulthood: implications for substance abuse prevention. *Psychol Bull.* 1992;112:64–105.

13. Dryfoos JG. *Adolescents at Risk: Prevalence and Prevention.* New York: Oxford University Press; 1990.

14. Tolan P, Guerra N. *What Works in Reducing Adolescent Violence: An Empirical Review of the Field. Report to the Center for the Study and Prevention of Violence.* Boulder, CO: Center for the Study and Prevention of Violence; 1994.

15. Hawkins et al. Predictors of youth violence. *Juvenile Justice Bull.* Washington, D.C.: Office of Juvenile Justice and Delinquency Prevention; 2000.

16. Catalano RF, Hawkins JD. *Risk-Focused Prevention: Using the Social Development Strategy.* Seattle, WA: Developmental Research and Programs; 1995.

17. Jessor R, Jessor SL. *Problem Behavior and Psychosocial Development: A Longitudinal Study of Youth.* New York: Academic Press; 1977.

18. Jessor R, Donovan J, Costa FM. *Beyond Adolescence: Problem Behavior and Young Adult Development.* New York: Cambridge University Press; 1991.

19. Donovan JE, Jessor R. The structure of problem behavior in adolescence and young adulthood. *J Consult Clin Psychol.* 1985;53:890–904.

20. Donovan JE, Jessor R, Costa FM. Syndrome of problem behavior in adolescence: a replication. *J Consult Clinic Psychol.* 1988;56(5):762–765.

21. Hirschi T. *Causes of Delinquency.* Berkeley: University of California Press; 1969.

22. Hawkins & Catalano, 1996.

23. DHHS, 2001.

24. NIH, 2004.

25. UNAIDS. *Preventing the Transmission of HIV among Drug Abusers: A Position Paper of the United Nations System.* Geneva: UNAIDS; 2000.

26. World Health Organization. *Principles for Preventing HIV Infection among Drug Users.* Copenhagen, Denmark: World Health Organization Regional Office; 1998.

27. Stimson G, Des Jarlais D, Ball A. *Drug Injecting and HIV Infection.* London: World Health Organization/UCL Press; 1998.

28. MacDonald M, Kaldor J, Hales J, Dore GJ. Effectiveness of needle and syringe programmes for preventing HIV transmission. *Int J Drug Policy.* 2003;14(5/6):353–357.

29. Lenton S. Policy from a harm reduction perspective. *Curr Opinion Psychiatry.* 2003;16(3):271–277.

30. Battaglia D, ed. *Rhetorics of Self-Making.* Berkeley: University of California Press; 1995.

31. D'Andrade R, Strauss C, eds. *Human Motives and Cultural Models.* Cambridge: Cambridge University Press; 1992.

32. Holland D, et al. *Identity and Agency in Cultural Worlds.* Cambridge, MA: Harvard University Press; 1998.

33. Holland D, Quinn N, eds. *Cultural Models in Language and Thought.* Cambridge: Cambridge University Press; 1987.

34. Shore B. *Culture in Mind: Cognition, Culture, and the Problem of Meaning.* New York: Oxford University Press; 1996.

35. Wertsch JV. A sociocultural approach to socially shared cognition. In: Resnick LB, Levine JM, Teasley SD, eds. *Socially Shared Cognition.* Washington, D.C.: American Psychological Association; 1991.

36. Foucault M. *Power/Knowledge: Selected Interviews & Other Writings, 1972–1977.* Gordon C, ed. Gordon C, Marshall L, Mepham J, Soper K, trans. New York: Pantheon Books; 1980.

37. Goffman E. *The Presentation of Self in Everyday Life.* New York: Doubleday Anchor; 1959.

38. Kelly GA. *The Psychology of Personal Constructs.* New York: Norton; 1955.

39. Oyserman D, Markus H. Possible selves and delinquency. *J Pers Soc Psychol.* 1990;59(1):112–125.

40. Oyserman D, Packer MJ. Social cognition and self-concept: a socially contextualized model of identity. In: Nye JL, Brower AM, eds. *What's Social About Social Cognition? Research on Socially Shared Cognition in Small Groups.* Thousand Oaks, CA: Sage; 1996.

41. Levi-Strauss C. *The Savage Mind.* Chicago: University of Chicago Press; 1966.

42. Bourdieu P. *Outline of a Theory of Practice.* Cambridge: Cambridge University Press; 1977.

43. Edberg M. *El Narcotraficante: Narcocorridos and the Construction of a Cultural Persona on the U.S.-Mexico Border.* Austin, TX: University of Texas Press; 2004.

44. Edberg M. The narcotrafficker in representation and practice: a cultural persona from the Mexican border. *Ethos.* 2004;32(2):257–277.

45. Edberg M. Street cuts: splices from project notebooks. *Anthropol Humanism.* 1998;23(1):77–82.

46. Edberg M. Drug traffickers as social bandits: culture and drug trafficking in Northern Mexico and the border region. *J Contemp Criminol.* 2001;17(3):259–277.

47. Liebow E. *Tell Them Who I Am: The Lives of Homeless Women.* New York: Free Press; 1993.

48. Herrera-Sobek M. *Northward Bound: The Mexican Immigrant Experience in Ballad and Song.* Bloomington: Indiana University Press; 1993.

49. Sonnichsen P. Texas-Mexican border music. Liner notes, Vols. 2 and 3, *Corridos,* Parts 1 and 2. Berkeley, CA: Folklyric; 1975.

CHAPTER 13

Evaluation: What Is It? Why Is It Needed? How Does It Relate to Theory?

LEARNING OBJECTIVES

By the end of this chapter, the reader will be able to:

- Understand the need for evaluation of health promotion programs and how theory and evaluation are linked
- Describe the basic types kinds of evaluation: process, impact and outcome
- Understand how to use a *logic model* to develop an evaluation
- Understand basic issues involved in doing a successful evaluation

> "You have first an instinct, then an opinion, then a knowledge, as the plant has root, bud and fruit."
>
> —RALPH WALDO EMERSON, JOURNAL ENTRY, JULY 21, 1836

INTRODUCTION

This is not a book on evaluation, and in this chapter we will not go into evaluation in great detail. However, it is so much a part of the program environment that it is important to gain some familiarity with what it means, because eventually you not only will learn more about it, but also will be using it in practice. It is also very much a part of using theory to design and implement a program.

Evaluation sounds formal. It sounds technical. But without getting into the details, evaluation is just the process of:

- Making sure you did what you proposed to do
- Determining whether your program had an impact based on what you were trying to achieve
- Assessing whether the program model, and the theory or theories you (or others) employed in the design of the program, were useful

Evaluation is very relevant to the entire scope of this book. It is the way in which you carry through your use of social and behavioral theory to the point where you can determine whether the whole process—of assessing a situation, identifying factors to address, and using the assessment together with relevant theory to plan and implement an intervention and relevant theory—*made a difference.*

EVALUATION AND THE CURRENT PROGRAM ENVIRONMENT

There is another very important pragmatic reason for evaluation as well. In the current and future environment of program funding, there is (and will be) a very strong emphasis on *evidence* and *accountability*. In other words, to maintain funding for a particular program, there needs to be some evidence that it is actually doing something to address the problem it is intended to address. This imperative is relatively recent. Serious evaluation of health promotion and behavioral interventions didn't really become the norm until a growing consensus developed among the research and practitioner community in the 1980s that better evaluation was needed to improve program planning and performance.[1-3] With the passage of the Government Performance and Results Act (GPRA) of 1993, accountability requirements have become an increasing element of federal, state, local, private, and global health promotion and intervention efforts. GPRA required agencies to develop and implement "performance monitoring" and accountability procedures to ensure that public funds were well spent. The influence of GPRA and the "accountability movement" of which it is a part has now been integrated into standard practice. It has also accelerated the degree to which agencies and organizations use strategic planning documents to set out their goals as a guide to action, and as a method for evaluating progress. So, if the planning document says "we will reduce the number of youth who smoke by 25%," then *documented* change in smoking behavior (compared to the goal of a 25% decrease) is the measure of success. Healthy People 2010 is a voluminous, comprehensive planning document of this type.

Maybe even a more profound change brought on by this trend is the move, within the public health field, to develop a body of *evidence-based practice* in the same way that the medical field has developed evidence-based standards of care. For health promotion and prevention interventions, this means the following:

- Evaluating the program becomes very important. Evaluation data is the *evidence*.
- Many agencies have begun to develop directories or listings of interventions that have this kind of evidence for effectiveness. Often, the directory will even "rate" programs or interventions on the basis of the quality of their evidence. So, a program that has been implemented in several places with different populations and shows evidence of being effective in all those situations will be rated more highly than a program that was tried just once, even if it

was effective that one time. The National Registry of Evidence-based Programs and Practices (NREPP) at the Substance Abuse and Mental Health Services Administration (SAMHSA), and the Centers for Disease Control and Prevention *Guide to Community Preventive Services* are two prominent examples. (See the boxes below for descriptions of these compendia of model programs.)

- Programs that demonstrate good evidence of effectiveness are typically called *model programs* or something similar. More and more, public and even private agencies are requiring, as part of the grant funding, that grant recipients use model programs or evidence-based programs—or if not, justify why there is no appropriate program of that type for the community, population, or situation to be addressed.

Because of this trend, a lot of research efforts are directed towards identifying model programs (developing or identifying the evidence base), and along with that, compiling evidence for the utility or inapplicability of different theoretical approaches used to structure such programs.

THE TYPES OF EVALUATION

As you start looking more closely at the theory and practice of evaluation, it begins to get a little more complex. There

Why Evaluate?

- *Accountability:* To respond to the public need to show that cost/resources invested in a program had some effect. More recently, because of the Government Performance and Results Act (GPRA), agencies are required to implement accountability and monitoring systems.
- *Learning and improvement:* As the program is being conducted, evaluation data can help determine what is working and what is not—feedback that allows you to make changes as you go.
- *Theory:* To test the validity of a theoretical linkage, or to test a model program/approach that has been demonstrated to be effective in some other situation.

The CDC Guide to Community Preventive Services

The *Guide to Community Preventive Services* (*Community Guide*) serves as a filter for scientific literature on specific health problems that can be large, inconsistent, uneven in quality, and even inaccessible. The *Community Guide* summarizes what is known about the effectiveness, economic efficiency, and feasibility of interventions to promote community health and prevent disease. The Task Force on Community Preventive Services makes recommendations for the use of various interventions based on the evidence gathered in the rigorous and systematic scientific reviews of published studies conducted by the review teams of the *Community Guide*. The findings from the reviews are published in peer-reviewed journals and also made available on the Internet Web site below.

From the Community Guide Web site: http://www.thecommunityguide.org/about/default.htm. Accessed August 6, 2006.

are, after all, many possible things to evaluate in any given program, and different goals for evaluation. To make this a little easier, let's start by understanding three basic categories of evaluation—*process, impact,* and *outcome.* (We first introduced these evaluation types in Chapter 7.) A project may employ one or all three at the same time, because each has a different purpose. There are also evaluations that look at cost effectiveness, evaluations used in program development (formative evaluation), quality assurance evaluations, and other specific types,[4] but for the purposes of this introductory discussion we will not cover those.

Process Evaluation

As its name implies, process evaluation means evaluating how the *process* of implementing a project fared. The basic process evaluation question is this: Were the components of the intervention implemented as planned? How do you answer the question? By keeping *records*—for example, of how many materials were developed and distributed, education sessions conducted, community coalition partners included, and so on. You can then compare what you actually did with what you planned to do.

For testing theory, process evaluation is also very important. If, for example, a theory-based intervention is based on the Stages of Change theory,[5,6] its effectiveness may depend in part on periodic assessment of intervention participants to identify their stage along a process of, say, changing diet, because the intervention components are tied to a stage for each individual. If the intervention is not as effective as expected, it would be very helpful to know, through process evaluation, if this was due to improper implementation of the assessments. If so, then at least you know that it may not be the theory or intervention design that is the problem, but the details of implementation.

In addition, a program that has shown evidence of effectiveness in one situation may then be *replicated*; that is, implemented in another situation. In order for that replication to serve as an additional test of the model, the program has to be replicated with *fidelity.* All program components have to be implemented according to the program design. A process evaluation will provide you with fidelity data. Related to the issue of fidelity is the concept of dosage. It may sound odd to use the term *dosage* when talking about something other than a medical intervention. What the term refers to in a health promotion/nonmedical public health intervention is "the amount of an intervention (e.g., number of education sessions, number of activities) that results in a particular impact or outcome."

The National Registry of Evidence-Based Programs and Practices

The National Registry of Evidence-based Programs and Practices (NREPP), formerly the National Registry of Effective Programs, is a system designed to support informed decision making and to disseminate timely and reliable information about interventions that prevent and/or treat mental and substance use disorders. The NREPP system allows users to access descriptive information about interventions as well as peer-reviewed ratings of outcome-specific evidence across several dimensions. NREPP provides information to a range of audiences, including service providers, policy makers, program planners, purchasers, consumers, and researchers.

From the SAMHSA Model Programs Web site: http://model-programs.samhsa.gov/template.cfm?page=faq. Accessed August 6, 2006.

Impact Evaluation

Now we start looking at the effects of a program. The question to be answered by impact evaluation is: What short-term or immediate effect did the intervention have? How do you answer this question? It depends on your program goals. What did you expect to happen in the short term? Was this expectation guided by theory and your assessment? In order to determine impact, the typical process is to collect data about the issues you expect to impact in the short term before your project begins, then collect the same kind of information at one or (preferably) more points after the intervention is in place, to measure change. This process is also known as collecting pre- and post-test data, or collecting baseline and follow-up data.

As we will discuss below in more detail, the expected impact has everything to do with theory, assessment, and how these are incorporated into your program design (as in the PRECEDE-PROCEED process reviewed in Chapter 7).

Based on specific program goals, the impact data you collect might include pre-post test data on knowledge change, changes in health service utilization, policy changes, or other data (e.g., educational, ecological, policy data). It is the kind of change you could expect from a program that was funded for, say, three or four years.

Outcome Evaluation

Now we get to the real health impact of a program, and to theoretical links you may have made between short-term impact and long-term outcome. The question to ask is: Did the intervention affect the health problem/issue that was the ultimate target? In other words, let's say you put in place a smoking intervention that includes several activities designed to increase individual awareness of risks and prevention options. You are hypothesizing (based, for example, on the Health Belief Model) that if there is a change in awareness among a particular group of people about their own susceptibility to cancer as a result of smoking, as well as options for quitting that don't present an insurmountable challenge, that they are likely to quit. So, you are *linking awareness change to health behavior change, and to a reduction in cancer.*

- What are the short-term impacts?
- What is the long-term outcome?

Long-term outcome is something you can measure if you: 1) have a project that is in place for an extended amount of time (e.g., more than three or four years); or 2) you can follow people who participated in your program (a "cohort") over an extended period. To measure these changes, you collect *baseline and follow-up data* like you would for short-term impact, except they are data related to the long-term outcomes you expect—for example, cancer morbidity and mortality. And you will likely be collecting follow-up data for a number of years to collect the kinds of information useful in understanding outcome.

USING A "LOGIC MODEL" TO SET UP AN EVALUATION

One way to think about setting up an evaluation, and building it into an intervention, is to go back to the PRECEDE-

PROCEED planning approach. Recall that the PRECEDE segment goes through the following assessments:

- *Social assessment:* The context and quality of life issues surrounding a community and its health problems
- *Epidemiological assessment:* The actual health problems from morbidity/mortality data
- *Behavioral/environmental assessment:* The environmental and behavioral risk factors associated with the actual health problems (morbidity/mortality)
- *Educational/ecological assessment:* Social norms, attitudes, awareness, policies, and other issues, understood in terms of predisposing, enabling, and reinforcing factors, that contribute to the behavioral and environmental risks
- *Administrative/policy assessment:* The resources available to support an intervention (e.g., people, funds), community politics, and structures that can help or hinder implementation of an intervention

Do you see the way in which the educational/ecological, behavioral/environmental, epidemiological, and social assessments form a kind of "logical chain"? (See Figure 13-1.) That is, where health problems result from risks, which result from predisposing/enabling/reinforcing factors (along with the community politics and environment)? In the real world, things may not actually line up that well. However, for the purposes of developing an intervention and an evaluation, it is a useful way to set things up, because your intervention can be viewed as *going back up the chain.* You have identified predisposing, enabling, and reinforcing factors that lead to risk, which leads to a particular health problem, and your intervention may target several of those factors, which, *logically,* should impact on risks, and therefore the health problem itself (see Figure 13-2).

This way of thinking can be summarized in what is known as a *logic model.* A logic model is a diagram or structure that links what you plan to do with its expected impacts and outcomes. More specifically, a logic model links the following:

- *The health problem to be addressed:* From the epidemiological assessment—the problem, such as HIV/AIDS, cancer, malaria, diabetes, or some other issue. More specifically, you might want to include the factors contributing to the problem that you want to address—relevant behavioral or environmental risks; or predisposing, enabling, or reinforcing factors; or community/policy factors.

> ## Process, Impact, and Outcome Evaluation: The Questions
>
> *Process evaluation:* Were the components of the program implemented as planned?
>
> *Impact evaluation:* What short-term or immediate effect did the program have? (What does your logic model and theory tell you *should have happened*?)
>
> *Outcome evaluation:* How did the program affect the health problem/issue that was the ultimate target? (What does your logic model and theory tell you *should have happened*?)

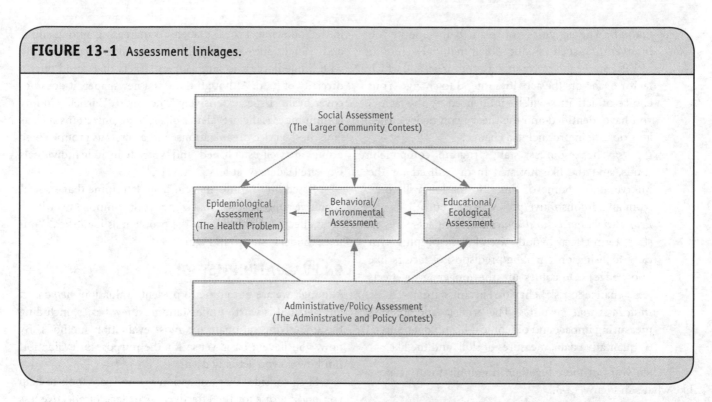

FIGURE 13-1 Assessment linkages.

In Figures 13-1 and 13-2, can you see that if you address educational/ecological factors, you will (hopefully) impact behavioral/environmental factors, and then impact the health problem itself (as documented in epidemiological data)?

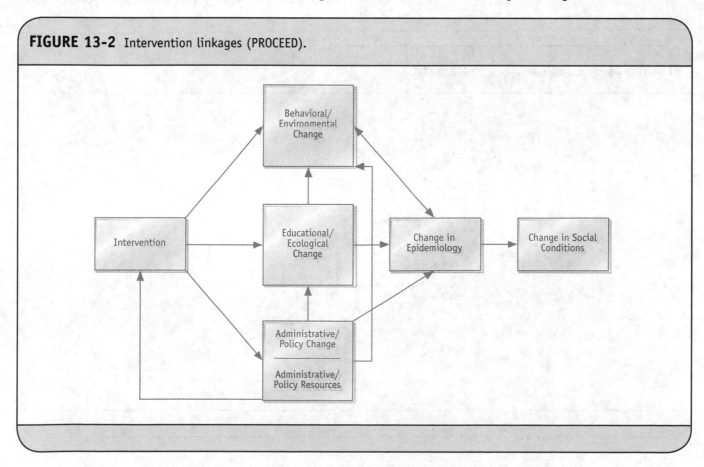

FIGURE 13-2 Intervention linkages (PROCEED).

- *Outputs:* The activities you plan to include in your intervention, such as educational materials, community events, health screenings, or trainings, and which factor or factors the activities intend to change. Your choice of activities will be influenced by the factors you have identified and the theory you believe to be appropriate in producing a change.
- *Inputs:* The resources, staff, program components, funds, and the like invested in or utilized for the intervention. (Some of this information will come from an administrative/policy assessment.)
- *Projected impacts and outcomes:* Impacts are the short-term effects hypothesized for the outputs (typically focusing on enabling/predisposing factors like knowledge). Outcomes are the longer-term effects (e.g., change in risk behaviors, health status).
- *Indicators and measures:* The criteria and tools for measuring impact and outcome—health data, survey or qualitative data, measures of skill, and the like.

When you put these together in graphic form, it looks like what's in Figure 13-3.

Now think of any health issue—diabetes, for example. Let's assume that a PRECEDE-type assessment has resulted

in the following: Type 2 diabetes is increasing among adults and young adults in Harfield County. It is a rural county, with limited access to large supermarkets that could offer a diversity of food. Although there is a newspaper, it does not cover health issues extensively. The key to Harfield County communities is the prevalence of social organizations such as churches, service organizations, and a veterans group. These groups are well-established, and typically include individuals who are leaders or at least "movers."

Based on this information, you determine that a social-cognitive approach, with social network components, will be most effective in addressing the problem as identified. Your logic model is shown in Figure 13-4.

ON EVALUATION METHODS

Although we are not going to present evaluation *methods* in any detail, it is worth understanding a few basics, including the underlying rationale for most evaluation methods. By now, you have a basic sense for the purpose of evaluation. But how do you actually do it?

First, consider that evaluation methods are tools to help you *make a case* for the effectiveness or lack of effectiveness of an intervention. It's a little like being a lawyer. The various methods aim to provide you information that could support

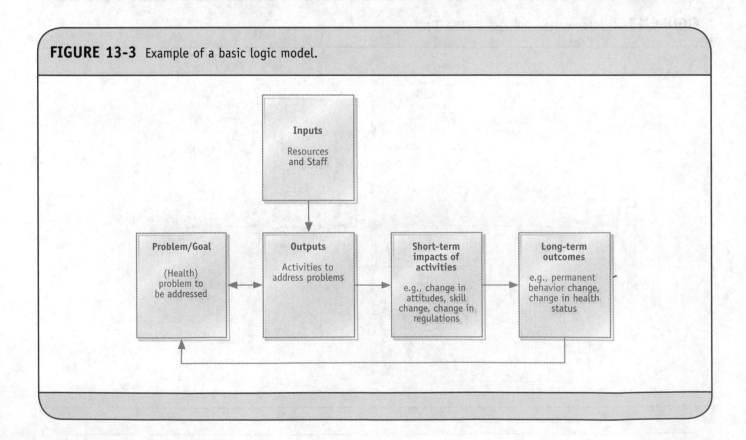

FIGURE 13-3 Example of a basic logic model.

FIGURE 13-4 The Harfield County Logic Model.

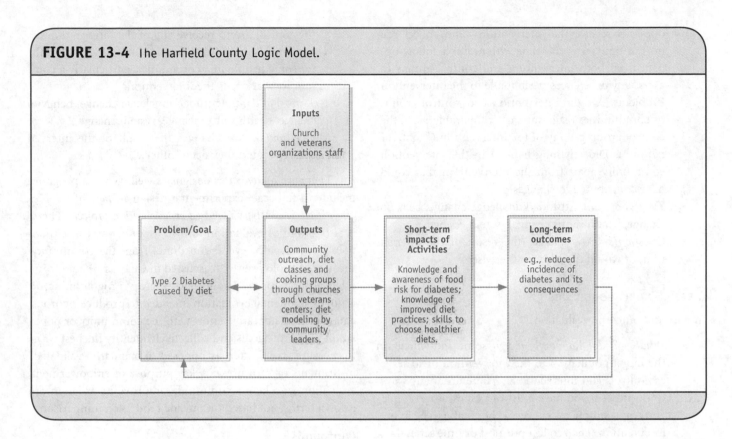

a claim that a particular intervention is responsible for a change—in attitudes, awareness, behavior, health status, or whatever the goal is. The more precise or *rigorous* the method, the more you will be able to argue that the intervention, *and nothing else*, was responsible for change. As you will see in the following discussion, as evaluation designs get more rigorous, they use control groups (people who do not get the intervention) for comparison, and in the most rigorous designs *randomly assign* people to the intervention or control group. The following is a selection of designs, from simple to rigorous.

Historical Recordkeeping Approach

A basic process evaluation method:

- *What you do:* Track project activities, client participation.
- *Type(s) of data:* Number of educational sessions conducted, health services delivered, calls taken, ads posted, client utilization, etc.
- *Question(s):* Are program inputs creating planned outputs?

Periodic Inventory/Time Series

Process and impact evaluation:

- *What you do:* At specified time intervals, beginning with a *baseline*, program data are tabulated and surveys are

completed to check progress towards program goals (e.g., number of people who quit smoking or changed attitudes about quitting). There is no comparison group.
- *Type(s) of data:* Attitude/knowledge change, program (client) participation, behavior change goals reached.
- *Question(s):* Are short-term goals being attained? Is progress being made towards goals?

Benchmarking

Process and impact evaluation:

- *What you do:* Assess program and participant impact data against some comparable "benchmark" standard (e.g., similar national or population-specific data).
- *Type(s) of data:* Attitude/knowledge change, program (client) participation, utilization, behavior change data, health status indicators.
- *Question(s):* Are program results comparable to other results as documented in comparison data?

Quasi-Experimental Design

Impact and outcome evaluation:

- *What you do:* Identify a community or population sample similar to your intervention sample—but that does *not* receive the intervention—and collect pre-post or time series (baseline with multiple follow-up) data from both intervention and control groups to assess any differences attributable to the intervention. Problems: Are the intervention and control groups or communities really similar (comparable)? Did the control group get any of the intervention ("contamination")? Did anything happen in the intervention community apart from the intervention that could have contributed to changes?

- *Type(s) of data:* Attitude/knowledge change, behavior change, health status change, system change.
- *Question(s):* Are changes the result of the intervention, or would they occur otherwise?

Classic Experimental Design

Impact and outcome evaluation:

- *What you do: Randomly assign* some individuals in the target population to the intervention or to serve as controls (no intervention). There are many ways to do this—if you have a list of names, for example, you could simply select every other name to be in the intervention. Then collect pre-post or time series data from both groups to assess any differences attributable to the intervention. Problems: Did people in

the control group receive any of the intervention by accident? Is it ethical to provide an intervention only for some people in a community, particularly a community that needs the intervention?

- *Type(s) of data:* Attitude/knowledge change, behavior change, health status change, system change.
- *Question(s):* Are changes the result of the intervention, or would they occur otherwise?

There are many other designs as well. When a program includes a full-scale experimental design *as part of the program itself*, it can be viewed as an *evaluation project*.[7] There is also a kind of evaluation known as *empowerment evaluation*.[8,9] This type of evaluation draws from the community theories of Paolo Freire[10] (discussed in Chapter 6), and from other general approaches to participatory programming. It is not experimental evaluation intended to produce rigorous data, but a collaborative effort with the community or population to identify goals, and collectively identify the best ways to measure goals (often as opposed to standard "validated" instruments or measures). A key purpose of empowerment evaluation is to help a community improve its program on its own terms, not based on outside models or comparison.

Confounds

Finally, when you are trying to *make a case* that a particular program or intervention is the cause of changes (that is, changes leading to better health outcomes), you will also have to address the kinds of things that could weaken your case. Some of these may have to do with methodology, and some may have to do with factors called *confounds*—unplanned occurrences that may affect an intervention and complicate claims that only the intervention caused a particular change. Here is a sampler of these confounds[1,7]:

- *History confound:* During the course of the intervention, something happens among or to the intervention or control groups/communities that is not connected to the experiment, leading to a change. This could be a highly publicized event; for example, a famous film star dies of HIV/AIDS.
- *Maturation confound:* During the intervention, some changes could occur—such as in behavior or attitude—just because subjects gain life experience.
- *Testing confound:* Some changes from baseline to follow-up data collection could be just the result of people becoming more familiar with the evaluation surveys or questions.
- *Regression to the mean:* When participants have characteristics or behaviors that are already extreme, these

Evaluation Design, Rigor, and the History of the Scientific Method

Recall that back in Chapter 3 we reviewed the history of positivist social science, its assumptions, and its connection to health promotion interventions

- What are some of the key assumptions from the Enlightenment that underlie the methods of science today, those methods that are viewed as *rigorous*?
- What do you think about the more rigorous evaluation designs described above and the rationale for them? When does it make sense to claim that in using those methods (for example, quasi-experimental designs and classic experimental designs) we are truly isolating and identifying just the effect of the program being evaluated?
- How else could you know whether an intervention program made an impact?

factors may change during the course of the intervention just because they were so extreme to start with. For example, with extreme poverty or extremely high risk behavior, pre-post scores may end up showing improvement, only because they can't get worse.

- *Selection bias:* When subjects are not a representative sample, for example, if answering your questionnaire is voluntary, then you have a selection bias because you are getting responses only from people who are motivated to participate.
- *Mortality or attrition confound:* When some people leave an intervention or research experiment over time, your post-test or follow-up responses are then only coming from those who stayed. Because of this, the responses may not reflect what happened with all respondents.
- *Diffusion of treatment:* When you cannot prevent the control group from getting some or all of the intervention; for example, in a public information campaign, when members of the control group (who are not supposed to be exposed to the campaign) move around to parts of the community where the intervention is being delivered, or where radio ads intended for the intervention community are picked up in the control community. In other words, you don't end up with a true comparison between people who received the intervention and others who did not, and your data may therefore not show much difference between the two.

There are often ways of offsetting these confounds that are included in evaluation designs, with the purpose of strengthening the argument.

WHAT KINDS OF IMPACT OR OUTCOME?

Finally, different types of evaluations provide different types of results. Just because all results are not rigorous evidence via a classic experimental design, it does not mean they are without merit. Programs are implemented in the real world, and success has many levels. For example, when just getting a program in place and operating is an achievement in itself, then a process evaluation may be all you need to do at that point. When the time period for your program is short, or when there are many barriers and the program can expect only a limited effect, an impact evaluation may be the best you can do. When a program can realistically expect to attain longer-term outcomes—because it is a 10-year program, or includes a long-term follow-up study—then looking for these outcomes would be appropriate. When the program includes a clinical intervention, clinical outcomes may be appropriate.

Independent and *Dependent* Variables

These are very important terms used in evaluation. Basically,

- An *independent variable* is a characteristic of an individual or situation that you are *not* trying to change in a health intervention. It is something that "just is." *But*, such variables are important because they tell you a lot about who and what your program can change.
- A *dependent variable* is a characteristic of an individual or situation that you *are* trying to change in an intervention. That is what you measure in an evaluation of impact or outcome.

For example: An intervention seeks to change diet and exercise behavior in women who are recent immigrants.

- The *independent variables* are: Being a woman and being a recent immigrant.
- The *dependent variables* are: You guessed it, diet and exercise behavior.

There are also different types of data that provide evidence of change, specifically, quantitative vs. qualitative data. *Quantitative data* refers to information that can be expressed numerically and analyzed statistically—the kind of data typically obtained from a survey where there are specific answer choices and you select one, or the kinds of data you can get from official records, such as demographic or epidemiological data. *Qualitative data* refers to data that are more *narrative, descriptive,* and *subjective* in character—the information typically obtained from extended interviews, focus groups, and observation, where there is not a precise set of questions, and where people have time to explain actions, beliefs, and interpretations. Because quantitative data are collected in the exact same way from a large number of people, they are useful in making comparisons and generalized conclusions about a population or group. On the other hand, because qualitative data are usually collected from a smaller number of people (because more time is required), they are useful in revealing the details and meaning of social interactions and events, the ways in which people interpret situations and events, and, for example, the dynamics of how interactions (e.g., patient–doctor) take place.

In other words, there is no cookie-cutter standard. Evaluation is tailored to the situation, the program, and the kinds of evidence needed. There are many other issues to be covered under the subject of evaluation. The key issue for this book, however, is the importance of evaluation in understanding the effect of interventions and the theory that guides them.

Chapter Questions

1. What are three basic reasons to evaluate a program?

2. How does evaluation help you understand whether a theory is applicable or useful?

3. What in the current public health program environment makes evaluation an imperative, on top of the other important reasons for doing it?

4. What are the three basic types of evaluation, and what is the purpose of each?

5. What is a "logic model," and how does a logic model help you connect theory to impact or outcome?

REFERENCES

1. Windsor R, Clark N, Boyd NR, Goodman RM. *Evaluation of Health Promotion, Health Education and Disease Prevention Programs.* 3rd ed. Boston, MA.: McGraw Hill; 2004.

2. World Health Organization. *Health Program Evaluation: Guiding Principles for Application of the Managerial Process for National Health Development.* Geneva: World Health Organization; 1980.

3. World Health Organization. *Development of Indicators for Monitoring Progress Toward Health for All by the Year 2000.* Geneva: 1981.

4. Pirie PL, Stone EJ, Assaf AR, Flora JA, Maschewsky-Schneider U. Program evaluation strategies for community-based health promotion programs: perspectives from the cardiovascular disease community research and demonstration studies. *Health Educ Res.* 1994;9(1):23–36.

5. Prochaska JO, Velicer WF. The transtheoretical model of health behavior change. *Am J Health Promotion.* 1997;12:38–48.

6. Prochaska JO, Redding CA, Evers KE. The transtheoretical model and stages of change. In: Glanz K, Rimer BK, Lewis FM, eds. *Health Behavior and Health Education.* 3rd ed. San Francisco, CA: John Wiley & Sons; 2002.

7. Bernard HR. *Research Methods in Anthropology: Qualitative and Quantitative Approaches.* 3rd ed. Lanham, MD: Altamira Press; 2002.

8. Fetterman DM. *Foundations of Empowerment Evaluation.* Thousand Oaks, CA: Sage; 2000.

9. Patton MQ. *Qualitative Research and Evaluation Methods.* Thousand Oaks, CA: Sage; 2002.

10. Freire P. *Pedagogy of the Oppressed.* New York: Seabury Press; 1970.

SECTION **IV**

Current Trends

CHAPTER 14

Culture, Diversity, and Health Disparities: Are Current Theories Relevant?*

* The author acknowledges information provided by the U.S. Office of Minority Health (Department of Health and Human Services) and backup research conducted by several staff members at Development Services Group, Inc. (DSG), a private research organization that supports evaluation activities at the U.S. Office of Minority Health. Some text is also derived from strategic planning efforts conducted by the author for DSG and the Office of Minority Health. However, the views expressed in this chapter are solely those of the author.

LEARNING OBJECTIVES

By the end of this chapter, the reader will be able to:

- Understand the current focus on health disparities and its relationship to diverse populations
- Understand the range of factors (within an ecological model) that contribute to health disparities
- Understand how social/behavioral theories can be employed to address this major public health issue

"Health is the first of all liberties."

—HENRY AMIEL, JOURNAL ENTRY, APRIL 3, 1865

INTRODUCTION

A lot has been said in recent years about the need to develop and implement "culturally competent" or "culturally appropriate" health interventions. Discussion about culture in this way has often been part of, or accompanied, the general issue of *disparities in health* among racial and ethnic minority populations. The second major goal of Healthy People 2010, in fact, is to eliminate health disparities.[1] Of course, not all health disparities have to do with racial/ethnic minority populations or cultural diversity. There are differences solely related to socioeconomic status or, for example, geography (e.g., living in a rural setting with little access to health care). However, the connection between diverse minority populations and health disparities is a primary aspect of the problem. In this chapter, we will take a brief look at this current and ongoing issue, because it raises many factors to be considered in the development of health interventions, and in the theory that guides them.

Why is this an issue? One reason certainly has to do with demographics. According to the U.S. Census Bureau, the two fastest growing population groups are Asian and Hispanic, with the Asian population growing 16% between 2000 and 2004, and the Hispanic population growing 17% during the same period.[2] Of the 100 million Americans added to the population since 1967, 53% are recent immigrants or their descendants.[3] This is a clear indicator that the population of the United States will be increasingly diverse, and it is common sense that the kinds of health interventions and programs developed and implemented should be responsive to this diversity.

Second, racial and ethnic minority populations in the United States have historically fared worse in terms of health than the majority population.[†] For example:

- African Americans die from diabetes at a rate more than twice that of European Americans. The rate for American Indian/Alaskan Natives is almost as bad.[4]
- Although African Americans comprise about 13% of the population, about half the new cases of AIDS from 2002–2003 were among African Americans. Hispanics are also disproportionately represented in the AIDS case rate.[4]
- Many Asian-American populations are at far greater risk for hepatitis than European Americans.[5]

---

† This is a general truism, and like all such truisms, it is not always true. For some health indicators, one or more minority populations fare better than the majority European-American population.

Racial and ethnic minority health disparities became a public policy issue in the United States following the publication of the Department of Health and Human Services (DHHS) Secretary's Task Force Report in 1985 (called the "Heckler Report," after then-DHHS Secretary Margaret Heckler).[6] The report identified six specific health issues that were the major cause of disparities between minorities and the majority European-American population: cancer, cardiovascular disease and stroke, chemical dependency (measured by deaths due to cirrhosis), diabetes, homicide and accidents, and infant mortality.[6(p4)] Although the report acknowledged that the health status of the U.S. population as a whole had improved significantly since the turn of the century as well as in more recent years since 1960, it concluded that "persistent, significant health inequities exist for minority Americans."[6(p2)] There was, for example, about a 30-year lag in health status improvement for African Americans as compared to European Americans, according to the report.

Twenty years after that report, a National Healthcare Disparities Report concluded that significant disparities still exist, even though these disparities have been the increasing focus of programmatic and research activity.[7] The report concluded that "disparities related to race, ethnicity and socioeconomic status still pervade the American health care system."[7] These disparities exist with respect to quality of health care, access to health care, levels and types of care, and many clinical conditions (e.g., cancer, diabetes, end stage renal disease, heart disease, HIV disease, mental health and substance abuse, and respiratory diseases). Disparities also persist with respect to the larger issue, overall disparities in the health status of minorities—referring to the differences in health status between the majority European-American population and each of numerous racial and ethnic minority[‡] populations in the United States and its territories. According to the American Public Health Association, these disparities can be identified across a range of health outcomes, including (but not limited to) the following[8]:

- Life expectancy
- Overall health status
- Infant mortality
- Cancer
- HIV/AIDS
- Violence
- Diabetes

The New Healthcare Disparities Report, for example, measured change in disparities by core measures that are utilized in the National Healthcare Quality Report (NHQR): Measures of health care *quality* (effectiveness, patient safety, timeliness, patient-centeredness) and measures of health care *access* (facilitators and barriers to health care, and utilization). The report not only confirmed the continued prevalence of disparities as noted above, but also documented the areas where there appeared to be improvement and where conditions were worse. Results included the following[7]:

- Fifty-eight percent of disparities in quality of care experienced by African Americans were becoming smaller, while 42% were becoming larger. Half the quality disparities experienced by Asians and American Indians/Alaskan Natives (AI/ANs) were becoming smaller while half were becoming larger.
- Forty-one percent of quality disparities experienced by Latinos/Hispanics were becoming smaller, while 59% were becoming larger.
- All disparities in access measures were becoming smaller for African Americans, Asians, and AI/ANs.
- Twenty percent of access disparities experienced by Latinos/Hispanics (and poor people) were becoming smaller, while 80% were growing larger.

WHY HEALTH DISPARITIES?

The reasons minority populations have fared worse are complex, and are difficult to separate from the historical experience of racial/ethnic minorities in this country, which has varied by population. The general experience of discrimination, social exclusion, lack of access to resources, higher exposure to environmental risk, and higher prevalence of poverty—to name a few factors—has contributed to patterns of living in which health-related beliefs, attitudes, expectations, and behavior have evolved that cannot help but reflect this experience. In addition, populations migrating to the United States from all over the world may come with different understandings about health and health care, as we discussed in Chapter 6.

Here is one way to think about this: What these historical circumstances produce is a *trajectory of health* for particular populations, which includes their vulnerability and exposure to disease, and the systems of knowledge, attitude, and practice related to health that developed in response to their vulnerability and historical experience within a larger society—or, you could say, a larger environment. This combination of *vulnerability*, *circumstance*, and *response* forms a larger set of forces that, together, contribute significantly to the differences in health status we refer to as health disparities.

Take, for example, attitudes towards use of health care and towards the "system" in general. Mistrust of doc-

---

‡ Understanding that much of the disparity related to race is intrinsically tied to race as a social, not genetic, category.

tors, scientists, and the government has been documented for African-American hospital patients.[9] A longstanding mistrust stemming from public knowledge about the infamous Tuskegee syphilis study has contributed to reluctance among African Americans to utilize HIV testing.[10] The Tuskegee study was an experiment conducted from 1932–1972 concerning the course of syphilis in which poor African-American men with syphilis were unethically left untreated in order to gain information about the progression of the disease! The author found attitudes very similar to this in a study and pilot project focusing on use of public health clinics for HIV testing—where the presence of HIV/AIDS was widely viewed as a conspiracy, and there was a strong reluctance to have blood drawn and tested at a public health clinic. In other projects, the author has encountered migrant worker populations, for example, from Central America, who come to the United States reluctant to trust government agencies and institutions (including public health clinics) due, among other things, to bad experiences during the years of civil conflict in Central America. If you add to this a long history of dealing with health problems outside of the mainstream health care system, because of a lack of insurance or other resources to cover the cost, or simply because of exclusion, it is not surprising that, for example, African-American and Latino men are less likely than European-American men to see a doctor, even when they are in poor health.[11]

In addition, populations that have experienced disproportionate poverty may be less accustomed to some of the lifestyle patterns that have become commonplace among wealthier and mainstream population segments. With this in mind it is again not surprising that African Americans and Hispanics are the population groups least likely to exercise even 20 minutes a day, three times per week.[12] Exercise as a discrete and popular activity, not just as part of life, is a relatively recent and largely middle or upper class phenomenon that accompanied the rise in living standards in the United States over the past century, and the increasing separation of work from physical activity in a post-industrial, technological society.[§]

Culturally specific experience accounts for some differences as well. There may be differences in knowledge and awareness between minority and majority populations. For example, a study of Mexican-American attitudes about screening and preventive medicine found a lack of knowledge about cancer, a tendency to avoid the disease, and fatalism

The Case of Lia Lee, Hmong Child

A well-known book entitled *The Spirit Catches You and You Fall Down*[16] describes the case of a young girl, Lia Lee, who was diagnosed with severe epilepsy. In the Hmong *ethnomedical system*, however, the symptoms that characterize what is called epilepsy in Western medicine were evidence of something very different for the Hmong. The Hmong are a people who come primarily from the mountainous areas in Laos, a Southeast Asian country bordering Thailand, Cambodia, Vietnam, Burma (Myanmar), and China. A significant number of Hmong were resettled in the United States after the Vietnam War, in large part due to their role in providing important support for U.S. efforts there. In the Hmong ethnomedical system at the time of this story, one cause of illness was that a person's soul was lost and wandering, possibly after a sudden event. To cure this and return the soul, a shaman (called a *txiv neeb*) would conduct a "soul calling." Epilepsy was known to the Hmong as *qaug dab peg*, or, literally, *a spirit catches you and you fall down*, and was viewed, among other things, as evidence of power to perceive things other people cannot see, a quality of distinction. The ensuing story is one of tragedy and conflict between the Hmong and Western way of understanding and treating Lia's condition, in which both parties eventually came to some understanding of how the other viewed the situation.

with respect to the consequences.[13] Avoidance of discussion topics related to sex and HIV/AIDS is viewed as characteristic of some Asian and Pacific Islander populations.[14]

As described in Chapter 6, health knowledge is also related to different ethnomedical systems[15]—that is, cultural systems of knowledge and practice that define illnesses and diseases, their causes, appropriate treatments, and appropriate treatment providers. Where these culturally specific systems vary from Western biomedical knowledge and practice, and where immigrant and refugee populations (for example) maintain strong adherence to these systems, a significant gap in understanding and utilization of standard medical care may result.

Even when there is access to health care, a number of studies have documented differential treatment for racial/ethnic minorities in the health care system. A recent Institute of Medicine (IOM) report, for example, described such disparities, including a lack of culturally and linguistically competent

---

§ Exercise and health "fads" have existed for some time, and of course, it has always been a part of life for athletes. I am referring to the popularization of exercise as part of a modern lifestyle, where it has become a significant commercial enterprise and consumer choice (fitness centers, gyms, running paths, sports apparel, etc.).

care.[17] The Kaiser Family Foundation has issued numerous briefings and reports addressing provider bias and differences in quality of care,[18,19] as has the Commonwealth Fund.[20]

The lack of *cultural competency* in health care and services has been identified in numerous documents as one cause of health care disparities.[21,22] One effort to address this issue was the development and dissemination of the national CLAS (culturally and linguistically appropriate service) standards,[¶] which define cultural competency in practice. The CLAS standards are organized into three themes—culturally competent care, language access services, and organizational supports for cultural competence.

Socioeconomic status (SES) itself is also a key factor, because of its significant implications for health. Although racial/ethnic minority populations include members across socioeconomic categories, it is fair to say that these populations are over-represented in lower socioeconomic groups, which means that the consequences of low SES fall harder on minority populations. Low SES is widely associated with health risks and problems,[23] such as nutrition, smoking, injuries, environmental pollution, unemployment, low income, family dysfunction, psychosocial stress, presence of community violence, limited recreational space, and the like. Housing segregation by race/ethnicity (regardless of income) is associated with a range of health risks.[24,25(p1171)] Neighborhood characteristics intertwined with socioeconomic status also have an impact on such health conditions as obesity, violence, and substance use.[26–28] The presence or absence of a wide range of neighborhood characteristics ("assets") are said to be related to health.[29]

Several organized efforts to address disparities at the state or community level have focused primarily on these social and economic factors. The California Campaign to Eliminate Racial and Ethnic Disparities in Health,[30] for example, based its approach to resolving disparities on an analysis of multiple environmental (nonmedical) factors that contribute to the disparities. According to the California Campaign, sources of health disparities include housing, education, labor (employment), economics (socioeconomic status), technology (technology gap), criminal justice (disproportionate representation), transportation disparities, and environmental risk (exposure). The campaign identified 20 community factors that were viewed as significant contributors as well, grouped under four categories: the built environment, social capital, services and institutions, and social-structural factors. In its report entitled *Reducing Health Disparities Through a Focus on Communities*,

PolicyLink (a nonprofit focusing on community solutions to health and other disparities) grouped community effects on health into the following three domains[31]:

- *Social and economic environment:* e.g., cultural characteristics, social norms, social networks, level of community organization, civic engagement, "reputation of the neighborhood"
- *Physical environment:* e.g., physical features of the neighborhood, physical spaces (parks, workplaces), public safety, physical access to opportunities
- *Services:* e.g., access and quality of services, access and quality of support services (public services, transit, police/fire protection, community institutions, commercial services, etc.)

Another way to synthesize the impact of these broad social and economic factors in producing health disparities is to think of poverty and social marginalization as creating groups of people (defined by their socioeconomic status, race/ethnicity, etc.) with poor access to the interrelated systems of health, economic, and social resources. This general access-poor relationship generates patterns of living that focus more on survival and achieving social goals (e.g., family needs, access to resources) within a very limited sphere, as opposed to maximizing health. This view is expressed in the literature on *vulnerable populations*,[32–35] and, for example, the research of medical anthropologists such as Dressler and colleagues.[36] It is also similar to the idea of disparities as an indicator of different *health trajectories*, mentioned earlier in this chapter.

Finally, there are also issues related to the lack of systems set up to address racial/ethnic minority health disparities. Before such disparities can be addressed, for example, *they have to be identified*; that is, data need to be collected and maintained on health status and disparities among racial-ethnic minority populations. Currently, this is often not the case. Many populations are lumped together under general designations like "Asian," which obscure significant differences; for example, people from Vietnam and India are both included in that category. And when disparities are identified, the information needs to go to someone or some agency that is designated to take action, and there has to be leadership, an organizing mission, coordination, and the allocation of resources—among other factors—for the issue to be addressed.[37]

WHAT TO DO: HOW IS THEORY CONNECTED TO RESOLVING HEALTH DISPARITIES?

Resolving the complex issues behind racial/ethnic disparities in health is not easy, and identifying appropriate action has been a challenge. In addition, national strategies and the

---

¶ Available from the Office of Minority Health Resource Center at www. omhrc.gov.

The Cultural and Linguistically Appropriate Service (CLAS) Standards

Standard 1 Health care organizations should ensure that patients/consumers receive from all staff members effective, understandable, and respectful care that is provided in a manner compatible with their cultural health beliefs and practices and preferred language.

Standard 2 Health care organizations should implement strategies to recruit, retain, and promote at all levels of the organization a diverse staff and leadership that are representative of the demographic characteristics of the service area.

Standard 3 Health care organizations should ensure that staff at all levels and across all disciplines receive ongoing education and training in culturally and linguistically appropriate service delivery.

Standard 4 Health care organizations must offer and provide language assistance services, including bilingual staff and interpreter services, at no cost to each patient/consumer with limited English proficiency at all points of contact, in a timely manner during all hours of operation.

Standard 5 Health care organizations must provide to patients/consumers in their preferred language both verbal offers and written notices informing them of their right to receive language assistance services.

Standard 6 Health care organizations must assure the competence of language assistance provided to limited English proficient patients/consumers by interpreters and bilingual staff. Family and friends should not be used to provide interpretation services (except on request by the patient/consumer).

Standard 7 Health care organizations must make available easily understood patient-related materials and post signage in the languages of the commonly encountered groups and/or groups represented in the service area.

Standard 8 Health care organizations should develop, implement, and promote a written strategic plan that outlines clear goals, policies, operational plans, and management accountability/oversight mechanisms to provide culturally and linguistically appropriate services.

Standard 9 Health care organizations should conduct initial and ongoing organizational self-assessments of CLAS-related activities and are encouraged to integrate cultural and linguistic competence-related measures into their internal audits, performance improvement programs, patient satisfaction assessments, and outcomes-based evaluations.

Standard 10 Health care organizations should ensure that data on the individual patient's/consumer's race, ethnicity, and spoken and written language are collected in health records, integrated into the organization's management information systems, and periodically updated.

Standard 11 Health care organizations should maintain a current demographic, cultural, and epidemiological profile of the community as well as a needs assessment to accurately plan for and implement services that respond to the cultural and linguistic characteristics of the service area.

Standard 12 Health care organizations should develop participatory, collaborative partnerships with communities and utilize a variety of formal and informal mechanisms to facilitate community and patient/consumer involvement in designing and implementing CLAS-related activities.

Standard 13 Health care organizations should ensure that conflict and grievance resolution processes are culturally and linguistically sensitive and capable of identifying, preventing, and resolving cross-cultural conflicts or complaints by patients/consumers.

Standard 14 Health care organizations are encouraged to regularly make available to the public information about their progress and successful innovations in implementing the CLAS standards and to provide public notice in their communities about the availability of this information.

U.S. Office of Minority Health, www.omhrc.gov.

policies of federal and other agencies are often caught in the middle of politics (think administrative/policy assessment), where decisions about whether to focus on social factors, economic factors, or only individual behavior and attitudes in addressing health disparities are difficult to separate from particular political viewpoints.

Let's take a look at some of the areas of possible action and their theoretical counterparts. As you think about the kinds of issues that need to be addressed to resolve health disparities, you will see that they amount to far more than just developing culturally competent programs, or information and materials that are language-appropriate.

First, you can see from our brief discussion above that the general *ecological model* is very much applicable to understanding health disparities, because there are many and varied causal factors forming an interrelated web or ecology. So, referring back to Chapter 7, it becomes necessary to "pick your battles" from a range of possible issues to address. It also depends on the specific population—a precise set of factors may be more relevant for disparities related to one population than for another. So let's touch on some of the possible uses of social/behavioral theory.

Individual Approaches

Because individuals are "behavers," there is always a role for individual-oriented approaches, even while we understand that individuals function within a larger social context. Recall from Chapter 4 that many theoretical approaches include *categories of information*—like social norms or perceived barriers—that are useful only when you fill them in with specifics related to a population. (Which norms? What perceived barriers?) That is the essence of using many of the individual theories in any work related to racial/ethnic minority health disparities. You have to use information related to these populations. So, for example, if you choose to use the Health Belief Model (HBM),[38,39] perceived barriers to using health care services may include, as we have discussed:

- Mistrust
- Concern that they will not understand the needs or practices of a minority culture (e.g., the need to consult family, traditional use of herb medicinals, differing ways of appropriately conducting examinations with older people, women, and men)
- Physical difficulties, such as lack of transportation
- Language—that the health provider does not understand a patient's language

Or, regarding attitudes—an individual must *intend* to change behavior, believe that there is a *positive or valued*

outcome to changing that behavior, and believe that he or she is *capable* of making the behavior change. So, if a certain risk behavior is related to social or cultural norms for "being a man" (for example, drinking, or not talking to health professionals about personal matters), intention may be low, and this may be the focus of a health promotion effort.[40–43]

Social, Community, and Group Approaches

You have also encountered, in this book, a wide range of theories focusing on the social, cultural, community, organizational, and political-economic context. Thinking about some of these contextual factors that contribute to racial/ethnic minority health disparities, and keeping in mind that such contexts vary by community and health problem and that what you do should be tailored to the situation and population you are working with, the following are some possibilities for integrating theory and action.

In order to create better access to health care, or remove an environmental risk that is affecting a minority community (and is therefore an important cause of health disparities), community mobilization and advocacy strategies may be useful. These strategies may increase general minority community capacity and empowerment as well.[44,45] Community mobilization is also among the recommended strategies in the Centers for Disease Control and Prevention (CDC) *Community Guide* with respect to tobacco intervention. Changes in local, state, or even national policy, and improved access to health care facilities can all result from mobilization and advocacy efforts, as well as *social marketing, media advocacy*, and communications campaigns.

To address norms, attitudes, and beliefs shared among a group or population, a number of health communications strategies, including social marketing[46] and mass media/communications campaigns,[47] focus on the process of disseminating information to individuals and maximizing the likelihood that individuals within a target population will adopt healthy behaviors. Addressing group norms is a different task than individual behavior change and includes working with key influencers within a group (community leaders, early adopters), working with social networks, and other strategies.[48–50] As with all theory, using any of these approaches first requires that you, for example, identify the key influencers or social networks for a particular social-cultural group, and themes/messages that will have meaning. Social networks for some immigrant populations may, for example, center around soccer or sports leagues, or exist in churches/faith organizations.

There is also the larger political-economic context. Reducing socioeconomic disparities is a longer-term issue, but some community/environmental approaches and strategies have attempted to address this as part of a coordinated community strategy. In Boston, for example, the Disparities Project specifically contemplates (though it has not yet implemented) efforts to address employment and socioeconomic issues for the target minority populations (see www.bphc.org). Working to ensure access to health insurance falls in this category.

Multilevel Programs

Several program efforts have tried to tie several of these strategies and practices together. The CDC REACH program, for example, focuses on the linkage among community organizational capacity, targeted action, knowledge and behavior change, and improved health outcomes. Figure 14-1 presents a model of the CDC sociocultural framework for addressing health disparities.

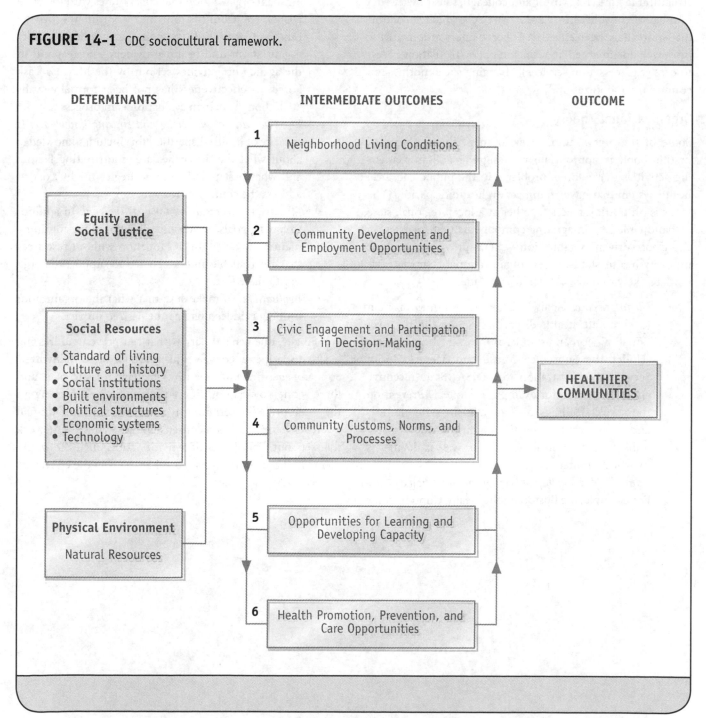

FIGURE 14-1 CDC sociocultural framework.

The THRIVE (Toolkit for Health and Resilience in Vulnerable Environments) program, developed by the Prevention Institute (in Oakland, California) under contract from the U.S. Office of Minority Health, focuses on building resilient communities.[51] THRIVE is based on four clusters (or domains) of factors within communities that are to be strengthened by program efforts. The four clusters are: built environment, social capital, services and institutions, and structural factors. Brownson and colleagues also reviewed a number of chronic disease areas where coordinated community efforts have been effective. Tobacco interventions are the most well documented, focusing on policy/regulation, access to care (e.g., cessation services), changing social norms, and community mobilization.[52]

Organizational Theory

Some of the organizational development theory discussed in this book is appropriate in designing and implementing activities that address problems in the public and local health system that have an impact on health disparities. The focus is on putting pieces together at a local, regional, state, or national level—integrating components that together, in a purpose-driven organization, will improve racial/ethnic minority health status. A few organizational characteristics that are likely to make a difference include:

- *Clear purpose:* Goals, mission, and values that aim to eliminate health disparities define the organizational mission and standards for evaluating progress. (Under the Substance Abuse and Mental Health Services Administration [SAMHSA] State Incentive Grants program, for example, a Strategic Prevention framework [SPF] is disseminated to state grantees and is expected to be the guiding framework for implementation of these funds, as well as the means by which grantees are evaluated.)
- *Committed leadership to keep the organization on track:* For example, the Boston Public Health Commission's

Disparities Project (www.bphc.org) is spearheaded by strong mayoral commitment and a Mayor's Task Force that set the agenda and defined the project.
- *Collaborations that include the participation of all levels of the system, including both public and private:* Nearly all model systems feature public and private partnerships. Again, the Boston Public Health Commission's Disparities Project is a good example: It is a local government organization that collaborates with the State Disparities Commission, and coordinates private funding that is used (via grants) to fund community organizations and health providers who respond to the agenda of activities set out by the Mayor's Task Force. Its effectiveness has not been formally evaluated, though such an evaluation is in process.
- *Effective ways of gathering and sharing knowledge:* In the case of health disparities, this includes knowledge about what the disparities are, contributing factors, and what best practices or strategies might exist to address the contributing factors.
- *Effective use of resources towards the goal:* In addition to having goals, leadership, collaboration, and information, no program can function without resources that are available and designated to support the organizational effort.
- *Evaluation:* To make sure that what the organization is doing is indeed having the desired impact.

Finally, one general barrier that can prevent addressing health disparities effectively is just the coordination involved. So many agencies and organizations have roles to play, and there is often overlap or different organizations working on the same problem without any communication or mutual awareness, and without a consensus approach or framework that sets out what kinds of activities and policies to implement. Without coordination, there are gaps in the effort that are not addressed at all.

Chapter Questions

1. What is meant by racial/ethnic disparities in health? Why is this an important issue?

2. What are some of the key factors contributing to these disparities?

3. Although the phrase "racial/ethnic disparities in health" covers many different situations, the idea of a *vulnerable trajectory* ties these together. Explain.

4. How can you use individual theories/approaches to address health disparities?

5. How can you use social, group, community, and organizational theories/approaches to address disparities?

REFERENCES

1. DHHS. *Healthy People 2010.* Rockville, MD: Department of Health and Human Services; 2010.

2. U.S. Census Bureau. Available at: www.census.gov/population/pop-profile/dynamic. Accessed June 2006.

3. El Nasser H. A nation of 300 million. *USA Today,* July 5, 2006:A-1.

4. U.S. Department of Health and Human Services. *Health, United States, 2005, with Chartbook on Trends in the Health of Americans.* Rockville, MD: U.S. Department of Health and Human Services; 2005.

5. Taylor, VM, Choe JH, et al. (2005). Hepatitis B awareness, testing, and knowledge among Vietnamese American men and women. *J Community Health* 30(6): 477-90.

6. U.S. Department of Health and Human Services. *Report of the U.S. Department of Health and Human Services Secretary's Task Force on Black and Minority Health.* Vol. I, Executive Summary. Washington, D.C.: DHHS; 1985.

7. Agency for Healthcare Research and Quality. *Third National Healthcare Disparities Report.* Rockville, MD: Agency for Healthcare Research and Quality, Department of Health and Human Services; 2005.

8. APHA Fact Sheet, "Racial/Ethnic Disparities"

9. Corble-Smith G, Thomas SB, Williams MV, Moody-Ayers S. Attitudes and beliefs of African-Americans towards participation in medical research. *J Gen Intern Med.* 1999;14:537–546.

10. Thomas SB, Quinn SC. The Tuskegee Syphilis Study, 1932 to 1972: Implications for HIV education and AIDS risk education programs in the black community. *Am J Public Health.* 1991;81:1498–1505.

11. Brown ER, et al. *Racial and Ethnic Disparities in Access to Health Insurance and Health Care 2000.* Los Angeles, CA: UCLA Center for Health Policy Research and Henry J. Kaiser Family Foundation; 2000.

12. Centers for Disease Control and Prevention, 2005. Behavioral Risk Factor Surveillance System 2005. Atlanta, GA: Centers for Disease Control and Prevention, U.S. Department of Health and Human Services.

13. Puschel K, Thompson B, Coronado GD, Lopez L, Kimball AM. Factors related to cancer screening in Hispanics: a comparison of the perceptions of Hispanic community members, healthcare providers, and representatives of organizations that serve Hispanics. *Health Educ Behav.* 2001;28:573–590.

14. UCSF Center for AIDS Prevention. What are Asian and Pacific Islander HIV prevention needs? UCSF Center for AIDS Prevention Fact Sheet.

15. Brown P, ed. *Understanding and Applying Medical Anthropology.* Mountain View, CA: Mayfield; 1998.

16. Fadiman A. *The Spirit Catches You and You Fall Down: A Hmong Child, Her American Doctors, and the Collision of Two Cultures.* New York: Farrar, Straus and Giroux; 1997.

17. Smedley BD, Stith AY, Nelson AR, eds. *Unequal Treatment: Confronting Racial and Ethnic Disparities in Health Care.* Washington, D.C.: National Academy Press; 2003.

18. Lillie-Blanton M, Lewis CB. *Issue Brief: Policy Challenges and Opportunities in Closing the Racial/Ethnic Divide in Health Care.* Menlo Park, CA: The Henry J. Kaiser Family Foundation; March 2005.

19. Lillie-Blanton M, Rushing EO, Ruiz R, Mayberry R, Boone L. *Racial/Ethnic Differences in Cardiac Care: The Weight of the Evidence.* Menlo Park, CA: The Henry J. Kaiser Family Foundation; 2002.

20. SteelFisher GK. *Issue Brief: Addressing Unequal Treatment: Disparities in Health Care.* New York: The Commonwealth Fund; November 2004.

21. Anderson L, Scrimshaw S, Fullilove M, Fielding JE, Normand J. Culturally competent healthcare systems: a systematic review. *Am J Prev Med.* 2003;24(3S):68–79.

22. Geiger HJ. Racial stereotyping and medicine: the need for cultural competence. *Can Med Assoc J.* 2001;164(12):16–19.

23. Kawachi I, Kennedy BP, Wilkinson RG. *Society and Population Health Reader.* Vol I, Income Inequality and Health. New York: The New Press; 1999.

24. Williams DR, Collins C. Racial residential segregation: a fundamental cause of racial disparities in health. *Pub Health Rep.* 2001;116(5):404–416.

25. Richards CF, Lowe RA. Researching racial and ethnic disparities in health. *Acad Emerg Med.* 2003;10(11):1169–1175.

26. Morland K, Wing S, Diez-Roux A, Poole C. Neighborhood characteristics associated with location of food stores and food service places. *Am J Prev Med.* 2002;22:23–29.

27. Shihadeh ES, Flynn N. Segregation and crime: the effect of black isolation on the rates of black urban violence. *Sociolog Forces.* 1996;74:1325–1352.

28. LaVeist TA, Wallace Jr. JM. Health risk and the inequitable distribution of liquor stores in African-American neighborhoods. *Soc Sci Med.* 2000;51:613–617.

29. Kretzmann JP, McKnight JL. 1993. *Building Communities from the Inside Out: A PathToward Finding and Mobilizing a Community's Assets.* The Asset-Based Community Development Institute, Northwestern University. Chicago, IL: ACTA Publications.

30. California Campaign to Eliminate Racial and Ethnic Disparities in Health. *Health for All: California's Strategic Approach to Eliminating Racial and Ethnic Health Disparities.* Washington, D.C.: American Public Health Association. Oakland, CA: The Prevention Institute. Sacramento, CA: The California Health and Human Services Agency; 2003.

31. PolicyLink. *Reducing Health Disparities Through a Focus on Communities.* Oakland, CA: PolicyLink; 2003.

32. Sebastian JG. Definitions and theory underlying vulnerability. In: Sebastian JG, Bushy A, eds. *Special Populations in the Community: Advances in Reducing Health Disparities.* Gaithersburg, MD: Aspen; 1999.

33. Sebastian JG. Vulnerability and vulnerable populations. In: Stanhope M, Lancaster J, eds. *Community Health Nursing: Promoting the Health of Individuals, Aggregates and Communities,* 4th ed. St. Louis, Mo.: Mosby; 1996.

34. Aday LA. *At Risk in America: The Health and Health Care Needs of Vulnerable Populations in the United States.* San Francisco: Jossey-Bass; 1993.

35. Flaskerud JH, Winslow BJ. Conceptualizing vulnerable populations health-related research. *Nursing Res.* 1998;47(2):69–78.

36. Dressler WW, Oths KS, Gravlee CC. Race and ethnicity in public health research: models to explain health disparities. *Ann Rev Anthropol.* 2005;34:231–252.

37. Gibbs BK et al. 2006. "Reducing Racial and Ethnic Health Disparities: Exploring an Outcome-Orineted Agenda for Research and Policy." *Journal of Health Politics, Policy and Law* 31(1):185–218.

38. Becker MH, ed. The health belief model and personal health behavior. *Health Educ Monogr.* 1974;2:Entire issue.

39. Janz NK, Becker MH. The health belief model: a decade later. *Health Educ Q.* 1984;11(1):1–47.

40. Ajzen I. The theory of planned behavior. *Organ Behav Human Decision Processes.* 1991;50:179–211.

41. Ajzen I, Fishbein M. *Understanding Attitudes and Predicting Social Behavior.* Englewood Cliffs, NJ: Prentice Hall; 1980.

42. Bandura A. *Social Foundations of Thought and Action.* Englewood Cliffs, NJ: Prentice Hall; 1986.

43. Bandura A. *Social Learning Theory.* Englewood Cliffs, NJ: Prentice Hall; 1977.

44. Minkler M, Wallerstein NB. Improving health through community organization and community building. In: Glanz K, Rimer BK, Lewis FM, eds. *Health Behavior and Health Education: Theory, Research and Practice,* 3rd ed. San Francisco, CA: Jossey-Bass; 2002.

45. Freire P. *Pedagogy of the Oppressed.* New York: Seabury Press; 1970.

46. Kotler & Roberto, 1989.

47. Maibach & Parrot, 1995.

48. Rogers EM. *Diffusion of Innovations,* 4th ed. New York: Free Press; 1995.

49. Scott J. *Social Network Analysis: A Handbook,* 2nd ed. London: Sage; 2000.

50. Trotter RT II. Friends, relatives, and relevant others: conducting ethnographic network studies. In: Schensul JJ, LeCompte MD, Trotter RT II, Cromley EK, Singer M, eds. *Mapping Social Networks, Spatial Data, and Hidden Populations: Ethnographer's Toolkit 4.* Walnut Creek, CA: Altamira Press; 1999.

51. Prevention Institute. *THRIVE: Final Project Report Executive Summary.* Oakland, CA: Prevention Institute; 2004.

52. Brownson RC, Haire-Joshu D, Luke DA. Shaping the context of health: a review of environmental and policy approaches in the prevention of chronic diseases. *Ann Rev Public Health.* 2006;27:341–370.

CHAPTER 15

Career Choices and Social/Behavioral Theory In Public Health: A Brief Introduction

LEARNING OBJECTIVES

By the end of this chapter, the reader will be able to:

- Describe the kinds of career paths in public health for which knowledge and experience in applying social/behavioral theory are important
- Understand how social/behavioral theory is used in these different career settings

"Go before the people with your example, and be laborious in their affairs."

—CONFUCIUS, *ANALECTS*

THE POSSIBILITIES

A good working knowledge of social/behavioral theory and its real-world application is an increasingly important and useful qualification for work in public health. You have seen numerous examples in this book of programs and interventions that were theoretically based. More and more programs will follow this trend, because as we have noted, a great deal of importance is placed on developing programs that make sense and are effective. Using theory is, really, a key part of designing programs that make sense, because the theory—when appropriately connected to real-world circumstances and people—is what lends coherence to an intervention.

In addition, using theory to design and implement a program is what allows for a meaningful evaluation, because the theoretical base tells you what *ought* to change as a result

of a program, and therefore what to evaluate. (Remember the idea of a *logic model* in Chapter 13?) I can't emphasize enough that the combination of theory, appropriately connected to real circumstances and program components, and evaluation will provide the evidence needed to improve the knowledge base about what works.

And that, as the saying goes, is where the money is.

Let's review, briefly, some examples of career paths in public health for which knowledge and application of social/behavioral theory play an important role. These career paths can be categorized as follows:

- *Government or public agency (domestic and global):* Program design and management
- *Nonprofit and community-based organizations (domestic and global), and schools:* Program implementation
- *Private sector consulting organizations:* Program design and evaluation, technical assistance
- *Private industry:* Program design and implementation
- *Health care providers:* Program design and implementation
- *Academic setting:* Behavioral research, program design, program evaluation, research collaboration, training

Government or Public Agency

Typically, a government agency (at the federal, state, or local level, or in an international agency) disseminates and manages funds allocated to address a particular health problem, such as HIV/AIDS. In order to do that, the agency may develop grant or other funding announcements that solicit applications from nongovernment organizations to design, implement, and evaluate actual programs. The grant announcements will describe the purpose of the program, the kinds of activities requested, the amount of funds available, and the criteria for measuring the success of the

Program Officer Example

Nora Henderson, MPH
(Hypothetical individual, not a real case)

Position: Program Officer, U.S. Department of Health and Human Services

Background: Master's degree in Public Health, with a concentration in health promotion. Bachelor of Arts (B.A.) degree in social psychology. Worked for five years at an urban nonprofit organization that developed and conducted health education and outreach programs to diverse populations concerning cardiovascular health, diabetes, and HIV/AIDS. Then worked for another five years at the state's Department of Public Health managing several community-based programs before moving to her current position.

Job Responsibilities: Assists in the design, implementation and evaluation of a national community grant program to prevent obesity and diabetes in youth and families who live in urban areas where there are few recreation facilities. Based on her informed input, together with others involved in the program design, funded projects are intended to combine both education (to increase knowledge about risks) and environmental change (to increase recreation opportunities)—the latter through community mobilization and public/private partnerships. Ms. Henderson is one of four Project Officers, and her primary responsibility is for grants awarded to communities in the Southeast region. She monitors how each of the grants in her region are doing, provides technical support and advice, and prepares reports and analyses concerning these projects. She also works with an Evaluation Officer to make sure that all her grants are conducting effective evaluations, and participates in presentations about the program.

Quote: "After working at the community level, I got a good firsthand look at the way so many things are connected to any given health problem. It really helped when I was involved in designing the current program, where we really tried to deal with obesity from several directions."

program, among other things. Such announcements are increasingly based on a program framework or theoretical approach developed or adopted by the agency that is determined to be appropriate for the problem. *Program heads* and *program officers* are among the agency staff that make these decisions. They do not, however, actually carry out the program or evaluation. The organization (or organizations) that apply and are selected to do that are *managed* or *overseen* by a program officer.

Once applications are received from organizations that want to do the work, they are usually reviewed by a panel of experts in the field, as well as staff from the funding organization. Selection is made based upon a rating of the applications as to which one presents the best plan to complete the work, at the best price, and supported by adequate organizational capabilities.

Public agencies also engage in *policy* work, in support of the mission of the agency. The agency might, for example, issue guidelines and regulations (e.g., concerning air and water pollution, or secondhand tobacco smoke), or disseminate recommended policies regarding, for example, disparities in health. In these cases, staff in the policy office of the agency work to develop policies, build consensus, and disseminate the policy recommendations through meetings, conferences, or other methods. The process of developing such policies draws heavily on such approaches as the ecological model, communications strategies, and organizational mobilization.

Nonprofit or Community-Based Agency

These agencies typically are at the "other end" of the process described above with respect to the government agency/project officer. Agencies like this are in direct contact with people and populations, and have an intimate knowledge of the communities and situations surrounding health behavior. If you are working with an agency of this type, the use of social/behavioral theory typically occurs in conjunction with program design and evaluation, either:

- In response to a government or private solicitation asking for organizations to submit applications for grants or contracts to implement a public health/health promotion program, or
- After developing a program (or idea for a program) that you/your organization believes will meet an important need for the community, where you have to seek funding for that program

Once a program is implemented, you will also be involved in conducting the evaluation, or work with another organization that has expertise in that area.

Another type of nonprofit agency where the emphasis is somewhat different is an *advocacy organization*. The focus of advocacy organizations is to help increase public awareness about an issue or group of related issues, and to impact public policy about that issue. These organizations typically engage in media advocacy, social marketing, and other communications efforts, as well as direct policy work (e.g., drafting position papers, helping to draft legislation). Your work with an advocacy organization would involve the design and/or carrying out of these kinds of activities, as well as the backup research involved.

In either case, a common task for all these organizations is *writing and preparing grant applications*. A grant application usually contains the following:

- A description of the health problem to be addressed
- A plan for how to address the problem with a specific program or programs, justified based on theory and an analysis of the problem (a little like a PRECEDE-PROCEED-type analysis)
- A plan for how to evaluate the effectiveness of the program
- A description of the staff and agency resources that will be used, and the qualifications/capabilities of the staff and organization
- A description of the organization's experience doing the kind of work proposed
- A budget for how much it will cost, and a time line for implementation

An exception to this role is the *private foundation*, like the Ford Foundation or Kaiser Family Foundation. These are nonprofits, but in some ways act like public agencies, disseminating funds and managing grant programs, or developing and disseminating policy recommendations.

Private Sector Consulting Organizations

In recent years, more and more of the work of government agencies has been undertaken by private organizations that have specific expertise, under a contract or other arrangement. These organizations may have, for example, expertise in evaluation, program design, organizational development, cultural competency, logistics and meeting planning, accounting and finance, communications campaigns and materials development, and other areas important to the conduct of public health programs. If you work in an organization like this, you are typically part of a *project team* that is assigned to develop and carry out the work. And, just like nonprofit agencies, private consulting organizations have to compete for funds by writing and submitting applications or proposals, in a format similar to that described above. The differ-

ence is that private consulting organizations usually work on a contract basis, rather than under grant funding. Contracts

---

Private Organization Example

George R. Barkley, Ph.D., M.A.
(Hypothetical individual, not a real case)

Position: Research Director, Social and Health Programs, Advantage International, Inc.—a private consulting firm specializing in global health.

Background: Doctoral degree in Public Health, and a Master's degree in International Development and Communications. Before returning to complete a Ph.D., he was a Peace Corps volunteer in the Dominican Republic, where he helped develop local communications efforts to increase awareness about the risks of cholera and waterborne disease. Then, for two years, he taught English in Chile. His first "real job" was with Johnson & Brenner, a social marketing company that conducted research and developed communications and social marketing programs on global health issues (HIV/AIDS, immunization, family health), primarily funded by the U.S. Agency for International Development (USAID), the World Bank, and other multinational agencies. After eight years there he moved to Advantage International, a similar, but larger organization, where he recently assumed his new position.

Job Responsibilities: Leads the development of grant and contract proposals to funding agencies for global health programs, and as part of this process he keeps close track of current theory, research, and practice in global health. Serves as Project Director on numerous funded projects, particularly for those that have a strong research component – for example, research on attitudes and risk behaviors with respect to a specific population and health problem (e.g., migrant farmworkers in South Africa and risks for HIV/AIDS) that will inform the development and implementation of a prevention or intervention program. He also leads an evaluation team for each project, and prepares reports (for the funding agency), journal articles, and presentations about the work.

Quote: "When you mention theory in connection with the kinds of projects I work on, people sometimes roll their eyes. But really, I use it, and refer to it, all the time. To reduce it down, how else would we make the connection between the reality we see out there and what to do about it?"

typically involve more hands-on interaction with the funding agency (the project officer) than do grants. In any case, a good knowledge of social/behavioral theory and its relationship to program design, implementation, and evaluation is very important for working in this capacity.

Private Industry (Other Than Health Care Providers)

Private businesses are part of the process in several ways. First, medium and larger businesses (and many small businesses) usually provide health insurance to their employees. As part of managing their cost, they may run several health promotion programs at the workplace—for example, wellness screening and education, exercise programs, or providing membership in a health facility. If the business is large enough, it may have its own exercise facilities and its own health promotion staff.

Second, businesses belong to industry associations and trade groups that may develop and advocate workplace-related health policies. Some of the advocacy may include lobbying Congress for specific policy recommendations.

Also very important, in many workplaces labor unions handle some or all of the employee support tasks such as wellness and prevention programming. Unions may also develop and disseminate policy recommendations regarding workplace health issues, and may lobby as well.

Work in this setting involves many possible situations, from designing and managing workplace health promotion programs, to evaluating them, to developing policy and dissemination strategies.

Health Care Providers

Health care providers may be public or private, large (hospitals) or small (individual practitioners). They have several key roles, in addition to providing health care, including:

- Disseminating health information
- Providing interpersonal communication and role modeling

- Providing "real-world" feedback on public health approaches and strategies that work, and those that don't

Health care providers can also be the setting for research on health knowledge/beliefs, effective program approaches, barriers to treatment, and many other activities.

Academic Setting

Academic settings are very much involved with social and behavioral theory in a number of ways. One way is certainly in *generating theory* through research and analysis, and *evaluating* the effectiveness of theory-driven interventions. Academic institutions are also involved in evaluating programs and identifying evaluation methods that are useful. These are, by and large, *research* activities. To conduct research, academics still have to go through a process of obtaining research grants, much like community organizations that are trying to seek funding. This means preparing and submitting a detailed application, which will in all likelihood be reviewed by a panel of scientific peers. Such applications may involve partnerships between the academic institution and community groups or other organizations with specific expertise. Research results are usually shared within the academic community through publication in journals, or in papers presented at conferences and meetings. They are also shared with platforms in the field and with the partnering communities. This is important—it is how research gets transferred to practice.

Of course, another key function for academic settings is teaching and training. Teaching students—those who will continue the practice and evolution of public health—as well as adults and public health practitioners via the multiple kinds of professional seminars and conference presentations allows for a dialogue in the field. Academics are also involved (sometimes on a *consulting* basis) in providing specific advice or training to public and private agencies/organizations.

There are, as you can see, many, many possibilities, and they can only increase!

Chapter Questions

1. What are some key reasons why a knowledge of social/behavioral theory is useful across a range of public health careers?

2. In what way(s) would a government or public agency staff member use theory?

3. What are some examples of the use of theory within the private consulting field?

4. From the point of view of a private business (a company), why would it be useful to have someone with a grounding in theory and application for the company wellness effort?

5. What roles do academic institutions play in terms of social/behavioral theory in public health?

Index

Page numbers in italic denote figures; those followed by *n* denote footnotes, and those followed by *t* denote tables